IMAGES
*of America*

# TENNESSEE'S DIXIE HIGHWAY

## SPRINGFIELD TO CHATTANOOGA

**ON THE COVER:** The Henry Davis Garage was located on the Dixie Highway at the intersection of Hazelwood Drive in the community of Stewartsboro in Rutherford County. The date on the car license plate reads 1922. (Courtesy of the Albert Gore Research Center, Middle Tennessee State University.)

IMAGES
*of America*

# TENNESSEE'S DIXIE HIGHWAY

## SPRINGFIELD TO CHATTANOOGA

Leslie N. Sharp

ARCADIA
PUBLISHING

ISBN 978-0-7385-8687-8

Published by Arcadia Publishing
Charleston, South Carolina

Printed in the United States of America

Library of Congress Control Number: 2010930146

For all general information, please contact Arcadia Publishing:
Telephone 843-853-2070
Fax 843-853-0044
E-mail sales@arcadiapublishing.com
For customer service and orders:
Toll-Free 1-888-313-2665

Visit us on the Internet at www.arcadiapublishing.com

*To JLD, whose friendship and generosity made this book possible.*

# Contents

# ACKNOWLEDGMENTS

This *Tennessee's Dixie Highway* publication came together with the assistance of many others. Friends, colleagues, and helpful people at the libraries and archives deserve my sincerest appreciation. My friends provided images, lodging, expertise, editing, entertainment, and often distractions. They include: Jeffrey Lee Durbin, Lauren Wray Grisham, Allison McGoffin, Michael McGoffin, Tara Mitchell Mielnik, Elizabeth Moore, Teri Nagel, Anne-Leslie Owens, Lance Selva, Jane Townes, Carroll Van West, and Jaime Woodcock. The professionals in the libraries and archives who were generous with their time and expertise include: Jim Williams and Matthew Brown at the Albert Gore Research Center, Middle Tennessee State University; Karina McDaniel at the Tennessee State Library and Archives; Jim Reese at the Chattanooga–Hamilton County Bicentennial Library; Yolanda Reid at the Robertson County Archives; Lisa Ramsay at the Linebaugh Library in Murfreesboro; and John Lodl at the Rutherford County Archives.

I appreciate the earlier scholarship of my preservation colleagues: Martha Carver, Jeffrey Durbin, and Claudette Stager. Several other institutions deserve recognition, including the Center for Historic Preservation at Middle Tennessee State University, the Tennessee Civil War National Heritage Area, Nashville Public Library, and the Chattanooga History Center (formerly the Chattanooga Regional History Museum), for their dedication to telling the stories of the Dixie Highway. I also would like to thank Arcadia Publishing's southern publisher, Maggie Bullwinkel, who encouraged me to do this project and answered all my questions. Lastly, I would like to acknowledge my husband, Tyrone, and my family for their loving support.

# Introduction

Constructed between 1915 and 1927, the Dixie Highway, with its eastern and western branches, traversed the United States from Sault Ste. Marie, Michigan, to Miami, Florida. It began as a private venture promoted and supported by the Dixie Highway Association. The highway was the dream of capitalists and everyday citizens who believed good roads were the key to a "progressive New South" characterized by economic prosperity and cultural change. The highway led to an expansion of the financial base of the region through the promotion of the tourism industry and access to markets. Not only was the South's economy altered, so were its people, politics, and landscape. Along the highway, people constructed gas stations, tourist camps and later motor courts, stores, and other tourist destinations to serve the car-traveling public. The images in this book will show how the Dixie Highway changed the Tennessee landscape.

Fortunately for commercial-minded Tennesseans, both the eastern and western branches of the Dixie came through their state. The eastern division went south from Cumberland Gap through Knoxville, Rockwood, and Dayton to Chattanooga. The western division of the route proceeded south from Springfield through Nashville, Murfreesboro, Shelbyville, Tullahoma, Winchester, Monteagle, and Jasper to Chattanooga, where it met the eastern branch and headed into Georgia. The western branch through Tennessee was particularly important, as it was roughly the halfway point of the route; contained the headquarters of the Dixie Highway Association in Chattanooga; and included the seemingly insurmountable Monteagle Mountain in Marion County—the very last portion of the highway to be completed. The area covered by the western branch of the Dixie Highway in Tennessee includes the capital city of Nashville, three of the state's five largest counties in terms of population, agricultural and rural areas, and some of Tennessee's most spectacular views. The Dixie Highway corridor eventually provided access to some of the best known tourist destinations in the South, including Andrew Jackson's home, named the Hermitage; the Parthenon; Ryman Auditorium; Stones River National Battlefield; Chickamauga-Chattanooga National Military Park; Rock City; Ruby Falls; and Lookout Mountain.

Road building in Tennessee and across the country during the early 20th century involved boosterism, business, and political will. These early efforts created an infrastructure that laid the foundation for economic development, the eventual federal highway program, and ultimately a changed landscape of the region. Getting the road completed was a complicated, and at times exciting, social, economic, and legal process involving multiple communities with multiple agendas. Public discontent over the condition of roads in Tennessee translated into popular support for the Good Roads Movement. Historian Leland Johnson writes that Tennessee had become the "detour state," meaning that travelers avoided the state because of the poor roads.

Chattanooga citizens and especially the Chattanooga Automobile Club provided immense backing for the Dixie Highway. The newly formed Chattanooga Automobile Club was an enthusiastic supporter of the road and remained closely associated to the Dixie Highway Association throughout its history. Five local members of the Chattanooga Automobile Club and eight other men pledged $1,000 each for the formation of the Dixie Highway Association.

The first major organizational meeting for the north-south highway was held on April 15, 1915, in Chattanooga. The attendees elected C. E. James, a Chattanooga builder, as the first president of the Dixie Highway Association, but he refused to serve following a dispute about the route. The members elected Judge Michael Morrison Allison, also of Chattanooga, as vice president and then president when the position was refused by James. Allison remained an extremely active president until the Dixie Highway Association disbanded in 1927 after the completion of the highway. Other prominent men, such as Clark Howell, editor of the *Atlanta Constitution*, were elected to serve as officers and directors.

The directors of the association met again on May 22, 1915, in Chattanooga to establish the rules and regulations of the association. Its offices were to be located in Chattanooga—roughly the halfway point of the highway. After much debate led by Carl Graham Fisher and Clark Howell, the delegates gave the Dixie Highway multiple routes—a system of highways with eastern and western divisions. Each division was routed through both Atlanta and Chattanooga.

On the 10th anniversary of the formation of the Dixie Highway Association, the *Chattanooga Times* wrote that the highway "has been a work of education as well as a task of performance." The education campaign focused on the economic opportunity available for areas in the path of the Dixie Highway. The campaign for the highway was based in Chattanooga in the Patten Hotel. The incorporators, who were delegated to create a charter for the association, were all from Chattanooga. They were: T. R. Preston, president of the Hamilton National Bank; Richard Hardy, president of Dixie Portland Cement Company; C. E. James, president of Signal Mountain Land Company; M. E. Temple, secretary of Chattanooga Furniture Company; John A. Patten, president of Chattanooga Medicine Company; C. H. Huston, vice president of Chattanooga Trust Company; and W. R. Long, president of Model Laundry Company. These prominent businessmen, who stood to profit from the road, became the biggest proponents of the highway in Tennessee and continued to support the association through advertising in *The Dixie Highway* magazine, attending meetings, and speaking on behalf of the highway.

Each of the seven states involved in the highway had two directors representing the state. The two directors from Tennessee were Col. A. M. Shook, a capitalist from Nashville, and Judge M. M. Allison, a lawyer from Chattanooga. Allison was certainly the most important. His role in the Dixie Highway Association was memorialized by a stone monument erected on Walden's Ridge above Chattanooga on the highest point of the Dixie Highway. Other people, such as Judge Will Cummings, played a critical role in getting the road constructed.

Although the road became a "national necessity" during World War I to provide relief from the shortages of freight cars needed to carry the military, tourism was the most common and visible rationale used to build support for the road. Articles in Tennessee newspapers proposed convincing arguments for the support of the highway. A 1918 Murfreesboro *News Banner* article promoted the completion of the road so that tourists might come from all over the northwest on their way to Miami. The article also said that Murfreesboro and Rutherford County could prosper like Chattanooga and Nashville and "accrue all the advantages of those cities." The *Nashville Banner* wrote at the same time that the highway between Nashville and Chattanooga should have been completed years ago and the lack of such a road marked the state as "unprogressive." This tourism argument proved to be right on target; the Dixie Highway provided access to resorts, Civil War battlefields, parks, tourist attractions, and all sorts of leisure activities.

Men were not the only good roads advocates in Tennessee. Josephine Anderson Pearson and Mrs. Claude D. (Mary?) Sullivan were extremely active in the push for the Dixie Highway. They were involved in the Dixie Highway Auxiliary Association as well as the Tennessee Good Roads Association. Publicly women were concerned more with the social benefits of the highway than the economic benefits advocated by men. The *Chattanooga Times* wrote in 1923 that "women worked selflessly [for good roads] whereas men worked selfishly."

Sullivan, in her 1923 speeches, asserted that Tennessee was handicapped by a lack of modern highway systems and that the women were convinced that roads were the most important consideration in the agricultural, industrial, economic, and educational development in Tennessee. Pearson, chair of the Cumberland Division of the Dixie Highway Association in Monteagle, Tennessee, planned and organized auxiliary meetings to involve "female good roads enthusiasts" and wrote an article for *The Dixie Highway* magazine on the benefits of the highway to mountain women. The benefits included work for the men, goods and services more readily available to all, improved education, and a decrease in the isolation of the mountains.

North of Chattanooga, Monteagle Mountain along the Cumberland Plateau was the last section of the highway to be completed, and even then only after political wrangling, the changing of county borders, and finally state and federal infusions of funds. Following its completion, the Dixie Highway Association disbanded in 1927. Two years before, the U.S. Secretary of Agriculture appointed a joint board of state and federal highway officials to come up with a uniform system of designating interstate highway routes. The east-west highways were given even numbers, and north-south highways received odd numbers. At this time, the Dixie Highway became known by numbers such as U.S. Routes 31 and 41. Certain portions of the original route were bypassed in favor of more direct routes. Even with the federal numbering systems, the name "Dixie Highway" was still used along certain sections of the road either by itself or with the designated numbers. Today, there are bypassed sections of the road all along the route that still bear the name "Old Dixie Highway," as seen in Marion County, just north of Kimball.

The Dixie Highway became a unifying force. Capitalists such as Carl Graham Fisher, elected officials such as Judge Will Cummings, and everyday citizens such as Josephine Pearson fought for good roads and shared dreams of the Dixie Highway's completion. What followed the development of the Dixie Highway in Tennessee can be seen in the following pages. The people, the places, the businesses, and the attractions show the importance of the Dixie Highway in Tennessee's history and represent the foundations of progress and economic vitality that came to the region over the course of the 20th century.

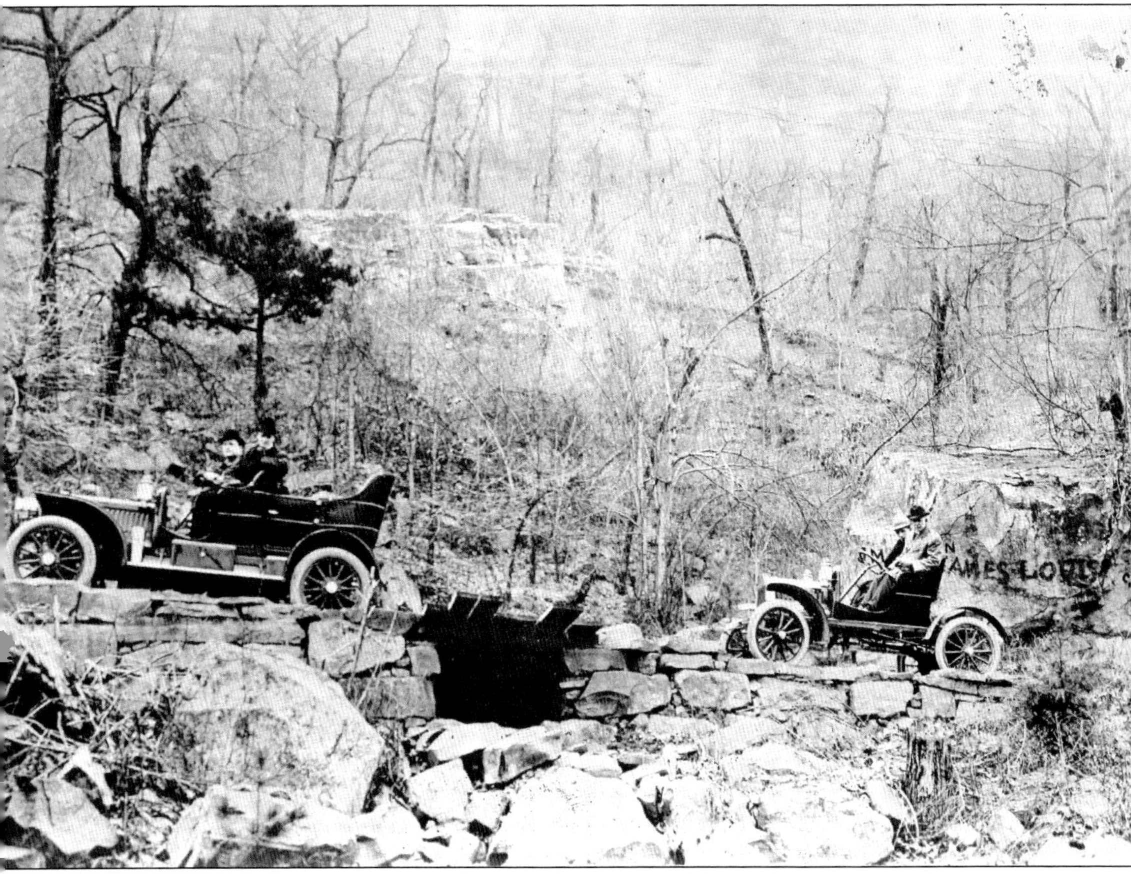

The conditions of Tennessee's roads at the beginning of the 20th century are depicted in this 1909 photograph of two Maxwell cars climbing Lookout Mountain. The steep terrain and the limestone composition of the area presented challenges to road building that were solved with great political will, state and federal financial support, and improvements in road building technology. Over the next two decades, Lookout Mountain became a destination rather than an impediment as the Good Roads Movement in Tennessee and across the country made great strides in passing legislation, getting roads funded, and getting roads paved. (Courtesy of the Chattanooga–Hamilton County Bicentennial Library.)

# One

# Getting Good Roads

The Good Roads Movement was considered one of the least controversial reform movements in American history and one of the most popular causes in the southern United States. Early proponents of good roads were cyclists, farmers, and railroad companies. The cyclists wanted good roads for touring on their bicycles. The farmer wanted improved roads in order to get their goods to market and as an alternative to rail transportation. The railroad companies backed the Good Roads Movement because it would extend the service area of their lines.

Congress enacted federal legislation in 1892 for the formation of a national highway commission, followed by the 1893 creation of an Office of Inquiry under the U.S. Department of Agriculture to focus on road-related needs. In 1902, the Brownlow Bill—sponsored by U.S. representative Walter P. Brownlow of the Tennessee First Congressional District—called for a federally supported highway program, but Congress rejected it as unconstitutional.

Like many other states, Tennessee's roads were in deplorable condition during this period. In 1890, Tennessee developed a Road Congress that determined road construction and maintenance programs should be the responsibility of counties and not the local precincts. This change in supervision alleviated political problems between communities within the counties. However, neither this effort nor other state legislation led to better roads, as a lack of financial resources continued to plague the counties and the state.

The campaign for improved roads had almost reached "religious fervor" by the 1910s. The rise in automobile traffic increased the need for good roads. Federal legislation passed during the 1910s and 1920s was especially beneficial to the South in general and Tennessee in particular. The Federal Highway Acts of 1916 and 1921, along with strong state leadership, finally earned Tennessee the good roads it so desperately wanted and led to the completion of the Dixie Highway in Tennessee.

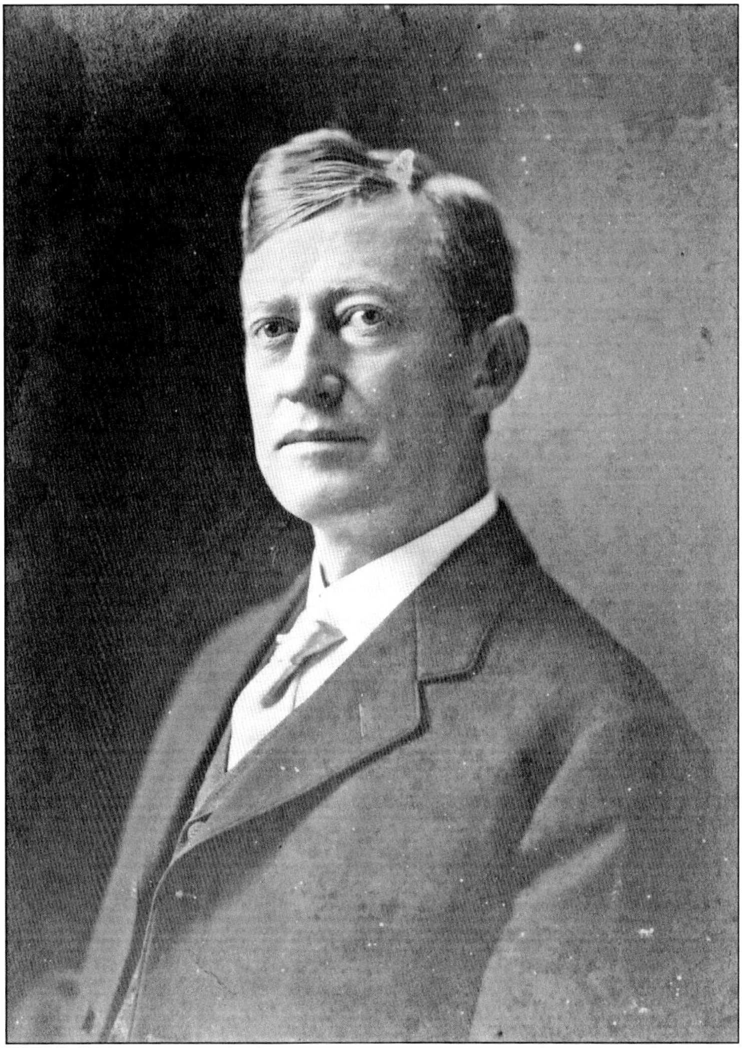

On April 15, 1907, Gov. Malcolm Rice Patterson approved a bill for the creation of a state highway commission. Patterson called the legislation the "beginning of a system of good roads building so much needed by the people of Tennessee," but in reality, this act was a feeble effort that did not include any money for the construction of the highways. (Courtesy of the Tennessee State Library and Archives.)

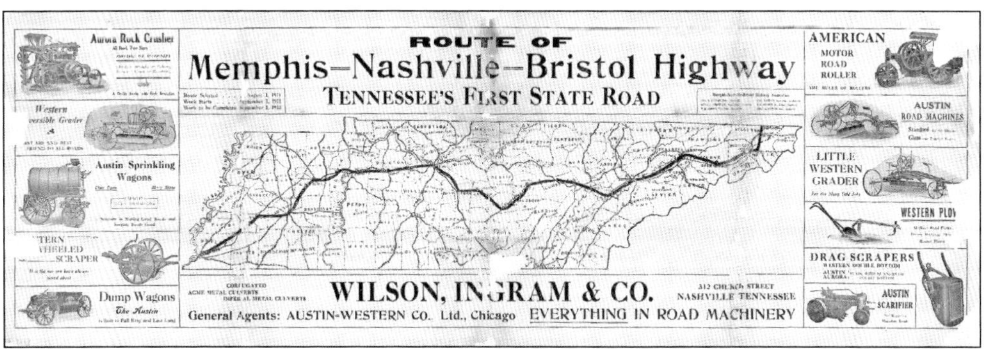


In 1909, Tennessee created a state highway commission to investigate how federal efforts in public roadwork could be used at the state level. This commission recommended that counties issue bonds to build roads, a Memphis-to-Bristol highway be built, state convicts be used in highway construction, and congress needed to create a standard tire width. (Courtesy of the Tennessee State Library and Archives.)

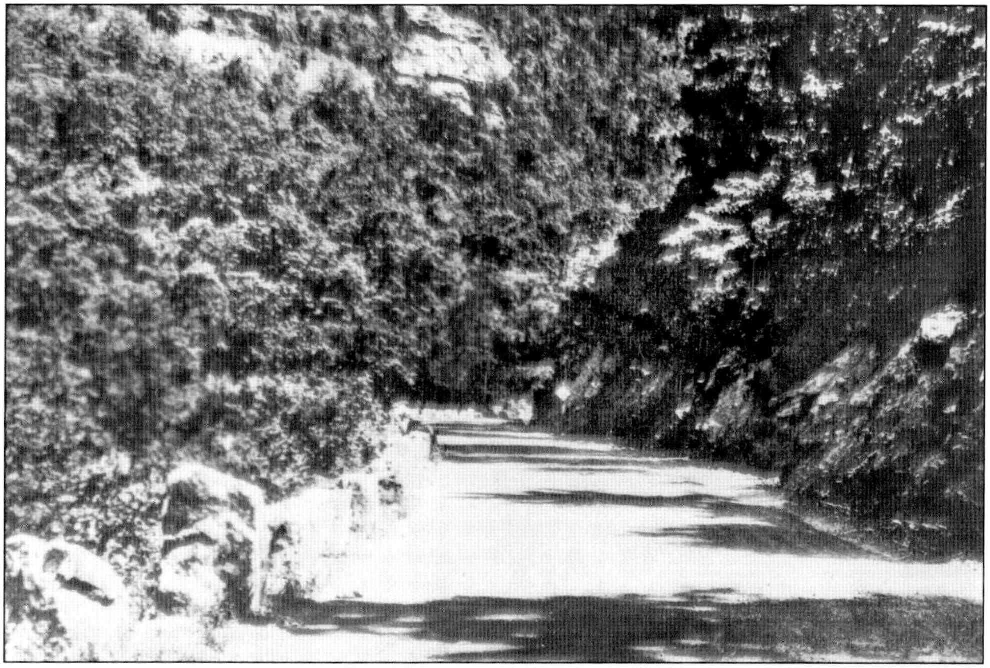

As more and more Tennesseans purchased cars, the support for good roads increased and the deplorable conditions of the roads became more apparent. According to the Tennessee Highway Commission, citizens had registered 25,000 vehicles by 1915 and 100,000 by 1920. (Courtesy of the Chattanooga–Hamilton County Bicentennial Library.)

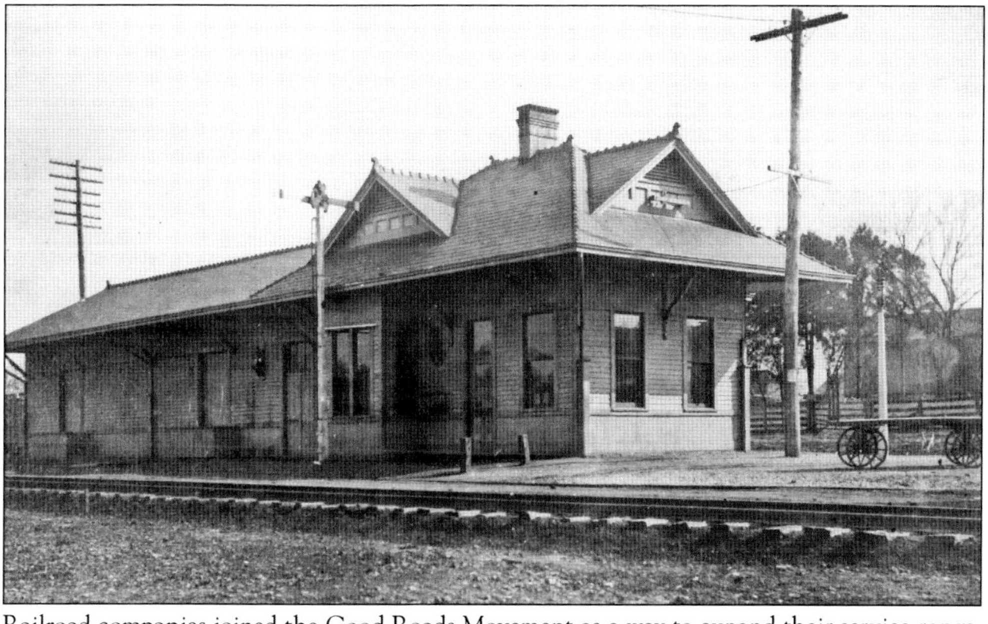

Railroad companies joined the Good Roads Movement as a way to expand their service range. The improvement of roads leading to the Louisville and Nashville Railroad Station in Adams, shown in this *c.* 1918 photograph, allowed Robertson County farmers to get their dark-fired tobacco and other agricultural products to the depot and to markets outside the region. (Courtesy of the Tennessee State Library and Archives.)

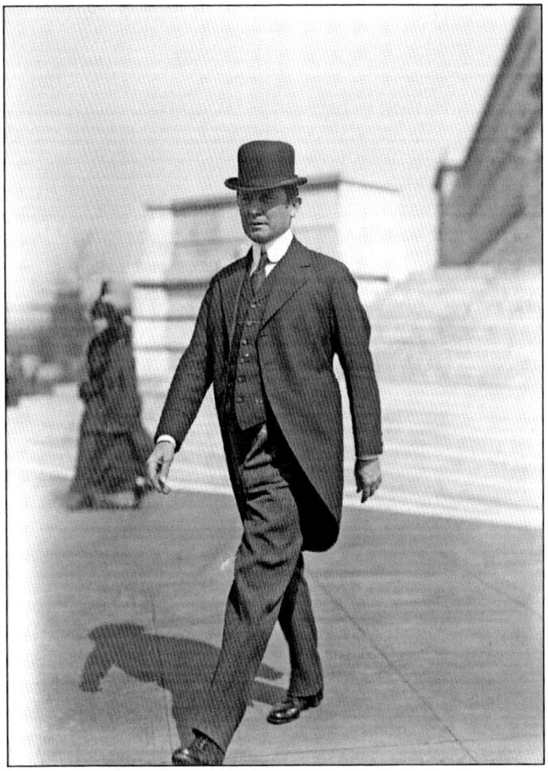

Tennessee congressman and good roads advocate Kenneth Douglas McKellar met with Pres. Woodrow Wilson to persuade him to approve the 1916 Federal Highway Act. Congress then passed the Federal Highway Act of 1921, which allowed federal funds to be used for a rapid improvement of interstate roads. The passage of these acts spurred road building throughout Tennessee and helped to complete the Dixie Highway. (Courtesy of the Library of Congress.)

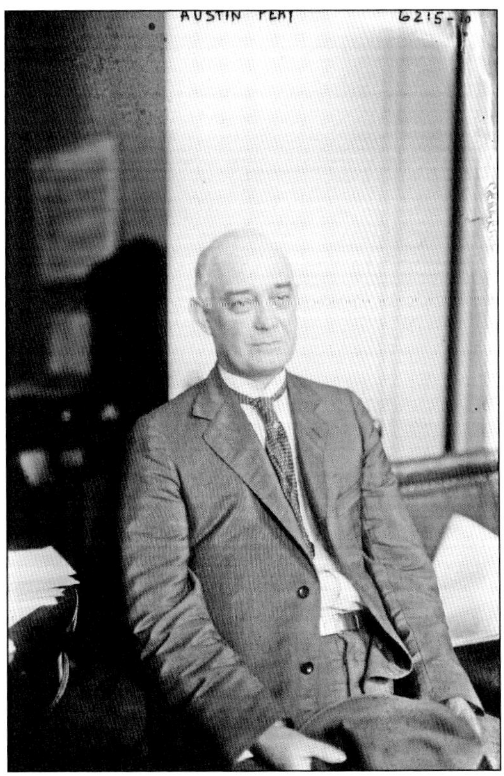


Austin Peay, dubbed the "Road Building Governor," was elected in 1923 on a platform to build highways, develop public education, and lower taxes. In order to pay for the highway and education improvements, taxes had to be raised. Peay advocated good roads through constant public appearances and political action. He spoke at the Dixie Highway Association's annual convention in 1923. (Courtesy of the Library of Congress.)

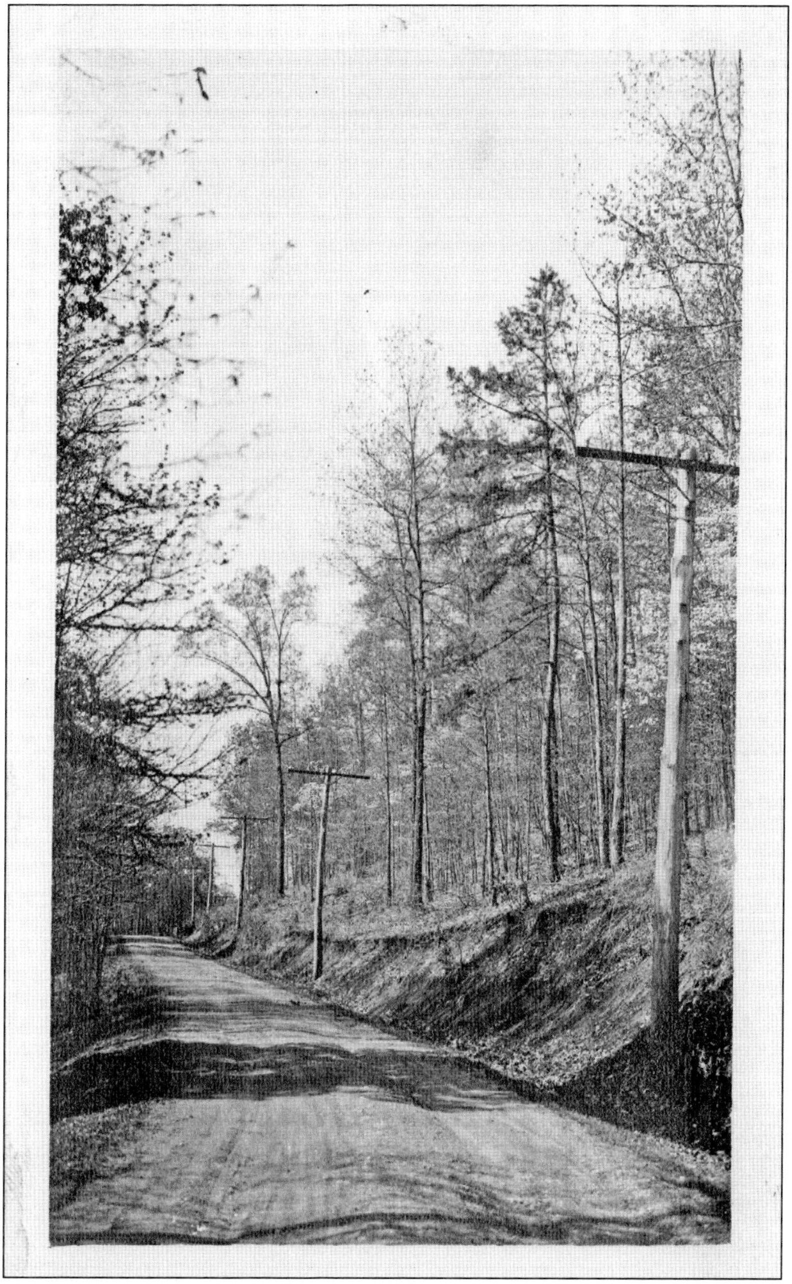

With the passage of the federal highway acts, Tennessee and other states had to pass state-enabling legislation in order to take advantage of the funding. Subsequently, counties had to pass local bills to receive their share. The result was improved macadamized roads, such as this 1920s one in Hamilton County, just south of Chickamauga Creek. Named for Scotsman John Loudon McAdam, who pioneered this method of hard-surfacing roads in the 1820s, the term "macadamized" refers to using layers of a single-sized aggregate bonded together with cement. All of this road construction led to people starting cement companies throughout the region, which was aided by the natural geology of the surrounding limestone mountains. (Courtesy of the Tennessee State Library and Archives.)

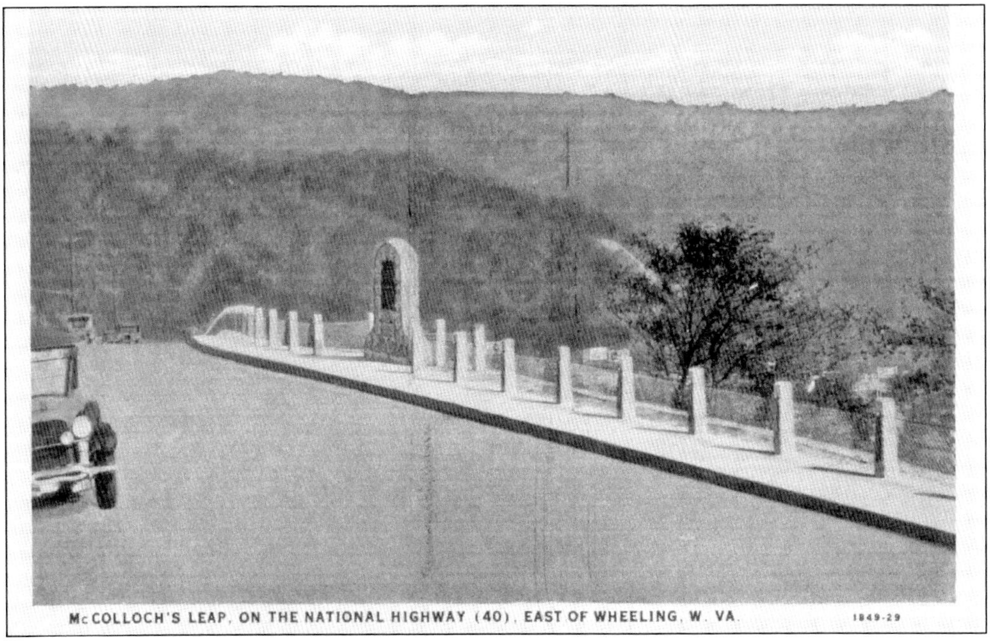


Parallel to and in conjunction with the governmental efforts to develop good roads, private citizens formed associations to get roads through their regions. The National Highway Organization opened its road, which went from Washington, D.C., through West Virginia and the Carolinas to Atlanta, Georgia, in 1909. (Courtesy of the author.)

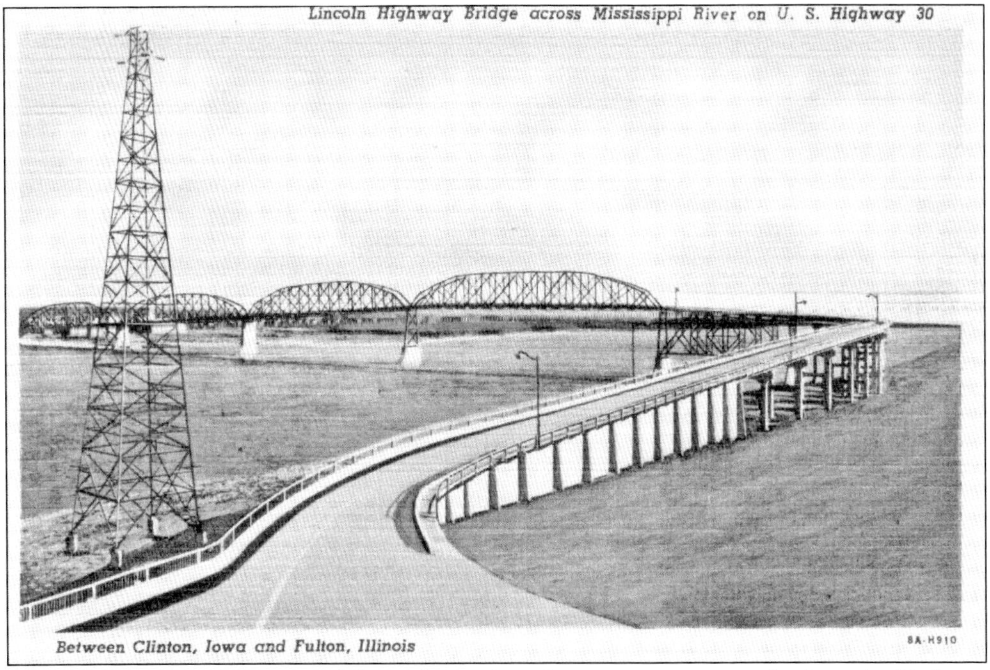


One of the most well-known of the early good roads organizations was the Lincoln Highway Association, which connected San Francisco with New York. Created in 1913, the Lincoln Highway intersected with the Dixie Highway in Illinois, Indiana, and Ohio, and provided a model for the Dixie Highway Association. (Courtesy of Jeffrey Lee Durbin.)

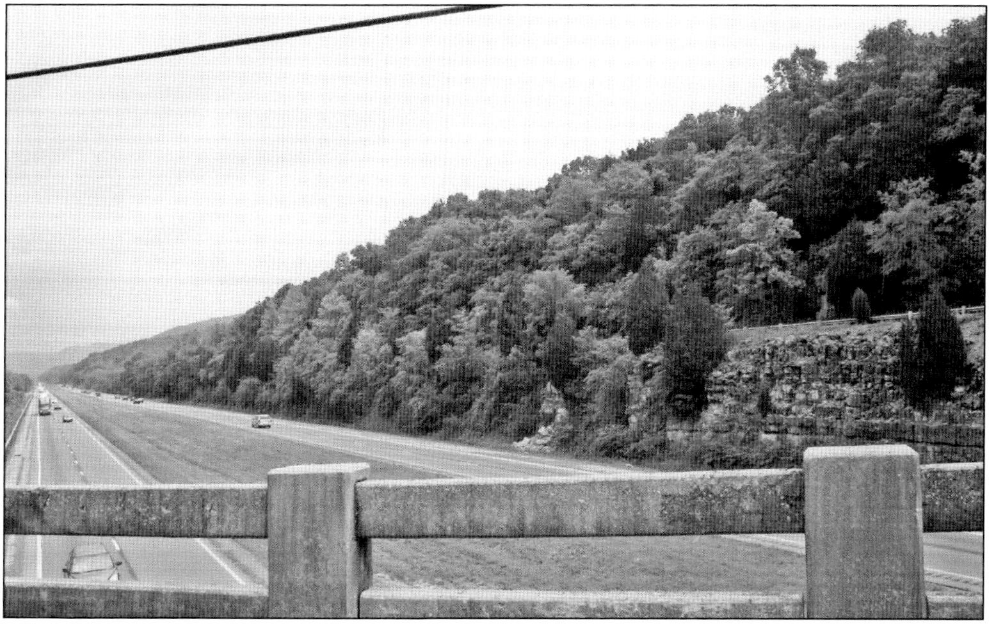

While the Good Roads Movement is linked to reform efforts in the early 20th century, the development of a national highway system continued throughout the 1900s. These earlier efforts established a precedent and created the infrastructure for federal investment at the state and local level for road building. This image shows Interstate 24 with the abandoned route of the Dixie Highway to the far right. (Courtesy of the author.)

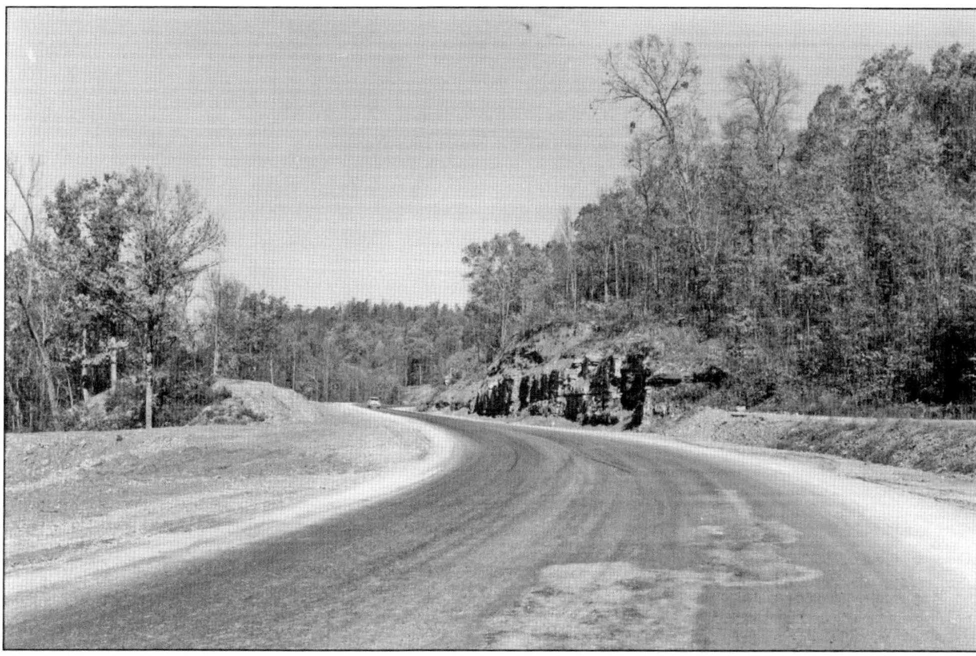

The development of the Dixie Highway demonstrates the success of the Good Roads Movement from both a private and public perspective. The road took more than a decade to finish but eventually was completed and brought change to the region. (Courtesy of the Tennessee State Library and Archives.)

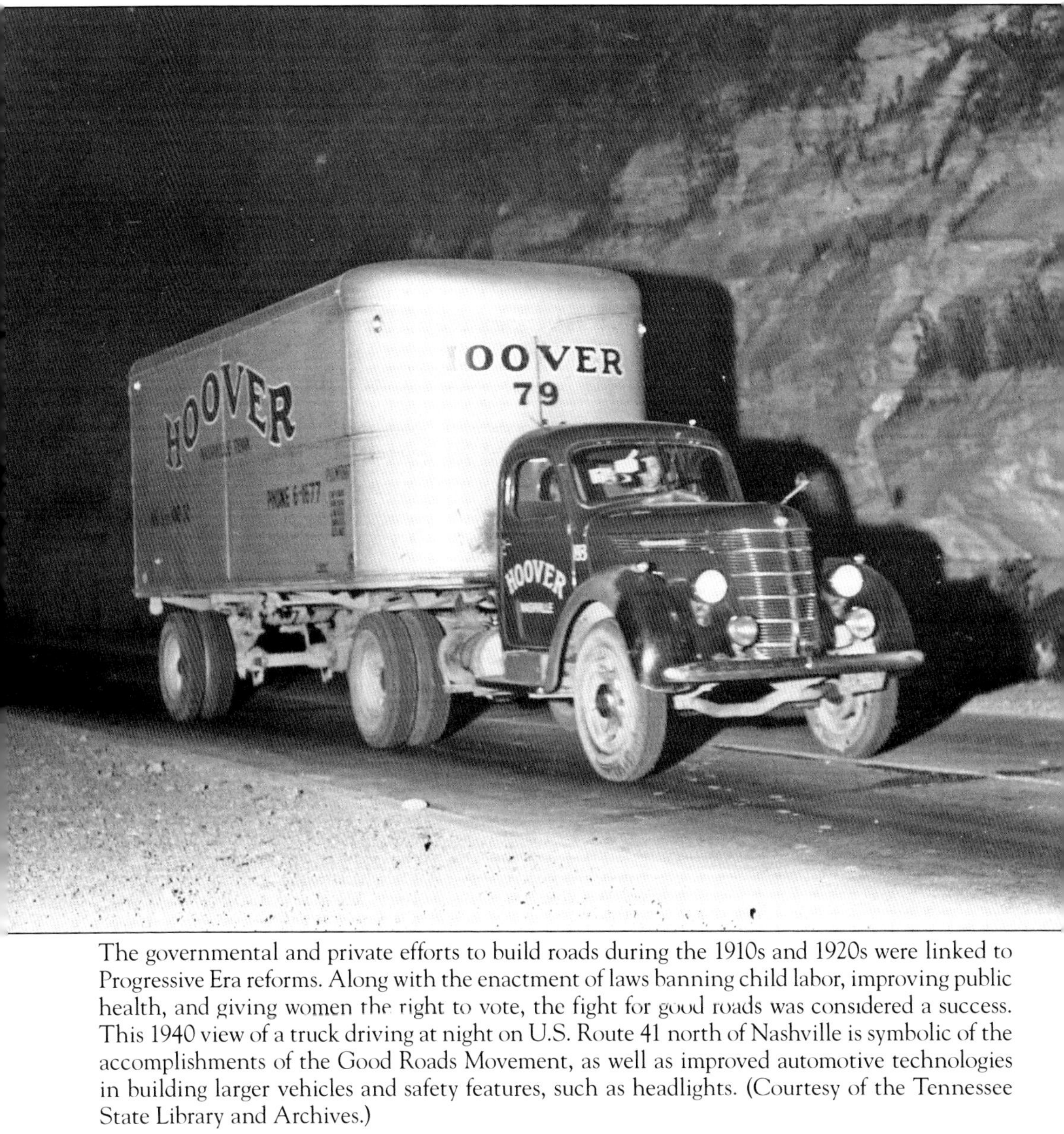


The governmental and private efforts to build roads during the 1910s and 1920s were linked to Progressive Era reforms. Along with the enactment of laws banning child labor, improving public health, and giving women the right to vote, the fight for good roads was considered a success. This 1940 view of a truck driving at night on U.S. Route 41 north of Nashville is symbolic of the accomplishments of the Good Roads Movement, as well as improved automotive technologies in building larger vehicles and safety features, such as headlights. (Courtesy of the Tennessee State Library and Archives.)

# *Two*

# Building the Highway

The Dixie Highway Association began as the dream of Carl Graham Fisher (1874–1939), a native of Indiana. Fisher was the founder of Prest-O-Lite Battery Company, which manufactured carbide battery–powered headlights for automobiles, and an owner of the Indianapolis Motor Speedway. Having already made a fortune in his earlier ventures, Fisher realized the potential for making money in anything automobile related.

After spending his honeymoon in Florida in 1910, Fisher began to purchase large amounts of land in south Florida for future development. Fisher knew that he had to get people to Florida in order to make money from his investments, which in turn meant there had to be roads connecting the North and the South. His goal was for people to be able to drive all the way to Florida with relative ease without being sidetracked.

As an early leader of the Lincoln Highway Association, Fisher knew how to promote roads. He used this experience to convince acquaintance W. S. Gilbreath, a businessman from Detroit, Michigan, to help launch a north-south highway. By the fall of 1914, Fisher and Gilbreath were gaining support for the project. Both Fisher and Gilbreath have been referred to as the "father of the Dixie Highway" for their role in its creation.

Indiana governor Samuel M. Ralston and Tennessee governor Tom C. Rye called an organizational meeting of the Dixie Highway Association for April 3, 1915, in Chattanooga. More than 5,000 people attended this first meeting, including governors from Indiana, Illinois, Ohio, Kentucky, Tennessee, Georgia, and Florida. The purpose of the meeting was to set the route and elect officers and directors of the Dixie Highway Association.

The meeting led to the creation of an organization whose purpose was to construct a permanent highway from a point on the Lincoln Highway near Chicago through Chattanooga to Miami. The route was soon extended to Mackinaw, Michigan, in May 1915 and again in 1917 at the request of Michigan governor Woodbridge Nathan Ferris to Sault Ste. Marie.

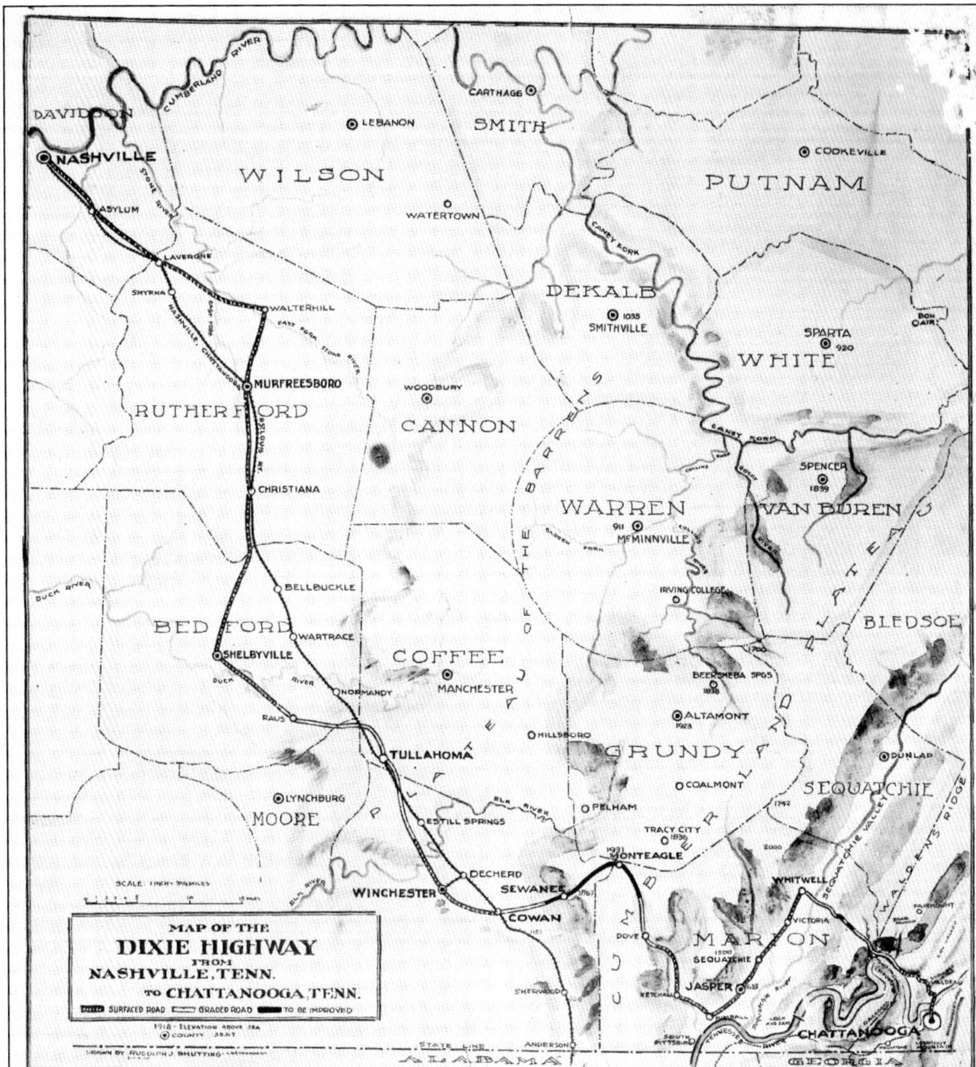


Rudolph Shutting (1878–1951) drew this 1918 map of the Dixie Highway from Nashville to Chattanooga. From Nashville to just south of Shelbyville, the road is surfaced, as are sections around Winchester, Jasper, Whitwell, and Chattanooga. The Monteagle section is designated as "to be improved" and the other sections as "graded." It was another nine years before the road was considered complete, with the section over Monteagle the last to be completed. The Nashville, Chattanooga, and St. Louis Railroad (NC&StL) is visible running roughly along the highway from Nashville to Cowan and then heading south into Alabama at Anderson, Tennessee. The artist Shutting worked as a draftsman for the U.S. Army Corps of Engineers and eventually opened his own business in Chattanooga, advertising himself as "R. J. Shutting Bird's-Eye View Artist," who could do high-quality drawings, maps, postcards, letterhead, and more. (Courtesy of the Tennessee State Library and Archives.)

Using his experience with the Lincoln Highway Association, Carl Graham Fisher garnered support for forming a north-south road association that became the Dixie Highway Association. He first contacted his business associates, and then together they began convincing elected officials to put their weight behind the road. (Courtesy of the Library of Congress.)

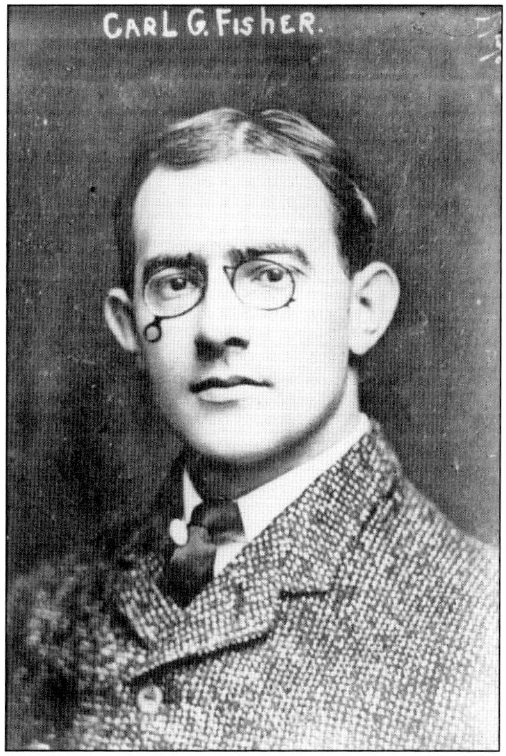


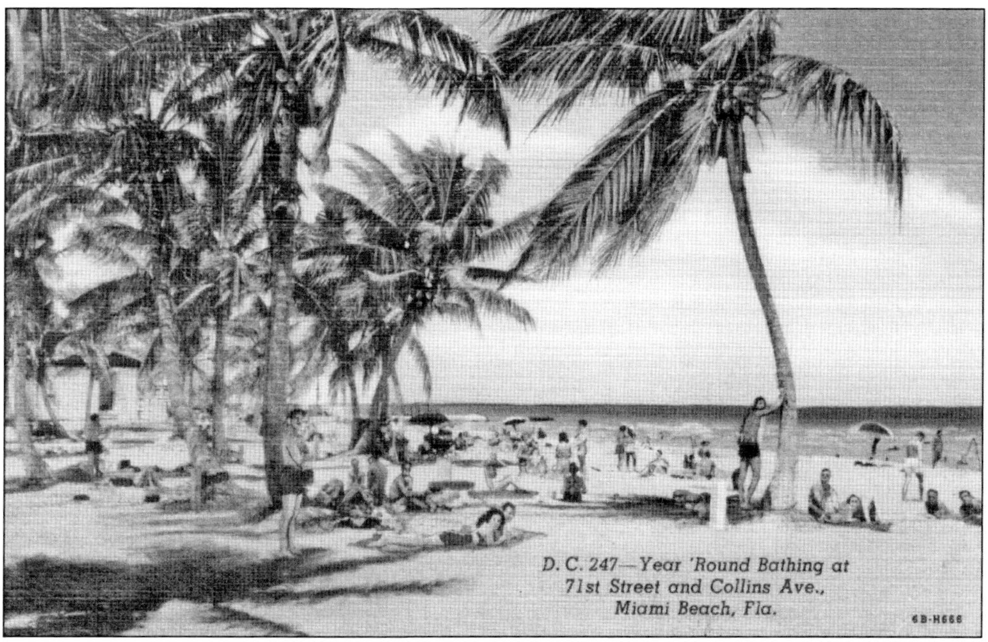


Carl Graham Fisher helped develop Miami Beach, located at the terminus of the Dixie Highway at the southern tip of Florida. Extremely successful, he was one of the biggest boosters of the 1920s real estate boom in Florida. The Dixie Highway aided in his success until he lost everything in the bust following the boom in the late 1920s and the stock market crash of 1929. (Courtesy of the author.)

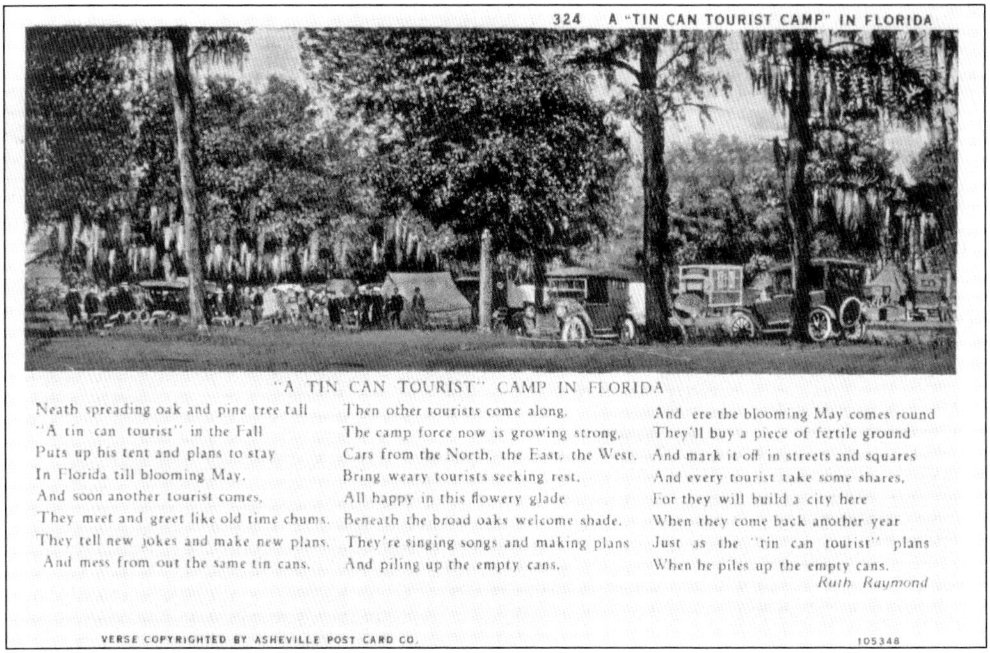


As Carl Graham Fisher envisioned, tourists flocked to Florida, traveling down the Dixie Highway from all across the Midwest. The "tin can" tourist was a popular site along the highway, loaded with luggage, often broken down, and leaving behind tin cans—so much so, that the lore was captured in postcards. (Courtesy of the author.)

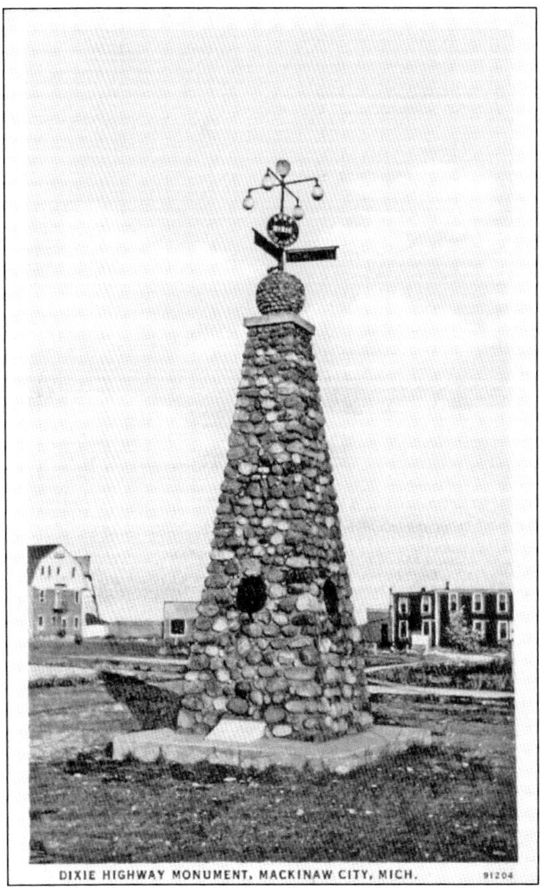


The original route was to be from a point on the Lincoln Highway near Chicago south through Chattanooga to Miami. The route was soon extended to Mackinaw City, Michigan, in May 1915 and again in 1917 at the request of Michigan governor Woodbridge Nathan Ferris to Sault Ste. Marie, and eventually to Ontario, Canada. This image shows the Dixie Highway monument in Mackinaw City. The sign on the top of the monument reads, "Apex Dixie Highway." (Courtesy of the author.)

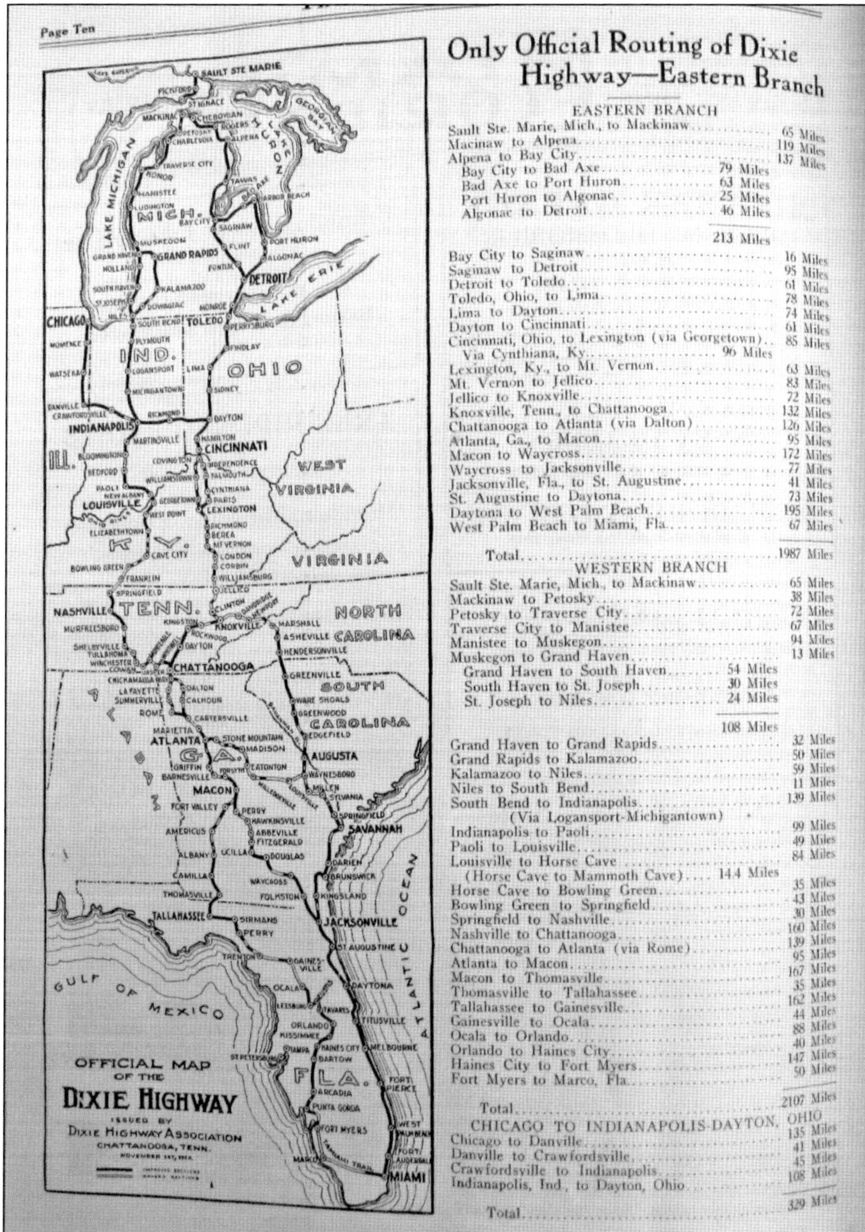

Page Ten

## Only Official Routing of Dixie Highway—Eastern Branch

EASTERN BRANCH

| | | |
|---|---|---|
| Sault Ste. Marie, Mich., to Mackinaw | | 65 Miles |
| Macinaw to Alpena | | 119 Miles |
| Alpena to Bay City | | 137 Miles |
| Bay City to Bad Axe | 79 Miles | |
| Bad Axe to Port Huron | 63 Miles | |
| Port Huron to Algonac | 25 Miles | |
| Algonac to Detroit | 46 Miles | |
| | 213 Miles | |
| Bay City to Saginaw | | 16 Miles |
| Saginaw to Detroit | | 95 Miles |
| Detroit to Toledo | | 61 Miles |
| Toledo, Ohio, to Lima | | 78 Miles |
| Lima to Dayton | | 74 Miles |
| Dayton to Cincinnati | | 61 Miles |
| Cincinnati, Ohio, to Lexington (via Georgetown) | | 85 Miles |
| Via Cynthiana, Ky | 96 Miles | |
| Lexington, Ky., to Mt. Vernon | | 63 Miles |
| Mt. Vernon to Jellico | | 83 Miles |
| Jellico to Knoxville | | 72 Miles |
| Knoxville, Tenn., to Chattanooga | | 132 Miles |
| Chattanooga to Atlanta (via Dalton) | | 126 Miles |
| Atlanta, Ga., to Macon | | 95 Miles |
| Macon to Waycross | | 172 Miles |
| Waycross to Jacksonville | | 77 Miles |
| Jacksonville, Fla., to St. Augustine | | 41 Miles |
| St. Augustine to Daytona | | 73 Miles |
| Daytona to West Palm Beach | | 195 Miles |
| West Palm Beach to Miami, Fla | | 67 Miles |
| Total | | 1987 Miles |

WESTERN BRANCH

| | | |
|---|---|---|
| Sault Ste. Marie, Mich., to Mackinaw | | 65 Miles |
| Mackinaw to Petosky | | 38 Miles |
| Petosky to Traverse City | | 72 Miles |
| Traverse City to Manistee | | 67 Miles |
| Manistee to Muskegon | | 94 Miles |
| Muskegon to Grand Haven | | 13 Miles |
| Grand Haven to South Haven | 54 Miles | |
| South Haven to St. Joseph | 30 Miles | |
| St. Joseph to Niles | 24 Miles | |
| | 108 Miles | |
| Grand Haven to Grand Rapids | | 32 Miles |
| Grand Rapids to Kalamazoo | | 50 Miles |
| Kalamazoo to Niles | | 59 Miles |
| Niles to South Bend | | 11 Miles |
| South Bend to Indianapolis (Via Logansport-Michigantown) | | 139 Miles |
| Indianapolis to Paoli | | 99 Miles |
| Paoli to Louisville | | 49 Miles |
| Louisville to Horse Cave | | 84 Miles |
| (Horse Cave to Mammoth Cave) | 14.4 Miles | |
| Horse Cave to Bowling Green | | 35 Miles |
| Bowling Green to Springfield | | 43 Miles |
| Springfield to Nashville | | 30 Miles |
| Nashville to Chattanooga | | 160 Miles |
| Chattanooga to Atlanta (via Rome) | | 139 Miles |
| Atlanta to Macon | | 95 Miles |
| Macon to Thomasville | | 167 Miles |
| Thomasville to Tallahassee | | 35 Miles |
| Tallahassee to Gainesville | | 162 Miles |
| Gainesville to Ocala | | 44 Miles |
| Ocala to Orlando | | 88 Miles |
| Orlando to Haines City | | 40 Miles |
| Haines City to Fort Myers | | 147 Miles |
| Fort Myers to Marco, Fla | | 50 Miles |
| Total | | 2107 Miles |

CHICAGO TO INDIANAPOLIS-DAYTON, OHIO

| | |
|---|---|
| Chicago to Danville | 135 Miles |
| Danville to Crawfordsville | 41 Miles |
| Crawfordsville to Indianapolis | 45 Miles |
| Indianapolis, Ind., to Dayton, Ohio | 108 Miles |
| Total | 329 Miles |



This map of the route of the Dixie Highway came from the May 1924 issue of *The Dixie Highway* magazine and shows routes of both the eastern and western branches of the road from Sault Ste. Marie, Michigan, to Miami, Florida. Maps were included in each issue of the magazine and included routing directions and advice to travelers. Readers had the opportunity to write in and ask questions regarding the best route to take. The maps also showed the progress of construction along both divisions. At the time of this publication, the road in Tennessee had not been completed in several sections, including north of Springfield, south of Murfreesboro, and between Monteagle and Whitwell. Notice that both the eastern and western divisions traveled through Chattanooga, Tennessee, and Atlanta, Georgia. (Courtesy of the Chattanooga–Hamilton County Bicentennial Library.)

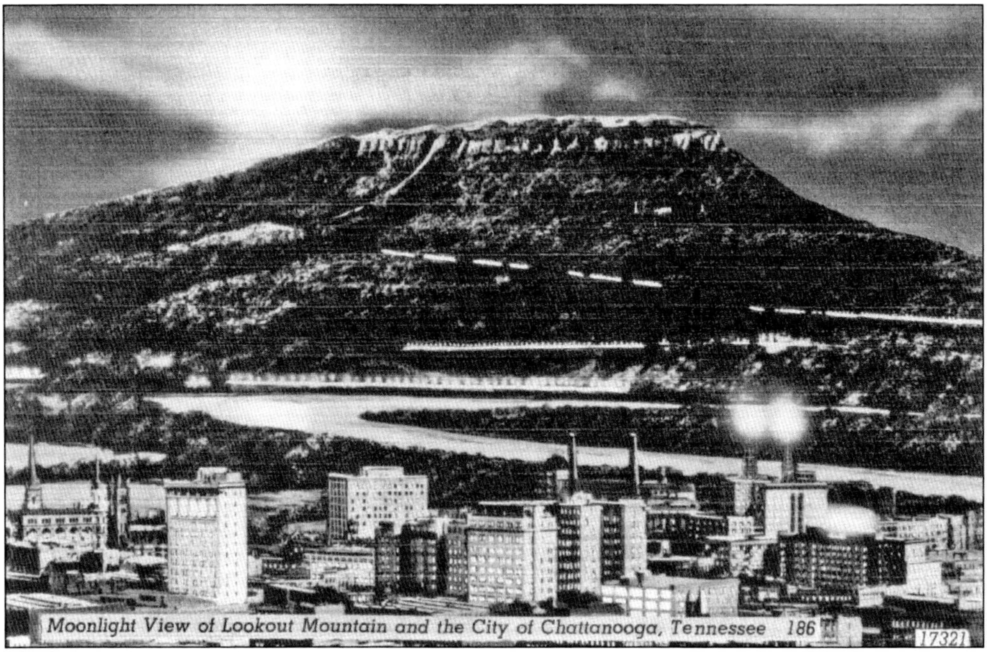


Roughly the halfway point of the Dixie Highway and headquarters for the offices, Chattanooga played a central role in the development of the road. Local businessmen made the majority of the initial investment to incorporate the Dixie Highway Association, bought advertisements in *The Dixie Highway* magazine, and promoted construction of the road across the region. (Courtesy of the author.)

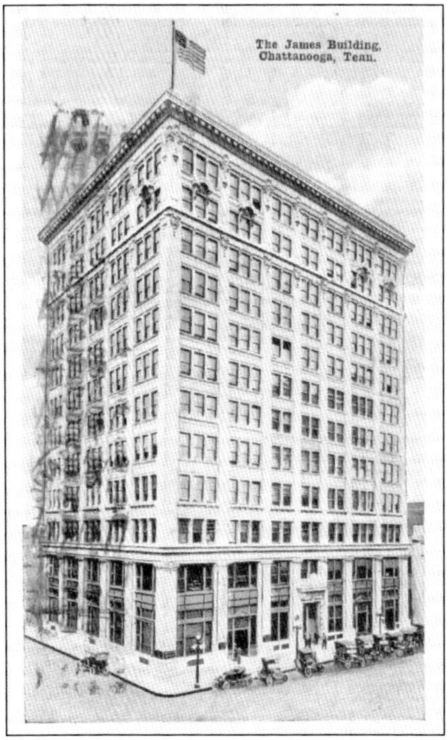


Located one block off the Dixie Highway, Chattanooga's first skyscraper—the James Building, constructed in 1907—was named for its developer, Charles E. James, president of the Signal Mountain Land Company. James was one of the original founders and incorporators of the Dixie Highway Association and was elected to be its first president but then refused to serve after a dispute over the route. (Courtesy of Jeffrey Lee Durbin.)

Chattanooga judge Michael Morrison Allison was elected vice president of the Dixie Highway Association and then became president when the position was refused by Charles E. James. Allison remained an extremely active president until the Dixie Highway Association disbanded in 1927 following the completion of the highway. (Courtesy of the Chattanooga–Hamilton County Bicentennial Library.)

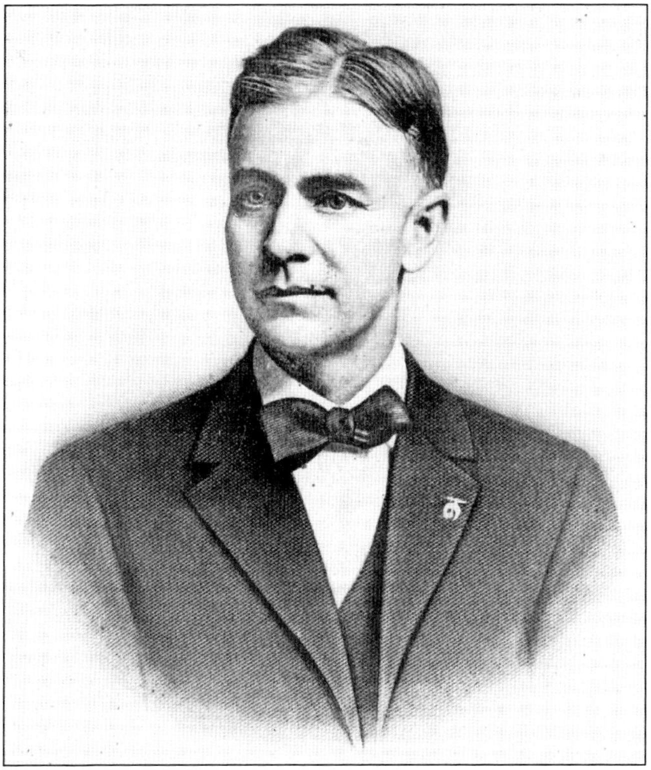

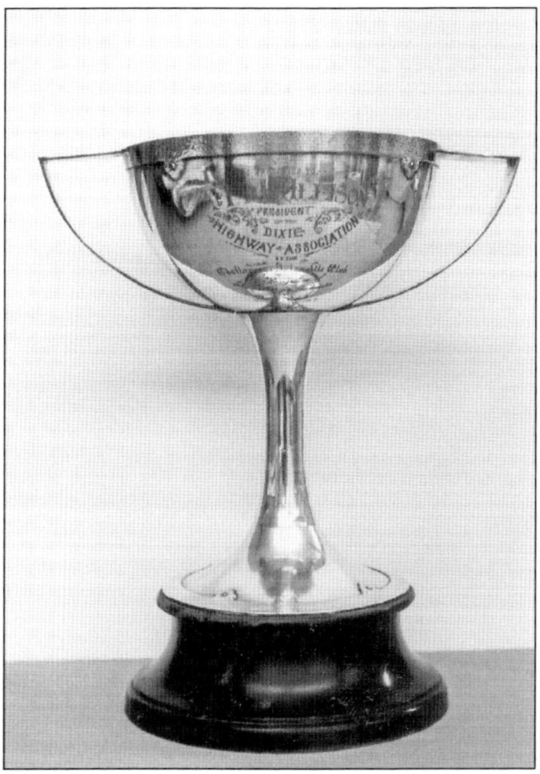


The Chattanooga Automobile Club presented this silver cup to Judge Michael M. Allison for his dedication and commitment to the Dixie Highway Association. The cup reads, "in recognition of his labors in the cause of better roads." (Artifact located in the Chattanooga Regional History Museum, now Chattanooga History Center. Photograph by the author with permission.)

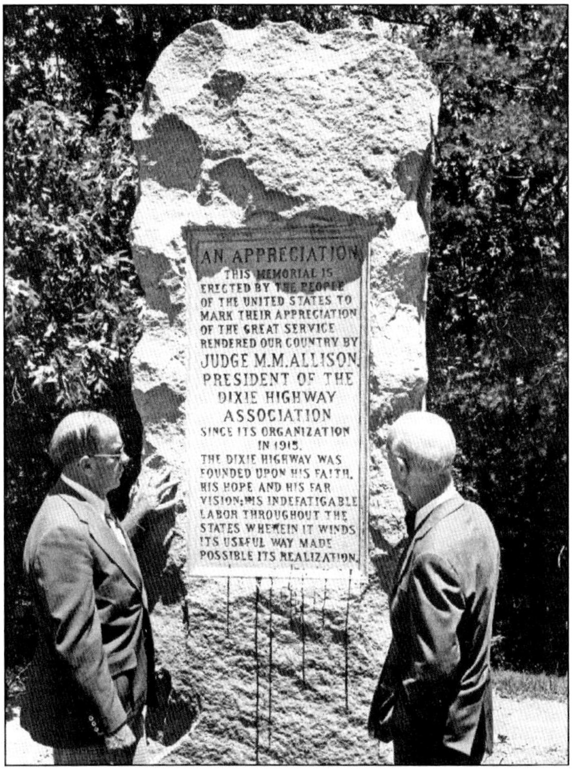


Allison's critical role in the Dixie Highway Association was memorialized by a monument erected on April 25, 1924, at Walden's Ridge above Chattanooga on the Dixie Highway. This 1976 photograph was taken on or around the time the Chattanooga Automobile Club merged with the Mid-South Automobile Club. Members Clarence Kolwyck and Ralph G. Lewis Jr. are in the picture. (Courtesy of the Chattanooga–Hamilton County Bicentennial Library.)

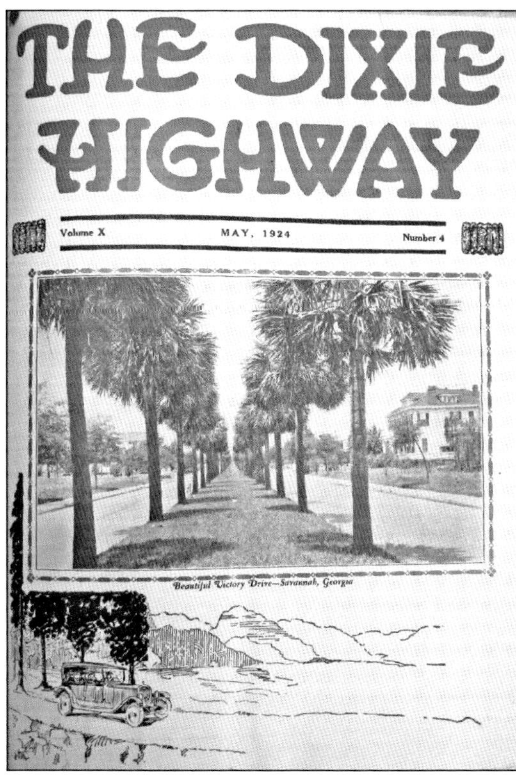


In 1916, *The Dixie Highway* magazine was published to stimulate interest in the road. Beginning as a semiweekly newspaper, it developed into a monthly publication that lasted until the death of Allison in 1931. Even though the Dixie Highway Association was essentially an all-male organization, the first and last editors of its publication were women—Nellie Perry Fyffe and Maude Roberts. (Courtesy of the Chattanooga–Hamilton County Bicentennial Library.)

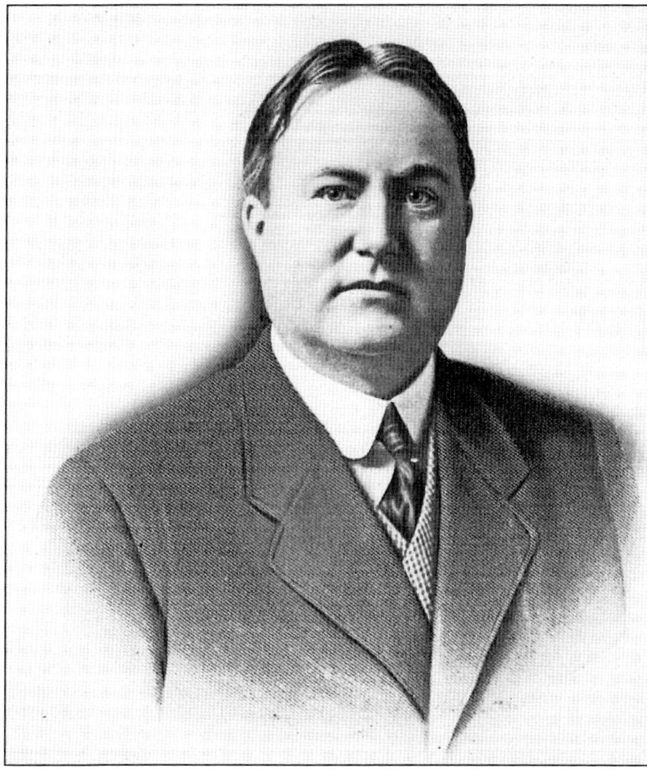

John A. Patten Sr. was president of the Chattanooga Medicine Company. He, along with 11 other men, was a founder of the Dixie Highway Association. Each of the founders was required to give $1,000 for membership. He was also one of the original incorporators of the association. (Courtesy of the Chattanooga–Hamilton County Bicentennial Library.)

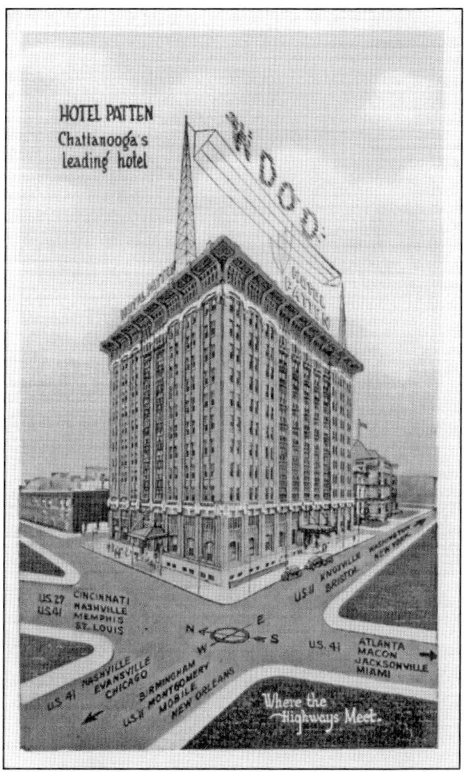


The Hotel Patten opened in 1908 on Market Street along the path of what became the route of the Dixie Highway. The Chattanooga hotel was named after John A. Patten and his wealthy uncle after they helped finance its construction. Not only was the hotel located at the junction of highways 41, 11, and 27, it served as the headquarters of the Dixie Highway Association and the Chattanooga Automobile Club. (Courtesy of the author.)

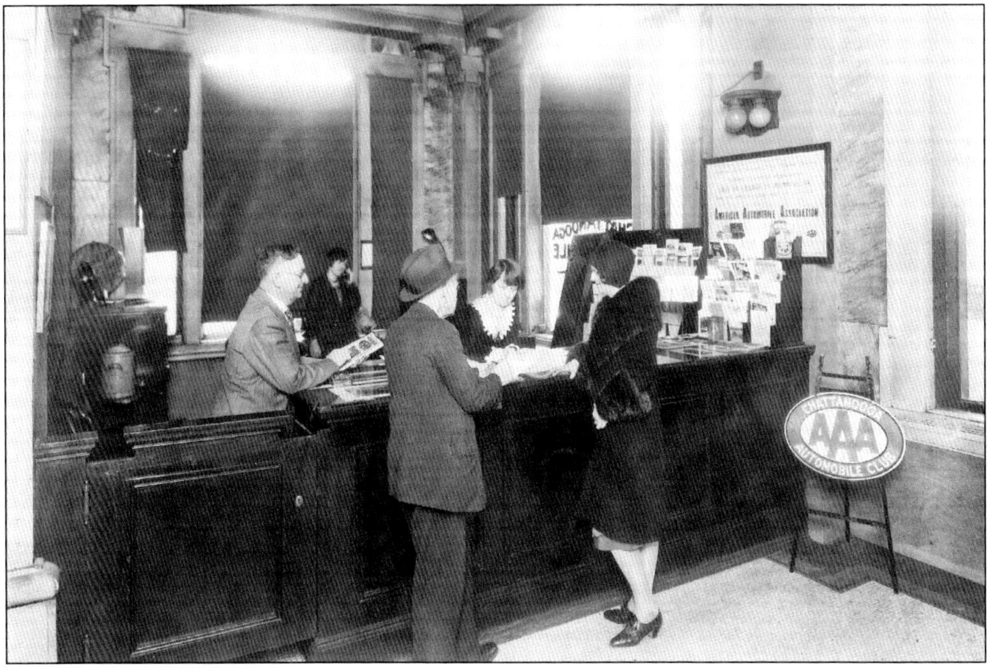


The interior of the Hotel Patten is shown in this image with the office of the Chattanooga Automobile Club, an affiliate of the American Automobile Association (AAA). Arguably the strongest supporter of the Dixie Highway Association, the club's members were extremely active in and generous to the Dixie Highway Association. (Courtesy of the Chattanooga–Hamilton County Bicentennial Library.)

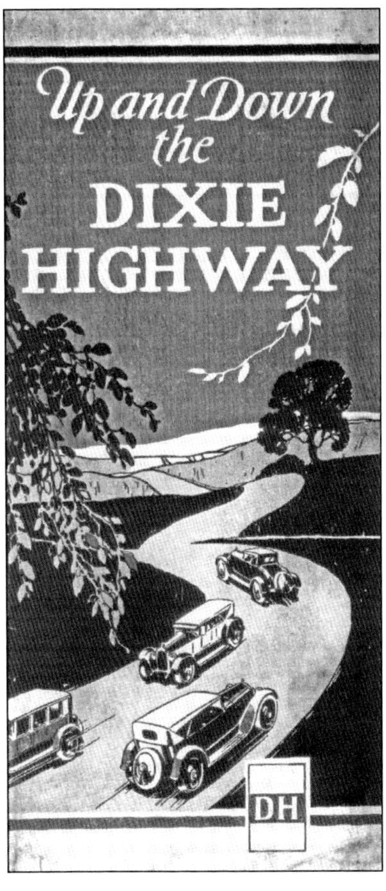


Travel brochures, such as this one entitled "Up and Down the Dixie Highway," were critical in promoting the highway to tourists. Frequently, these brochures featured advertisements, travel advice, and the hotels along the route. Note the official Dixie Highway logo in the bottom right corner. (Courtesy of the Chattanooga Regional History Museum.)

T. R. Preston, president of the Hamilton National Bank at Seventh and Market Streets along the Dixie Highway, was one of the original founding members of the Dixie Highway Association. Shown in this photograph, his bank was a neighbor of the Dixie Highway. (Courtesy of the Chattanooga–Hamilton County Bicentennial Library.)

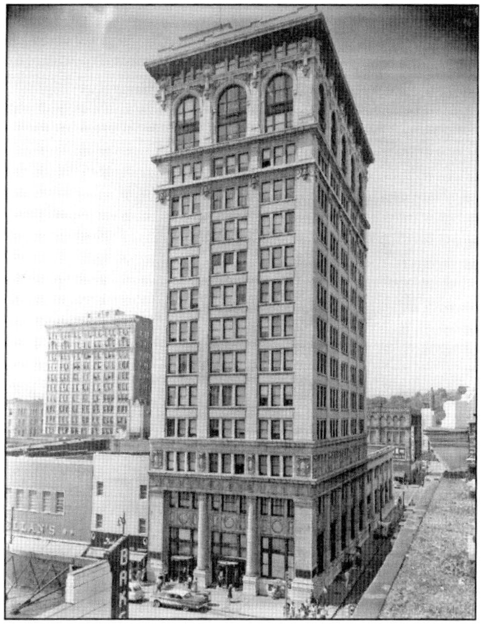

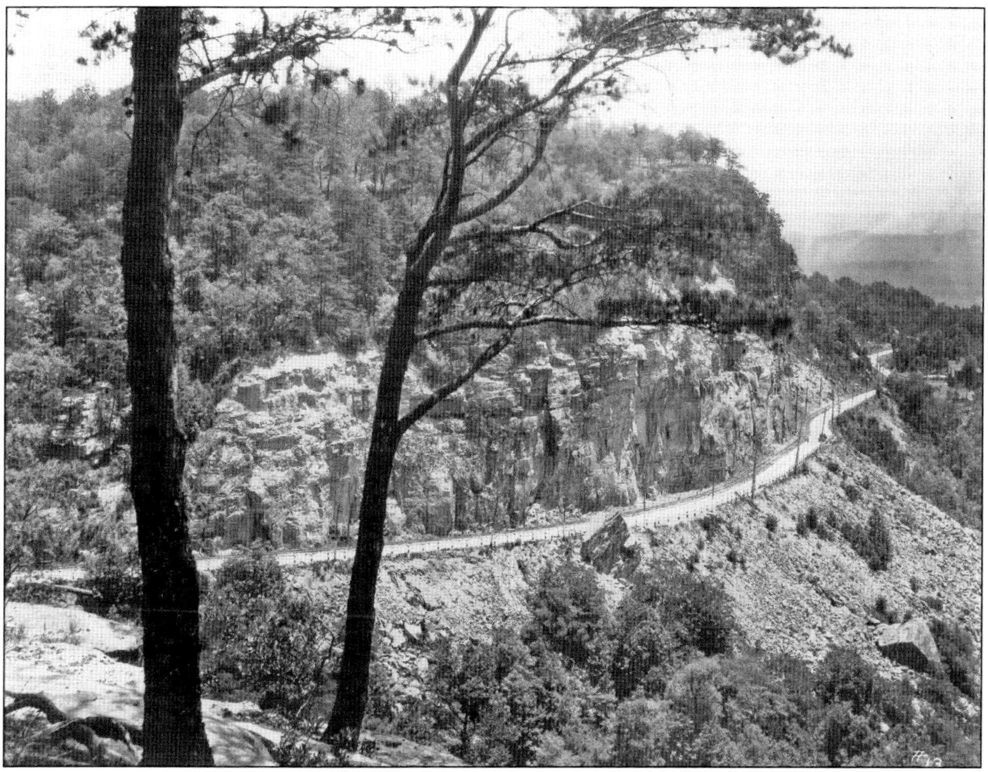

This photograph shows the improved road to Signal Mountain, a result of the efforts of many people like Mayor Richard Hardy (1868–1927) of Chattanooga. Hardy was president of Dixie Portland Cement Company and a founding member of the Dixie Highway Association. Mayor Hardy was extremely supportive of road-building projects. (Courtesy of the Chattanooga–Hamilton County Bicentennial Library.)

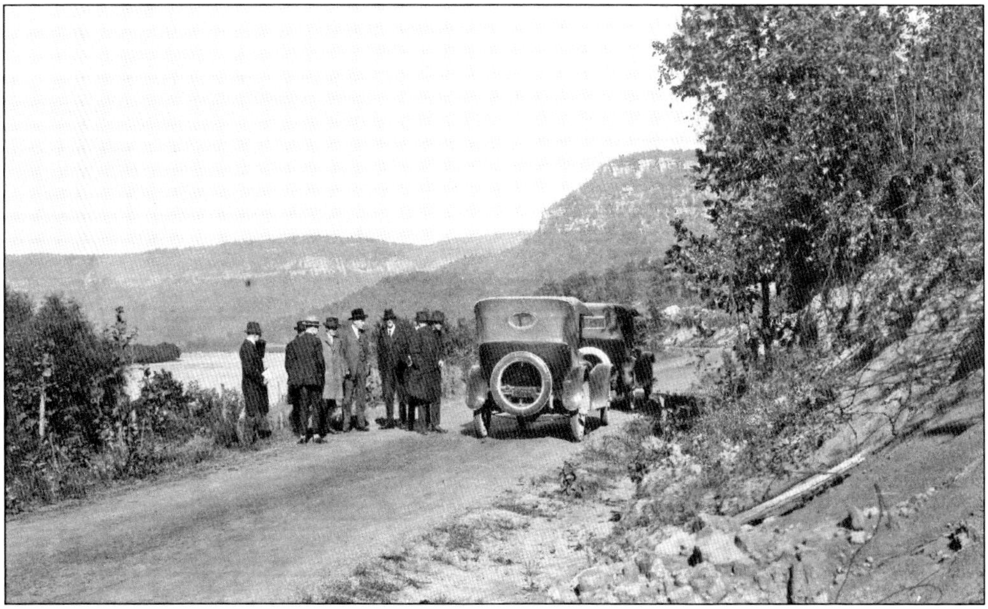

The Chattanooga Automobile Club was made up of road enthusiasts and businessmen who enjoyed traveling by car and saw the economic value of good roads in their community. This 1916 photograph depicts a club scouting trip to Nashville, during which participants traveled to check out road conditions and document the duration of their trips. (Courtesy of the Chattanooga–Hamilton County Bicentennial Library.)

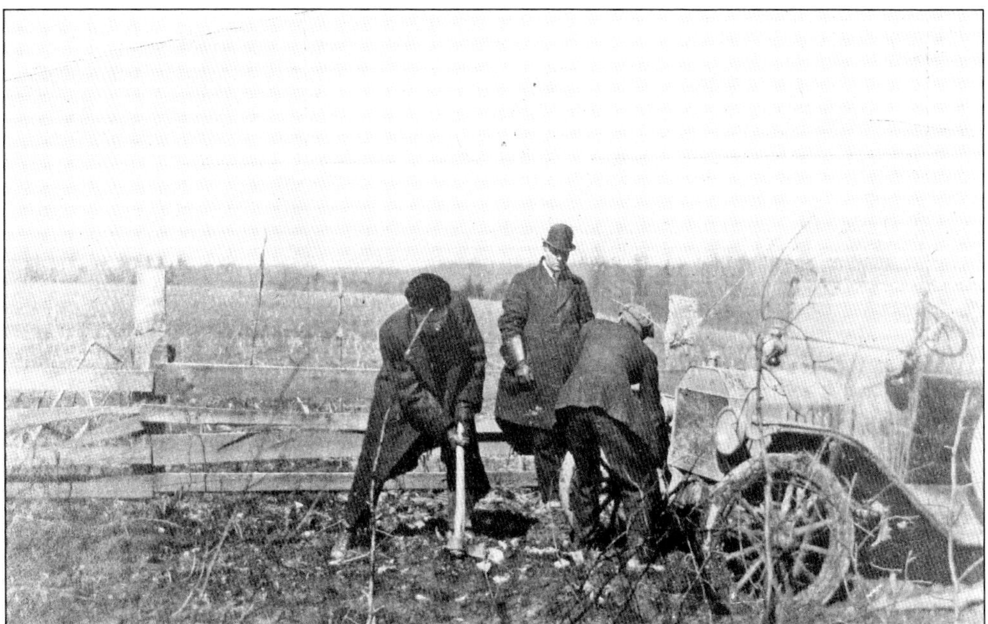

This photograph depicts a common scene along the highway—getting the car unstuck. These men are digging out a car on the road to Nashville. They are probably on a Chattanooga Automobile Club outing. Club member Fred Cautrell is in the derby hat, and the other two men are unidentified. (Courtesy of the Chattanooga–Hamilton County Bicentennial Library.)

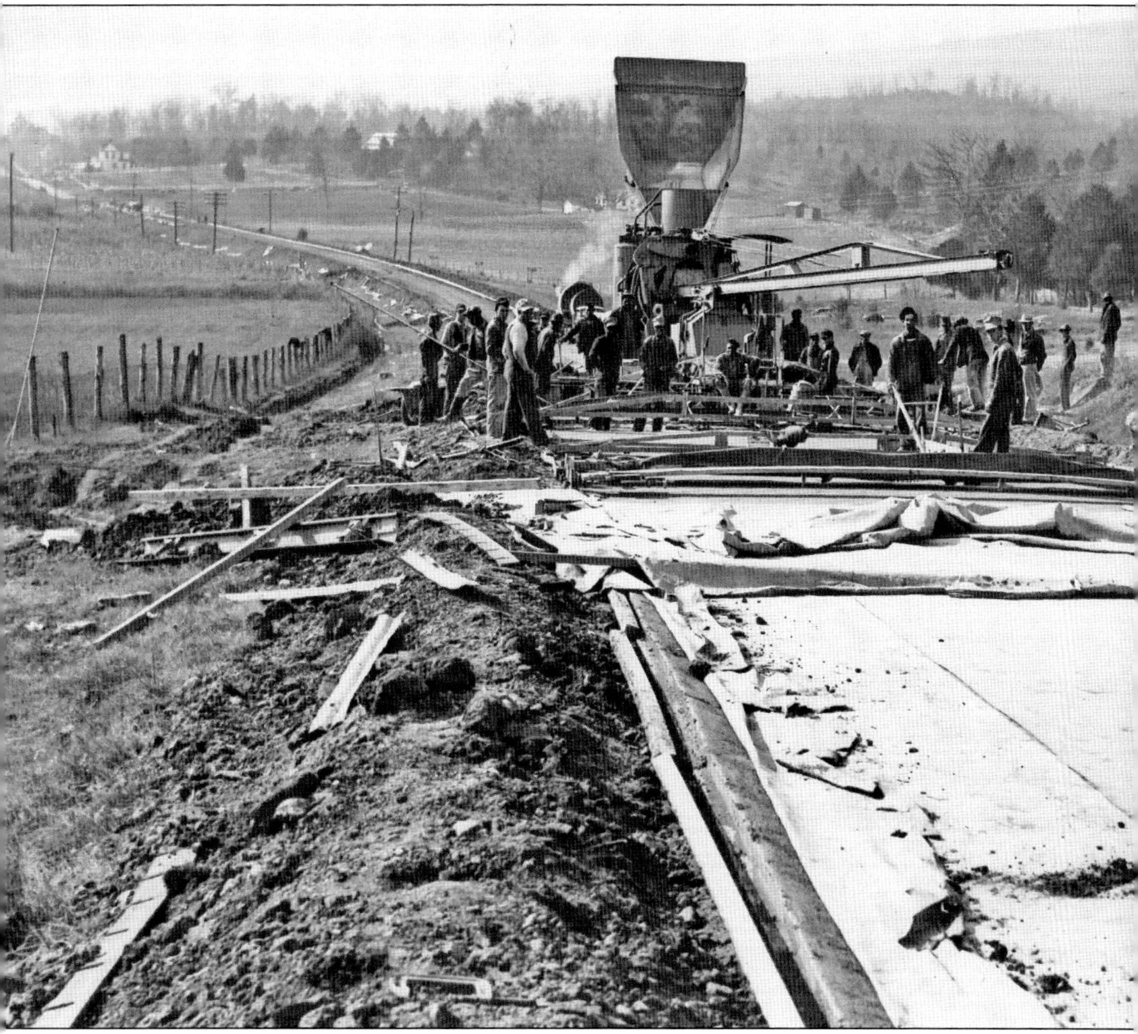

This *c.* 1917 photograph shows the actual construction of the Dixie Highway near Chattanooga. In some areas, the highway overlapped existing roads, but in other areas, a new road was built. The highway in both cases had to conform to the standards of the Dixie Highway Association. In the beginning, the association allowed local municipalities use the name Dixie Highway. However, the association soon began to require that the road be completed and meet all of its regulations before the road was officially designated. This required local governments to acquire land and right-of-ways to meet the standard road width. In Rutherford County, the quarterly court had to approve the purchase of land, address the complaints of citizens whose property had been damaged, and appropriate funds for new construction and maintenance of roads. (Courtesy of the Chattanooga–Hamilton County Bicentennial Library.)

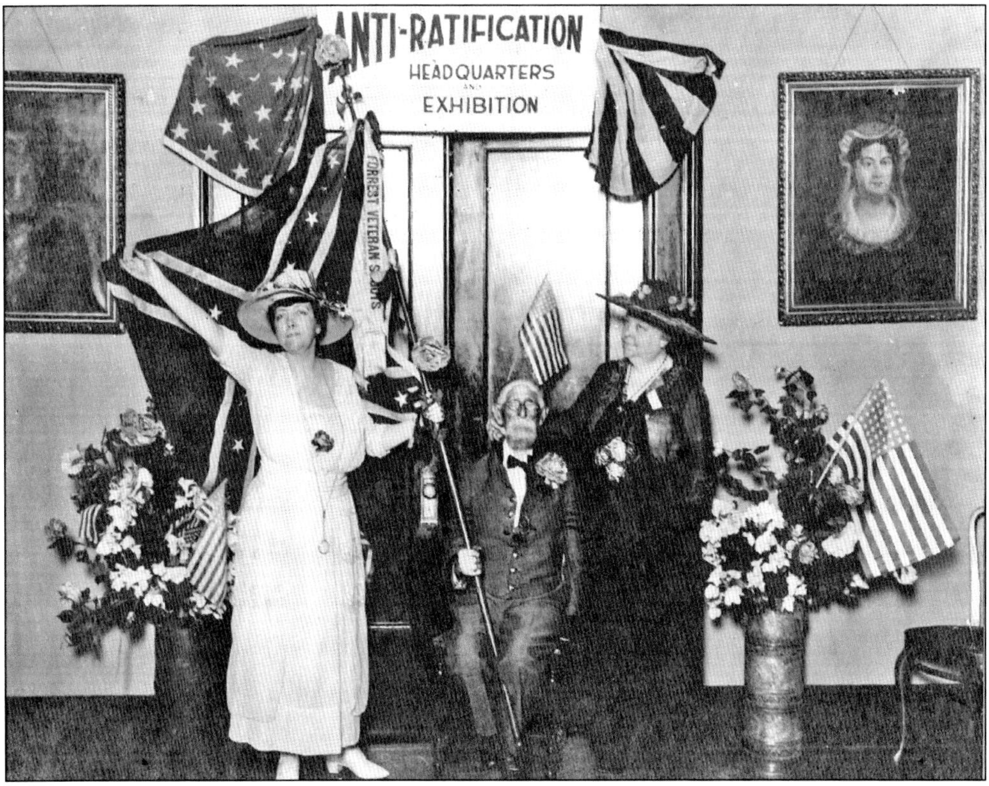


Josephine Anderson Pearson (1868–1944), chair of the Cumberland Division of the Dixie Highway Association, organized meetings to involve "female good roads enthusiasts" and wrote and spoke on the benefits of the highway to mountain women. Opposed to giving women the right to vote, this 1920 image shows Pearson with an unidentified man and Nina Pinkard, left, at an anti-suffrage event. (Courtesy of the Tennessee State Library and Archives.)

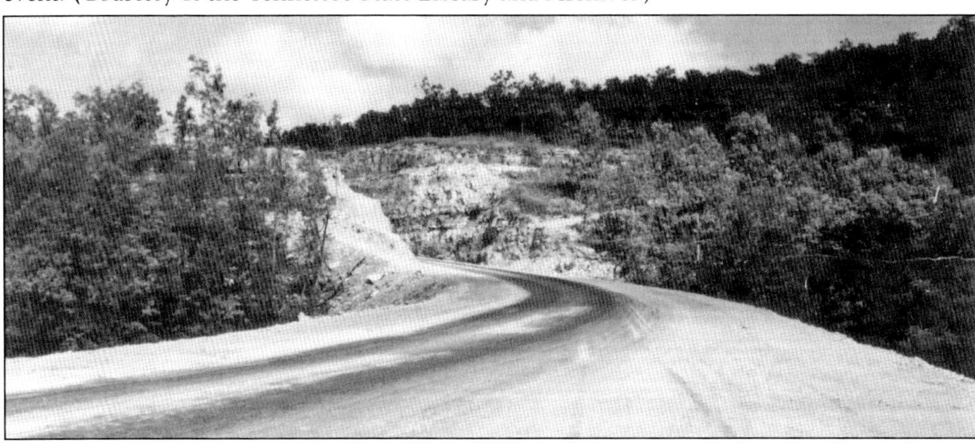

Living in Monteagle, Pearson sent out more than 6,000 letters to the residents of Marion County urging them to support the highway. Even though she had put in untold hours of work advocating for the highway in her region, when it came time to form a more formal organization in May 1918, the "men of Monteagle, Sewanee, and Tracy City desire[d] a strictly men's organization," as stated in a letter to Pearson from the secretary of the Dixie Highway Association. (Courtesy of Jeffrey Lee Durbin.)

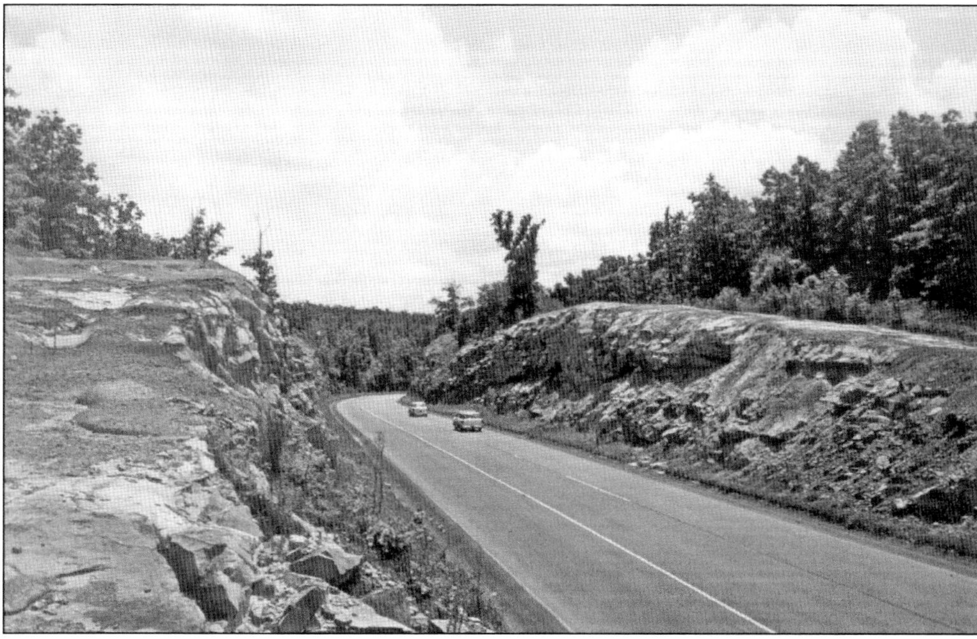

Completing the highway in Tennessee was especially difficult, because Monteagle Mountain blocked the completion of the Nashville-to-Chattanooga segment. The mountain itself was not the only obstacle preventing the construction of the road—Marion County did not have the means to finance the roads. (Courtesy of Jeffrey Lee Durbin.)

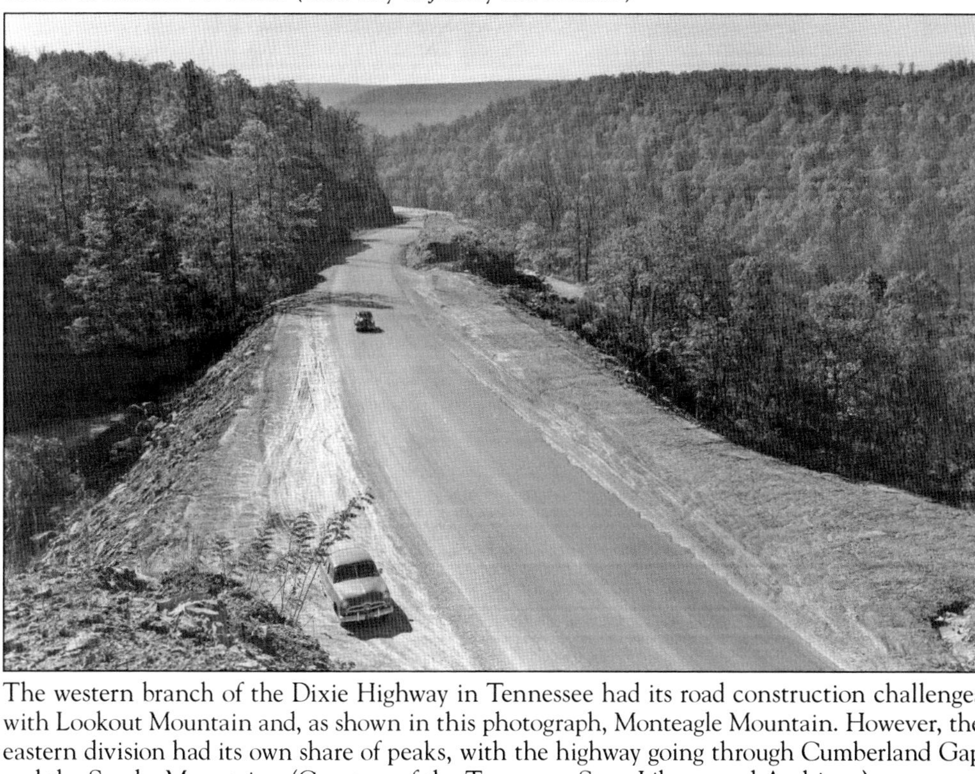

The western branch of the Dixie Highway in Tennessee had its road construction challenges with Lookout Mountain and, as shown in this photograph, Monteagle Mountain. However, the eastern division had its own share of peaks, with the highway going through Cumberland Gap and the Smoky Mountains. (Courtesy of the Tennessee State Library and Archives.)

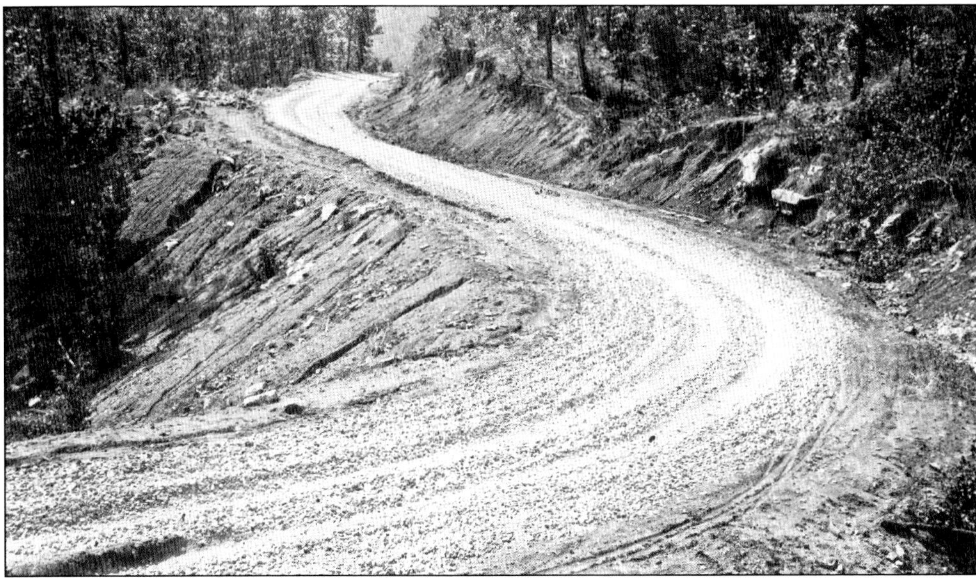

The Monteagle Mountain section of the highway in Marion County became the most widely known road problem in Tennessee, according to the "Biennial Report of the Commissioner of the Department of the Highways and Public Works for the Years of 1923 and 1924." In 1923, the State of Tennessee finally took over construction of this section of the highway, and after several more years, it was completed. It was the last link in the highway to be finished and was considered a nationwide concern because it linked the North with the South. A special state senate committee even made the trip from Nashville to Chattanooga in five-and-a-half hours, proving that the road was no longer a "mule hole." (Both, courtesy of the Tennessee State Library and Archives.)

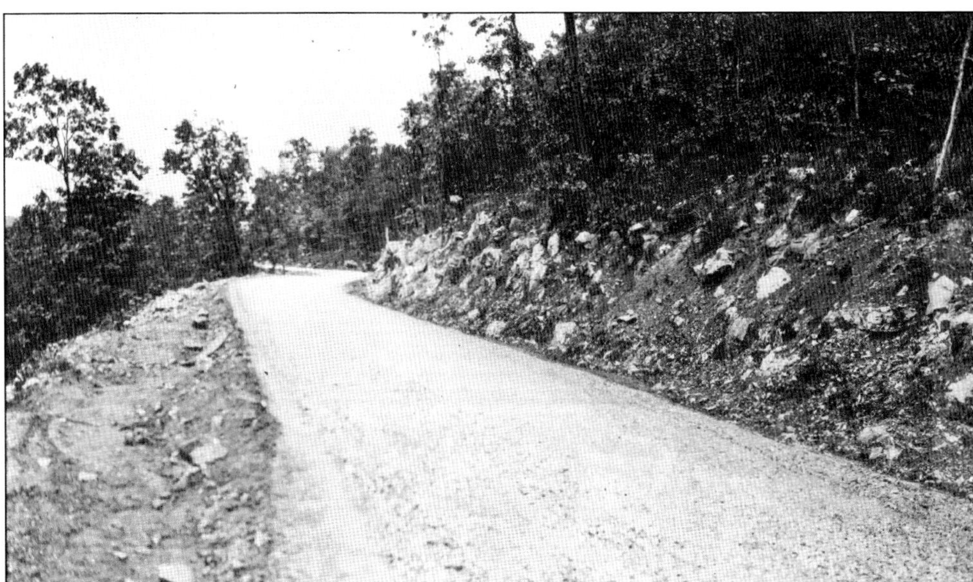

Under the leadership of Allison and Hamilton County judge Will Cummings, a 1919 state legislative act was passed to change the county line between Hamilton County and Marion County so that Hamilton County would finance the completion of the road. However, this section was not completed until the state provided assistance. (Courtesy of the Chattanooga–Hamilton County Bicentennial Library.)

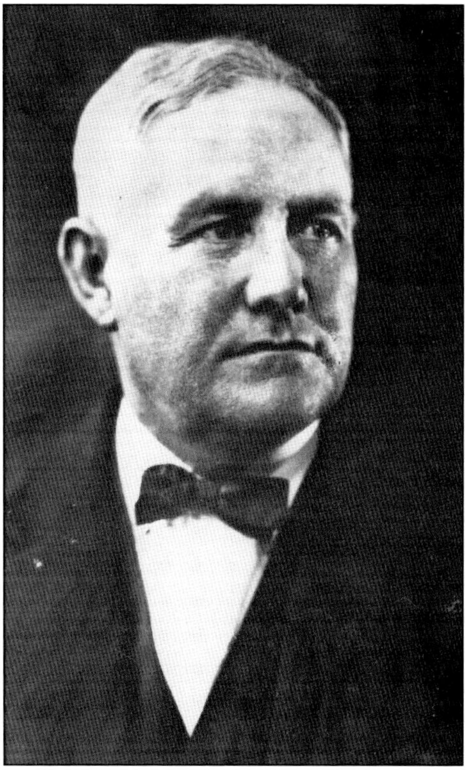

Located on the Cummings Highway, the Cummings House was the home of Judge Will Cummings (1870–1969), who was a Hamilton County judge from 1912 to 1918 and from 1926 to 1942. He was a strong proponent of developing roads and infrastructure in the region, including the Market Street Bridge, the Dixie Highway, the Chickamauga Dam, and the Bachman Tunnels. (Courtesy of the Chattanooga–Hamilton County Bicentennial Library.)

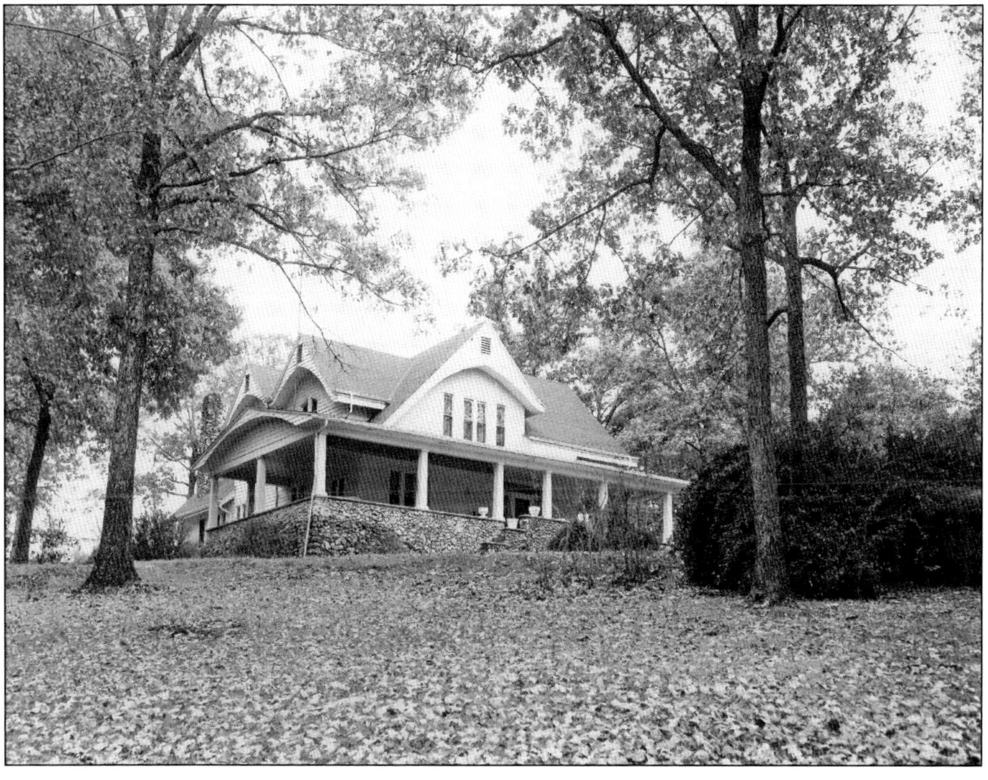

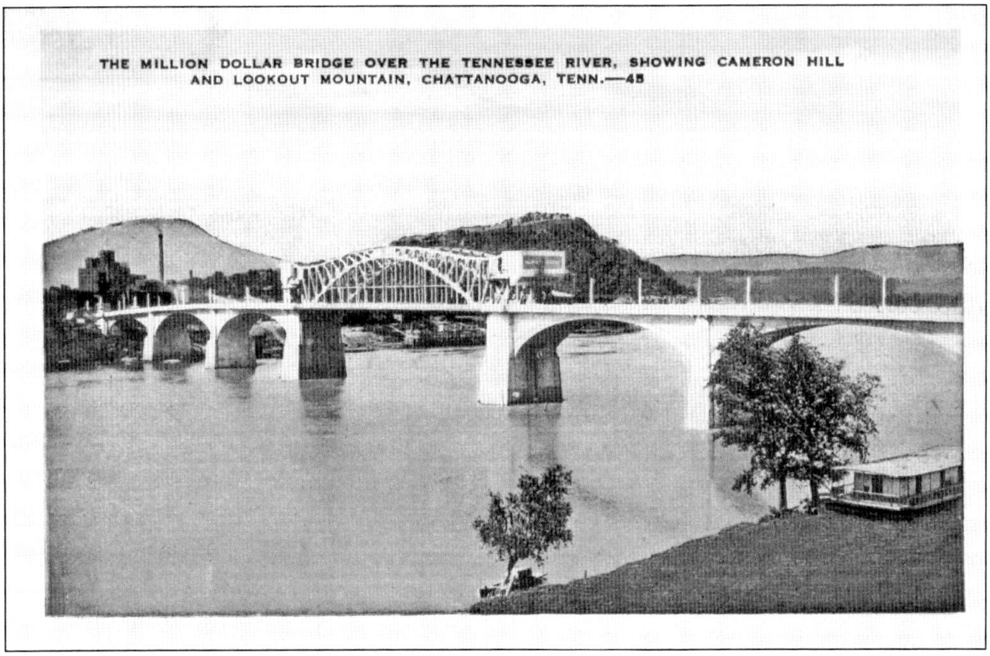


Elected to his judgeship in 1912, Cummings's first act as judge was to support the construction of the Market Street Bridge over the Tennessee River. In 1918, he lost his seat as his opponent accused him of wasting taxpayers' money, since the bridge ended up costing $1 million—hence its nickname on the postcard. (Courtesy of the author.)

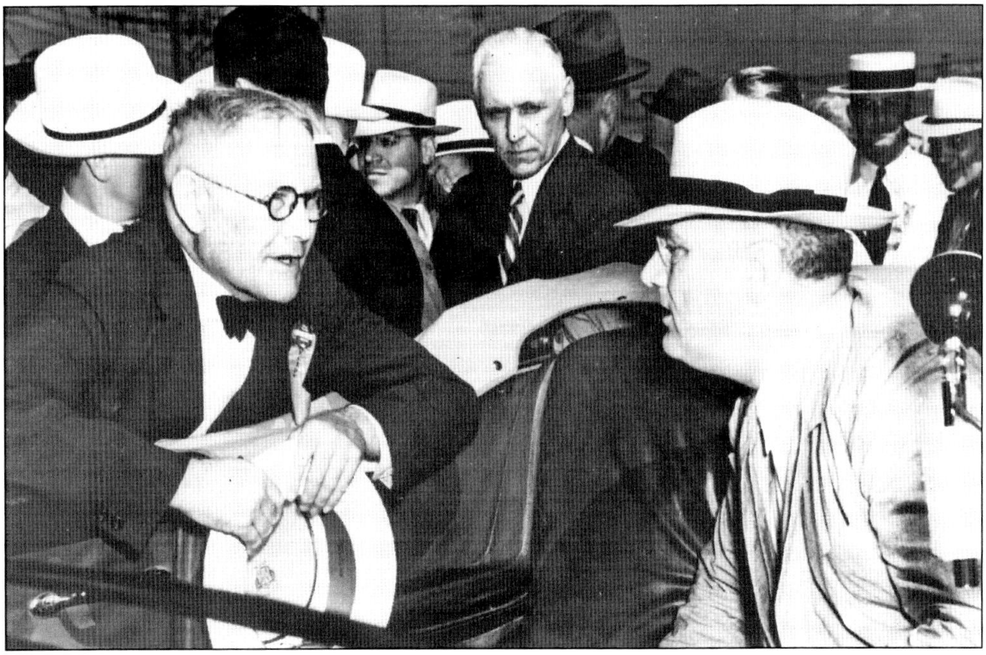

Cummings's commitment to improving his community continued from his early days as a member of the Dixie Highway Association to his 1930s work on getting the Chickamauga Dam completed. This photograph shows him with Pres. Franklin D. Roosevelt on the occasion of the dedication of the dam in 1940. (Courtesy of the Chattanooga–Hamilton County Bicentennial Library.)

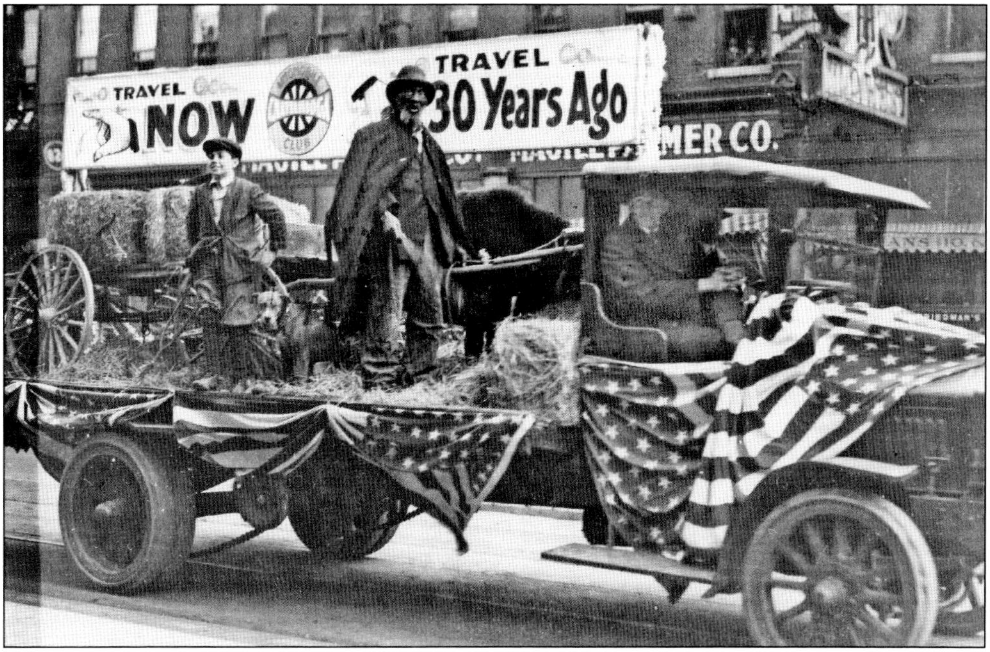


This photograph shows the Chattanooga Automobile Club float on Market Street in the Third Liberty Loan Parade in 1918. The float is an oxcart with banners reading "travel now, travel 30 years ago." Incorporated in 1907, the Chattanooga Automobile Club provided great support for the Dixie Highway Association. (Courtesy of the Chattanooga–Hamilton County Bicentennial Library.)

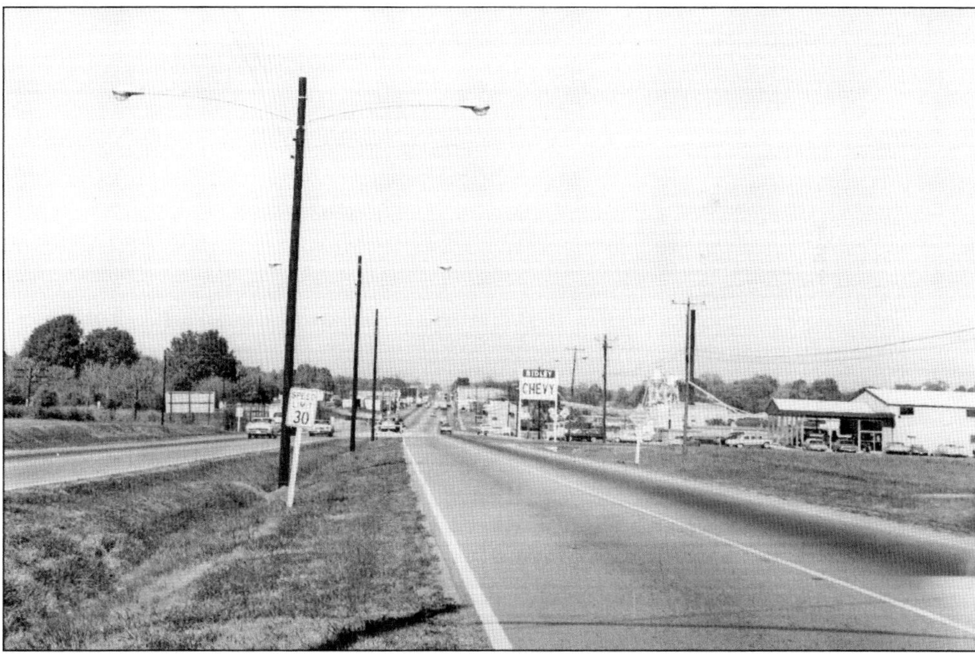


This 1965 view of U.S. Route 41 shows the nature of the road that bypassed the Dixie Highway in the 1950s in Rutherford County. The divided highway with grassy median and multiple lanes going in the same direction became common all over the country. (Courtesy of the Albert Gore Research Center, Middle Tennessee State University.)

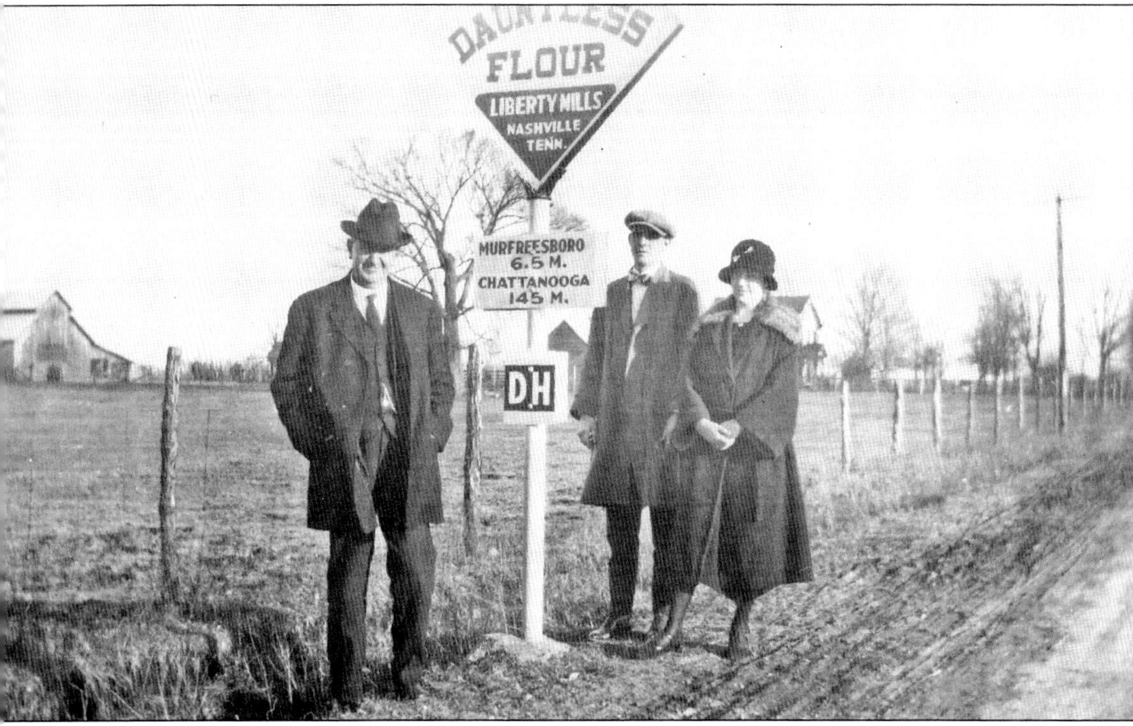


At the May 1916 Dixie Highway Association meeting in Detroit, Michigan, delegates decided to mark the Dixie Highway with white and red bands depicting the highway's initials, "D. H." These markers were to be placed on at least three telegraph or telephone poles on each side of all roads or at intersections with the signs 8 feet from the ground. This image shows an example of a Dixie Highway sign outside of Murfreesboro. This particular sign obviously did not meet the specifications outlined above. (Courtesy Lisa Ramsay.)

# *Three*

# Connecting the Places

Like other portions of the road, Tennessee's western branch took a circuitous route from north to south connecting cities to towns, crossroads to county seats, and nowhere to somewhere. The route of the Dixie Highway was not the straightest or most direct, but it was often the most practical considering the circumstances. Because there was little federal or state funding prior to 1916, all monies had to be raised locally. Therefore, counties and cities that could not or would not raise the money were bypassed, and the next county over was included on the route. Other reasons for the highway's crooked path were that each county determined the route within its own area and, in some Tennessee communities like Franklin and Marion Counties, the terrain mandated the path.

From the beginning, the route was the focus of heated debates among the proponents of the Dixie Highway. According to a 1925 *Chattanooga Times* article, delegates from counties, cities, and communities "bided, spoke, wrote, and begged" for the route to come through their area. These areas knew they were competing for the path to economic prosperity. When delegates stood up to speak for their communities, the *Times* article recorded that "representatives from rival communities hurled insults and taunting criticisms" at the speaker. Even families were willing to go to battle to get the road to come through their communities. In vying for the route to come through their counties, the four Fort brothers took competing sides, with two brothers wanting the road to come through Sumner County and the other two wanting it to come through Robertson County. Joel B. Fort, the president of the Good Roads Association of Robertson County, led the fight for the Robertson County route with his great oratory skills and hospitality, as he hosted a picnic for the Dixie Highway officials and 3,000 citizens from around the Springfield area in a show of support for the road. Joel Fort had multiple agendas for bringing the road through his county, including his intention, at the urging of his wife Jane, to open a tavern known as Mint Springs Tavern that would benefit from the Dixie Highway traffic.

The Dixie Highway connected people to many places. These places included schools, public buildings, and other communities. This chapter will show some of the hundreds of places that people could get to by driving the Dixie through Tennessee.

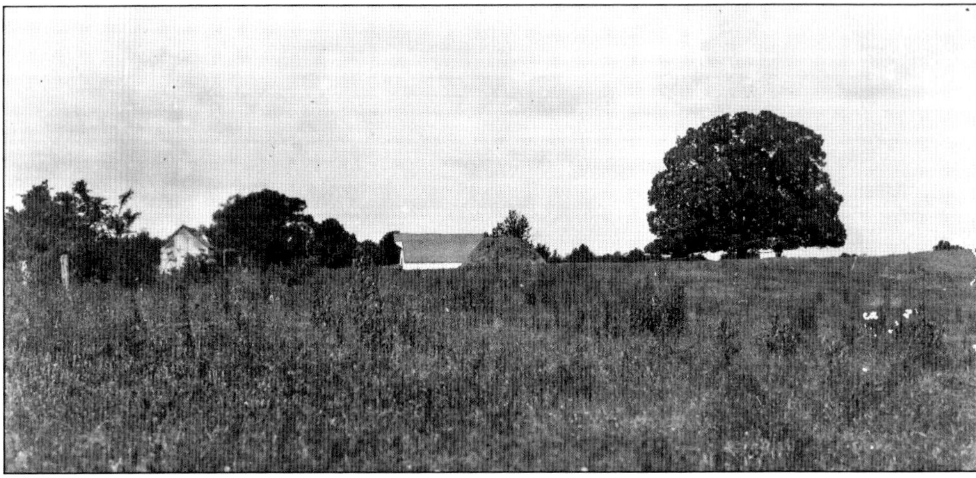

This photograph was taken around 1911 about 3 miles northwest of Adams, Tennessee. It shows the rural character of Robertson County as it was at the time of the Dixie Highway. Adams may be best known for the site of the legendary Bell Witch hauntings between 1817 and 1821 that reportedly resulted in the death of John Bell. (Courtesy of the Tennessee State Library and Archives.)

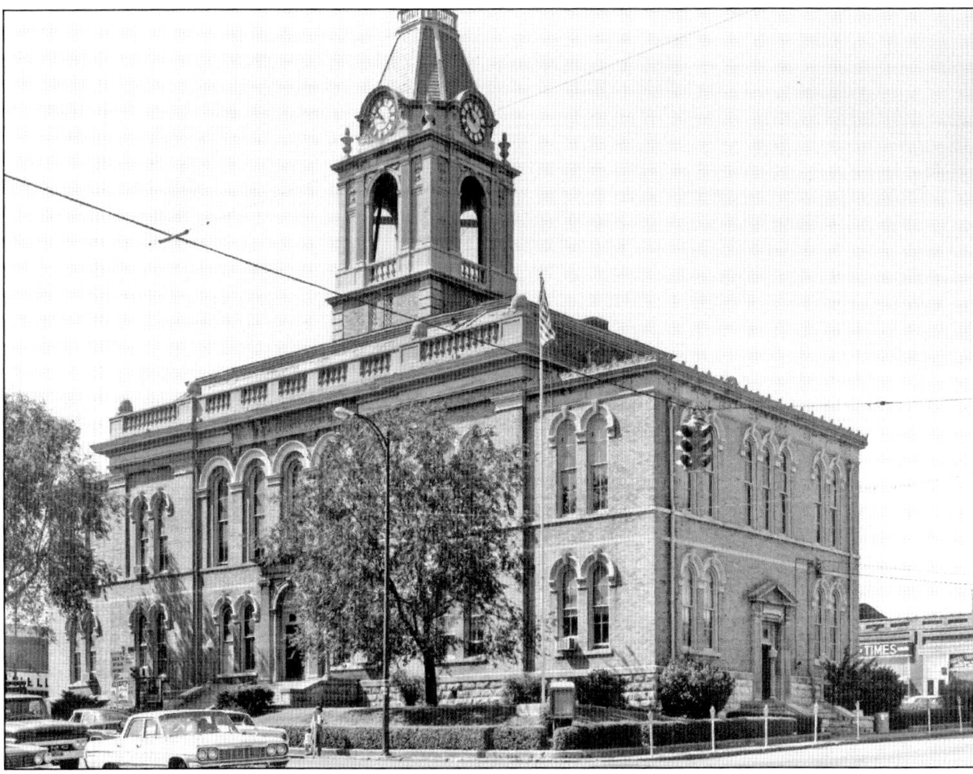


The Robertson County Courthouse is located on Main Street in Springfield. Designed originally by William C. Smith, it was completed in 1881 in the Second Empire style. In 1930, the prominent Nashville architectural firm of Dougherty and Gardner completed a major renovation of the building that included expanding the building and removing much of the Second Empire ornament. (Courtesy of the Tennessee State Library and Archives.)

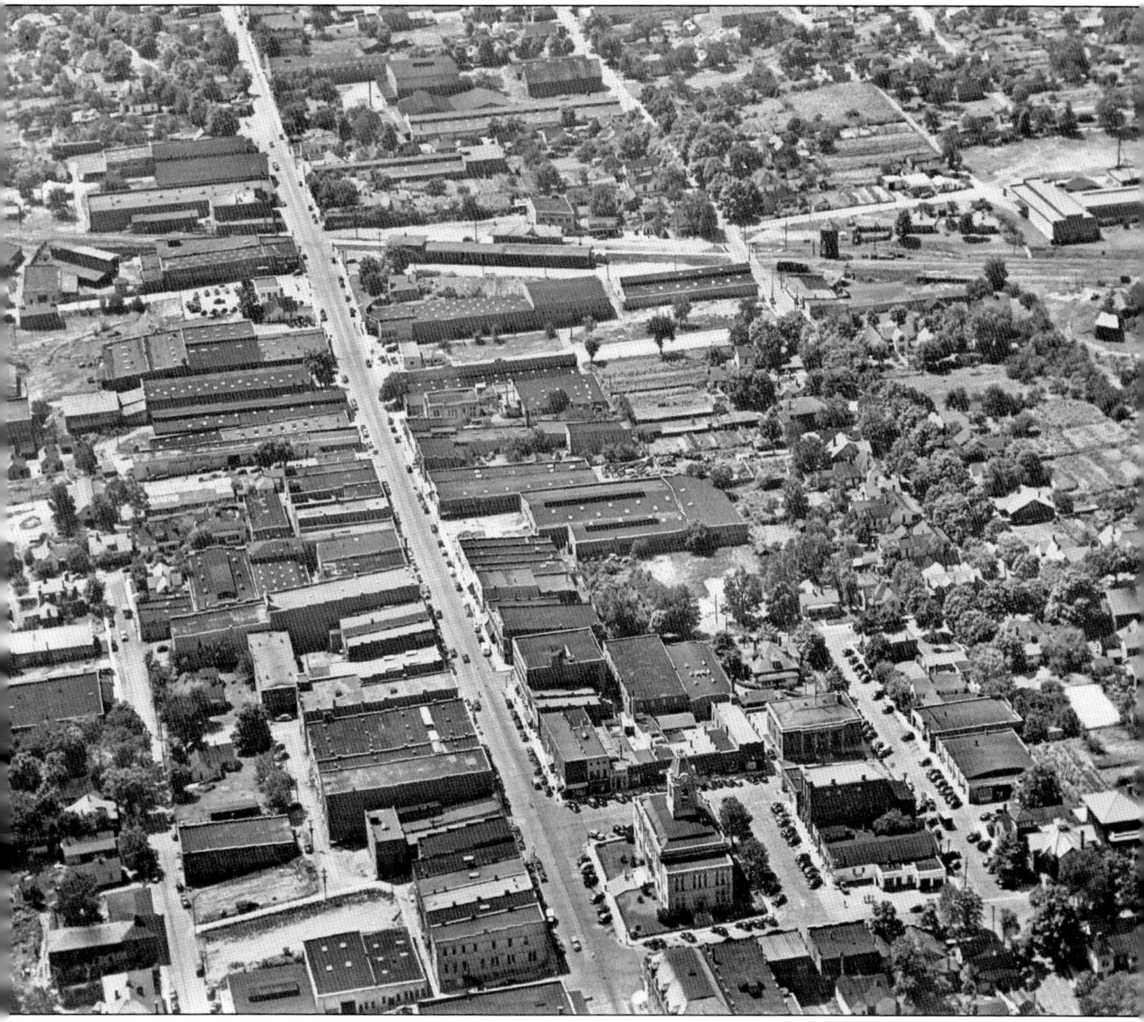

In 1796, the first General Assembly of Tennessee authorized Springfield as the county seat of Robertson County. However, the city was not founded until two years later. Historically and currently, Springfield has served as a commercial center for the surrounding agricultural area, which is known for its dark-fired tobacco. This aerial view of downtown Springfield shows the city in 1941. Main Street, which followed the route of the Dixie Highway through town, is the major thoroughfare that runs from the top to the bottom of the photograph. The railroad tracks run through the edge of downtown and cross the Dixie Highway at the top of the photograph. The agricultural warehouses can be seen along the tracks. The Robertson County Courthouse is visible at the bottom of the photograph. (Courtesy of the Tennessee State Library and Archives.)

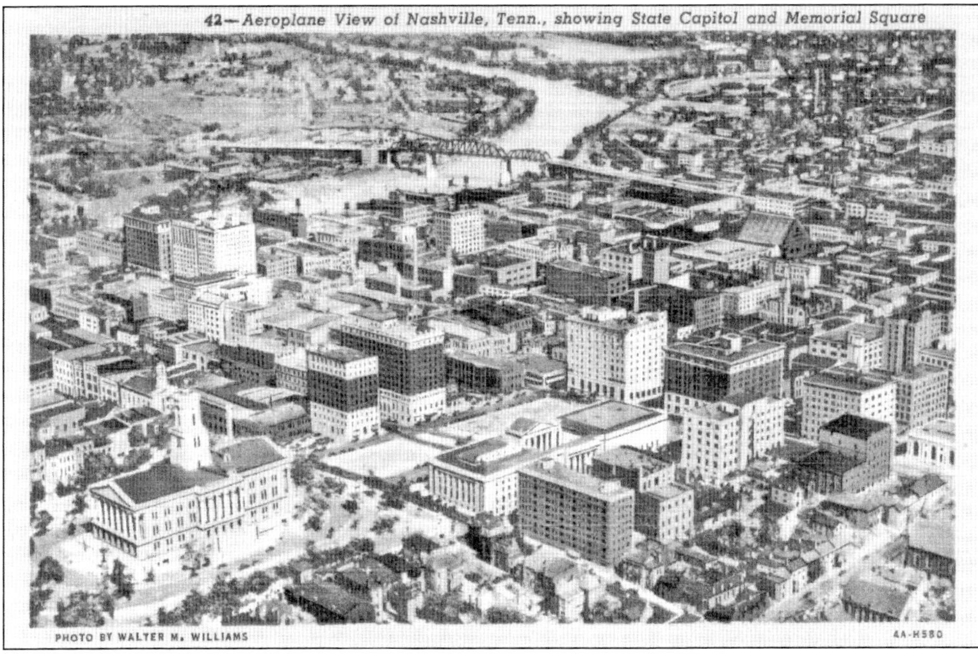


Nashville was founded in 1779 as Fort Nashborough after Revolutionary War hero John Nash. It was incorporated in 1806 as Nashville, the county seat of Davidson County. In 1826, Nashville became the temporary capital of the state, a decision the General Assembly of Tennessee made permanent in 1843. (Courtesy of the author.)

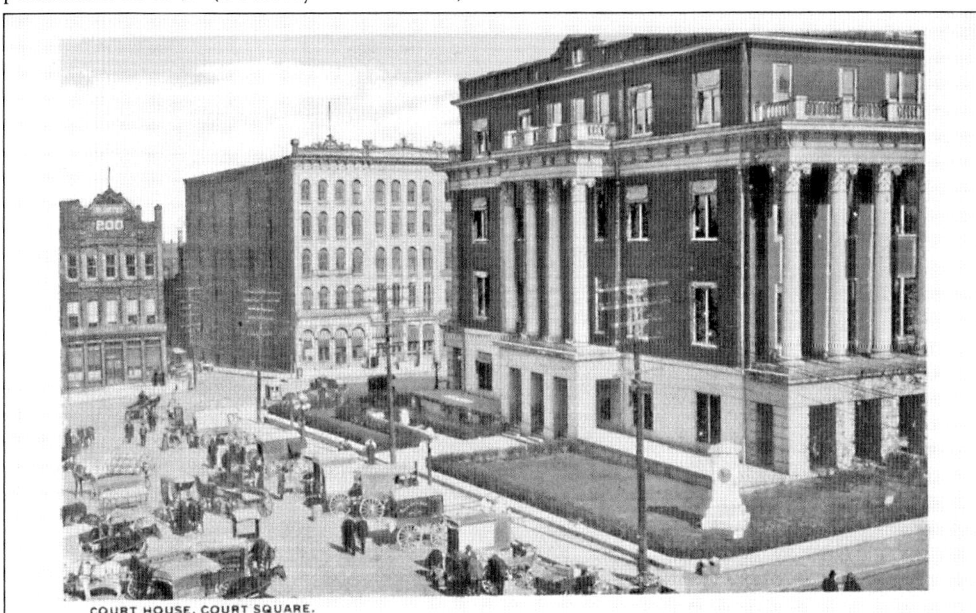


This postcard shows the fourth Davidson County Courthouse, which was designed by Francis Strickland, son of prominent architect William Strickland. A fire destroyed the previous courthouse in 1856, and this building was completed a year later. In 1910, the county expanded the courthouse to include a fourth story, as seen in this photograph. In 1935, this building was demolished for the current building. (Courtesy of the author.)

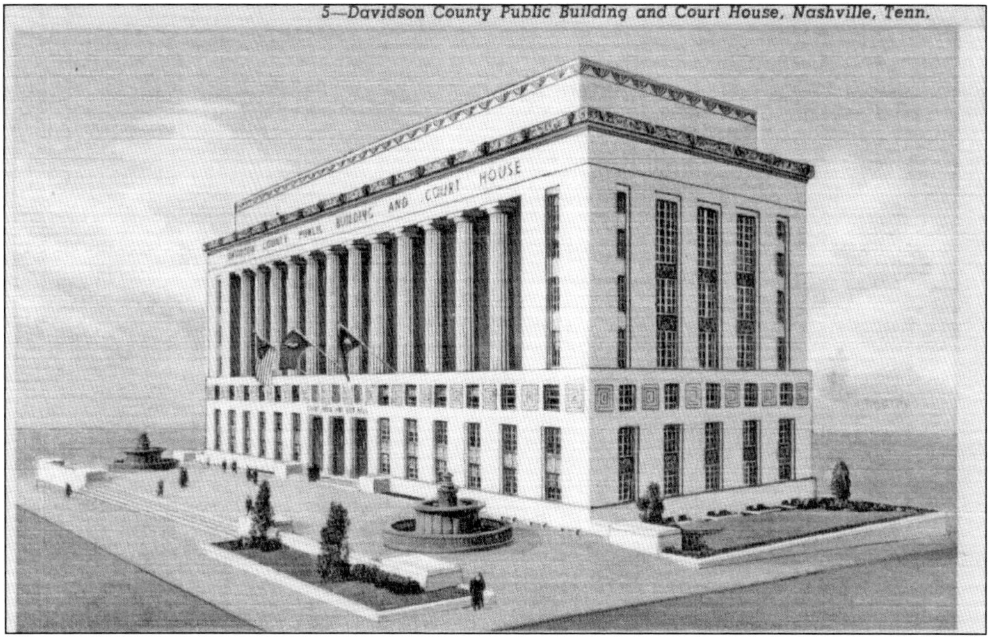


In 1937, Davidson County completed the current building with partial funding from the Federal Emergency Administration of Public Works, a New Deal agency that helped fund municipal buildings all over the country during the Depression. Local architect Emmons H. Woolwine in partnership with Frederick C. Hirons of New York designed the building. (Courtesy of the author.)

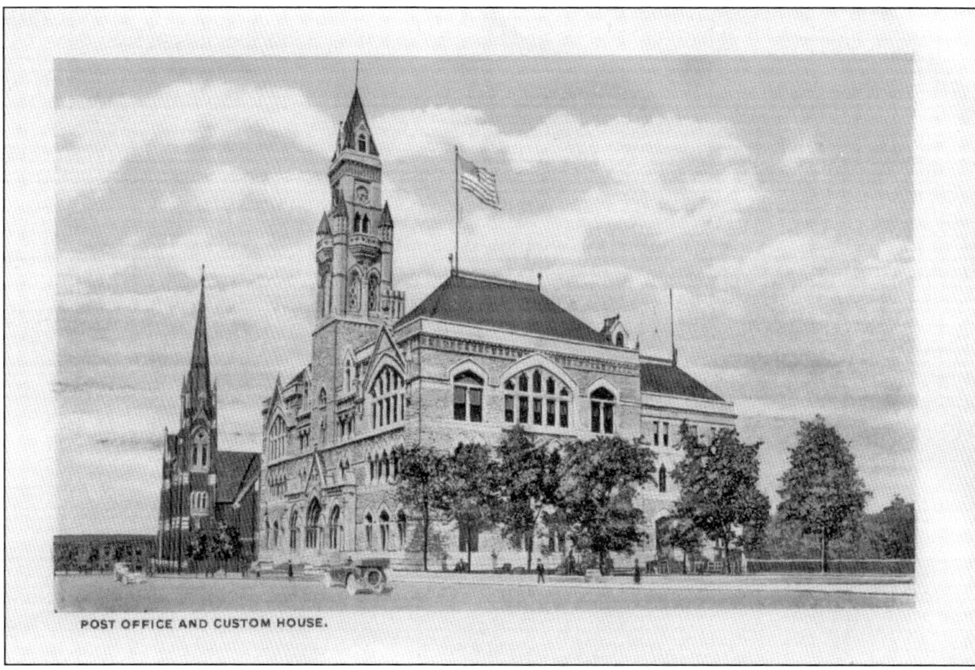


This 1916 postcard shows the post office and customhouse on Broadway Street in downtown Nashville. "Customhouse" was a general term used for a federal office building that housed multiple units with different uses. Architect William Potter designed this building, which was completed in 1882. The First Baptist Church is in the background. (Courtesy of the author.)

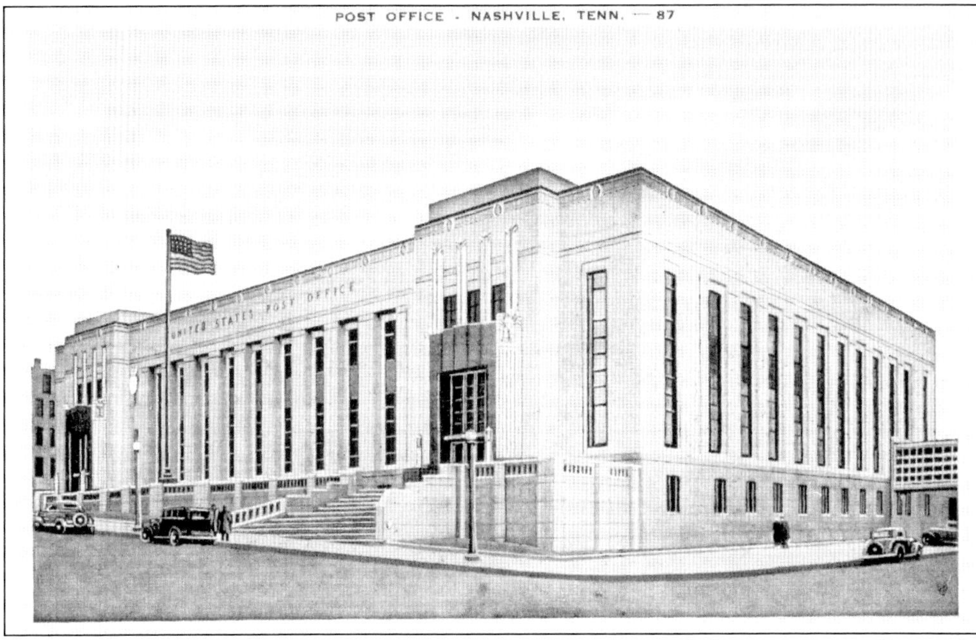


Prominent Nashville architectural firm Marr and Holman designed this U. S. Post Office in the stripped classical style. It was completed in 1934 using federal funds that had been appropriated by the Hoover administration. Located on Broadway Street in downtown Nashville, the building currently houses the Frist Center for the Visual Arts. (Courtesy of the author.)

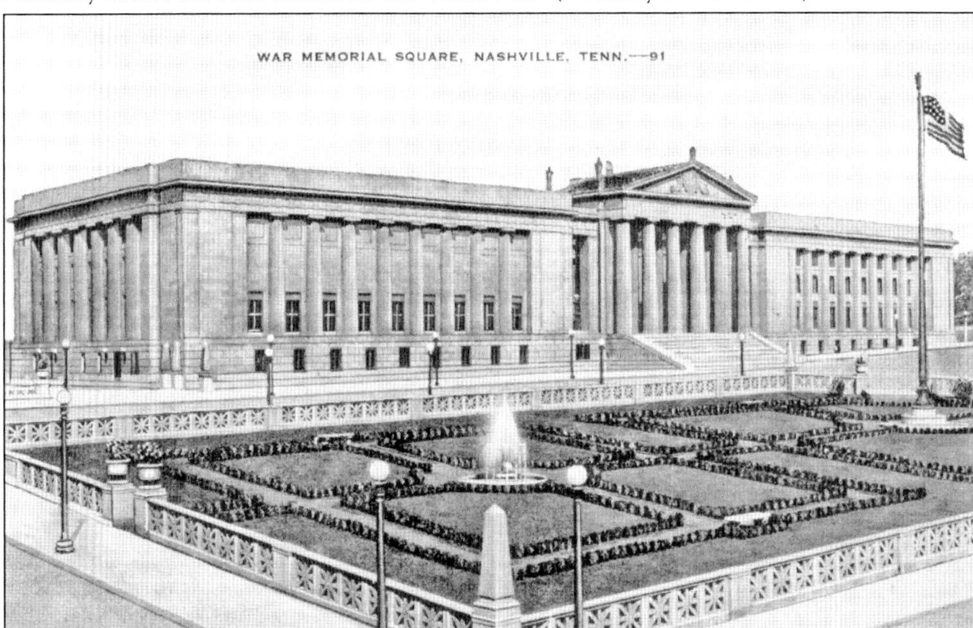


The War Memorial Building is located south of the Tennessee State Capitol. Completed in 1925, the building originally was constructed as a memorial to the people who died in World War I. Now it is a monument to all veterans in all wars. Local architect Edward Dougherty, in partnership with the nationally prominent firm of McKim, Mead, and White of New York, designed the building. (Courtesy of the author.)

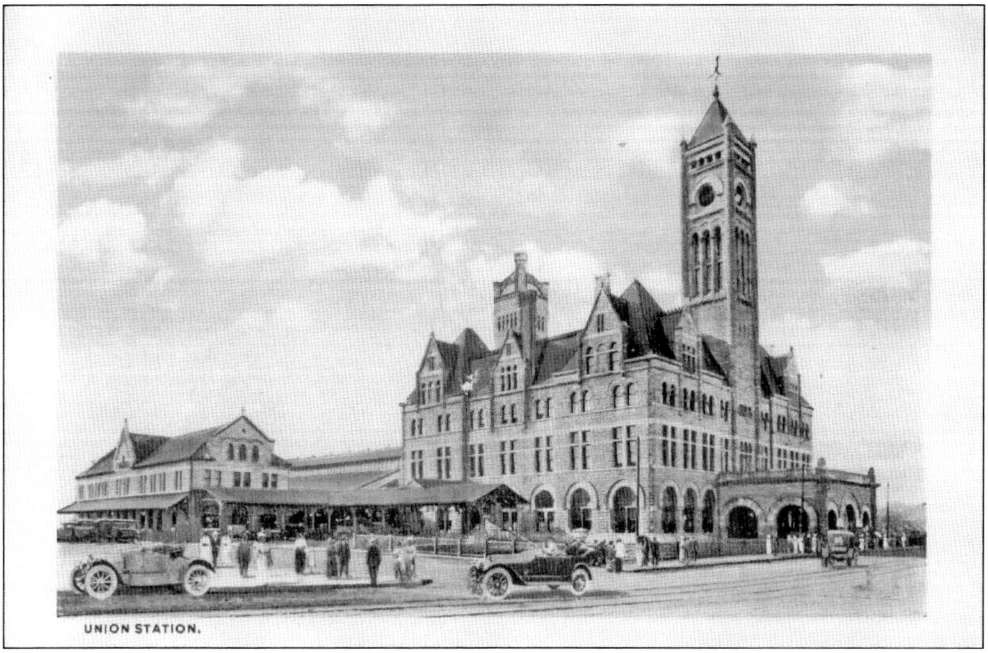


Union Station, a former passenger railroad station, was built in 1900 and served eight railroads and the Nashville trolley system. It continued to function as a train station until 1979. In the mid-1980s, it was converted into a hotel, and it remains so today. (Courtesy of the author.)

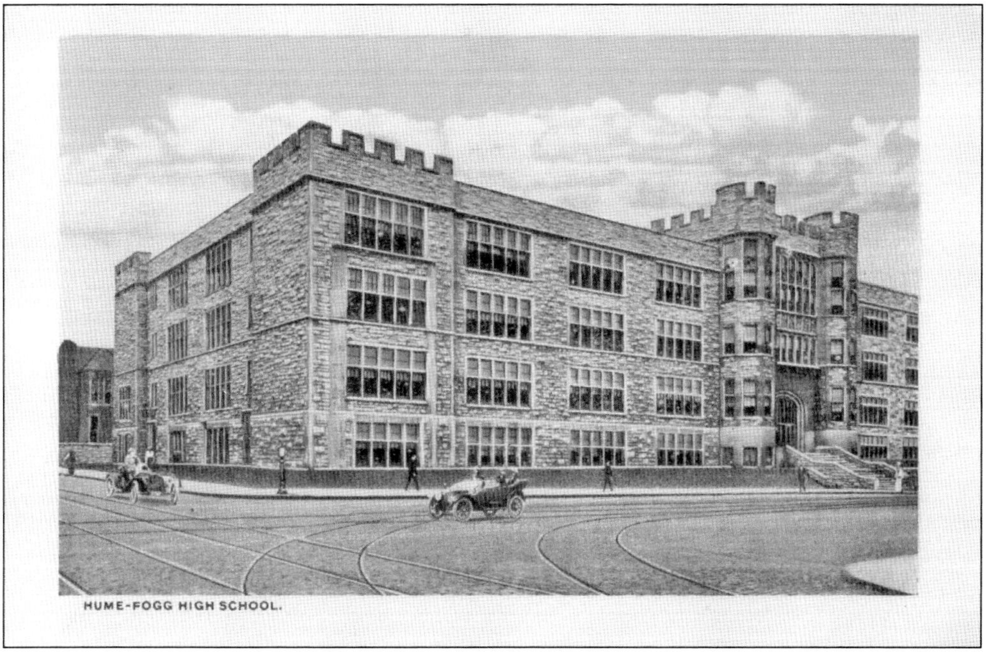


Architects William B. Ittner and Robert Sharp designed the Hume-Fogg High School, which opened in 1912 at this location when the Hume School—the first public high school in Nashville—combined with the Fogg School. In 1964, Hume-Fogg became the first public high school in Nashville to desegregate its athletic teams. It is located on Broadway Street in downtown Nashville and continues to function as a public high school. (Courtesy of the author.)

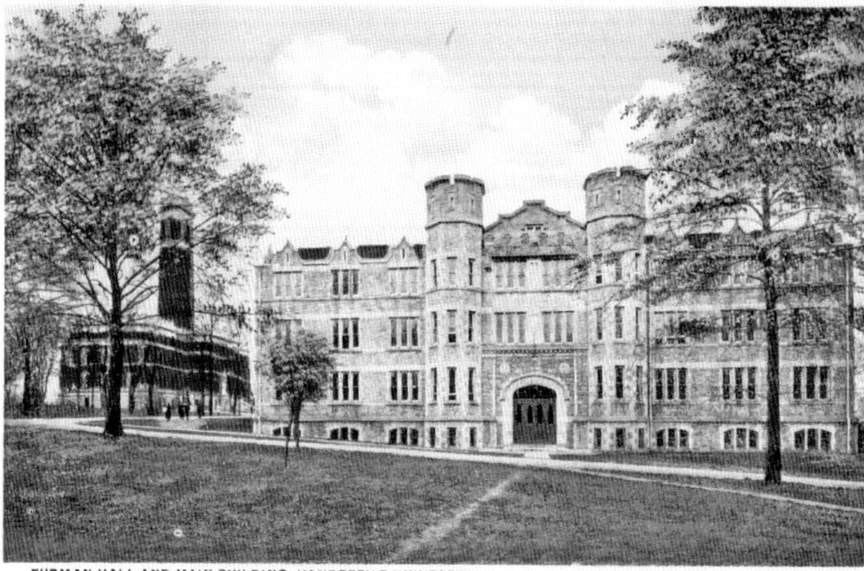

FURMAN HALL AND MAIN BUILDING, VANDERBILT UNIVERSITY.

Founded in 1873 as a gift from "Commodore" Cornelius Vanderbilt, Vanderbilt University is a private research university that offers baccalaureate, graduate, and professional degrees. Although intended as a men's college, women attended Vanderbilt from almost the beginning. The 1907 Furman Hall was originally the chemistry and pharmacy building. The Old Main Building was one of Vanderbilt's original buildings and housed classrooms, laboratories, and offices. The medical department was originally located not on main campus but on the University of Nashville campus, several miles away to the south. The Dixie Highway would have made getting to and from school much easier for students who did not live in Nashville. (Both, courtesy of the author.)

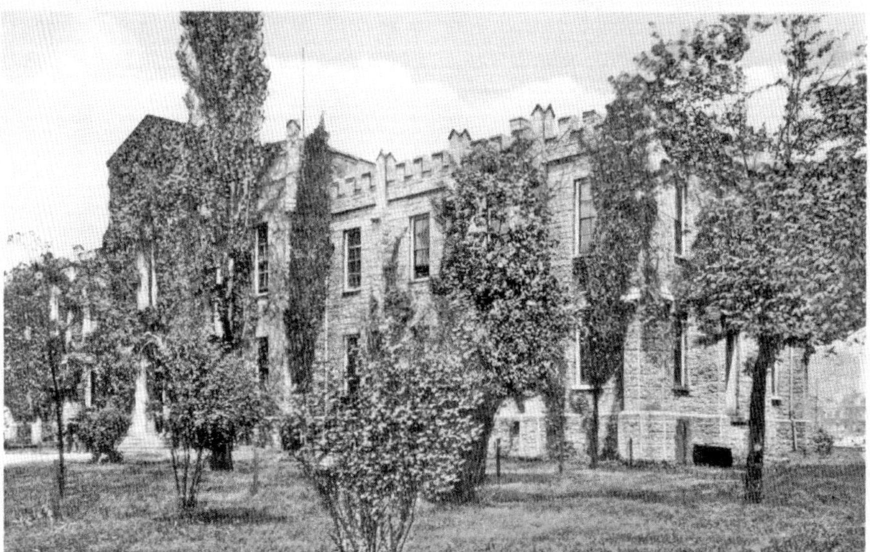

MEDICAL DEPARTMENT, VANDERBILT UNIVERSITY, SOUTH CAMPUS.

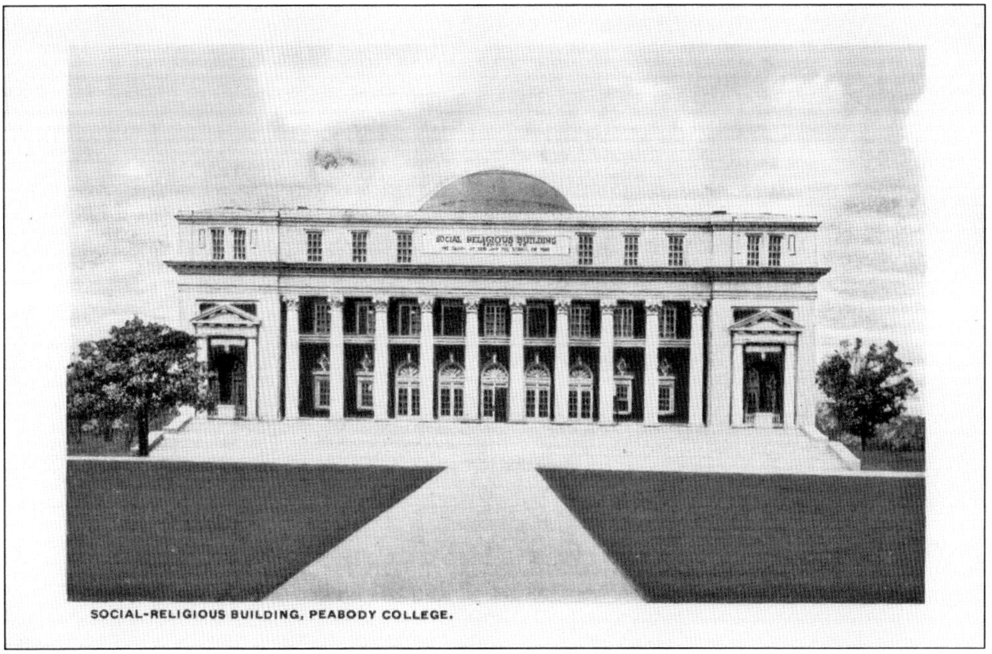


George Peabody College for Teachers was founded in 1875, when the University of Nashville split into a prep school and a college. In 1979, it became the Peabody School of Vanderbilt University. Since 1992, the Social-Religious Building shown in this image has served as an administration and technology education center. (Courtesy of the author.)

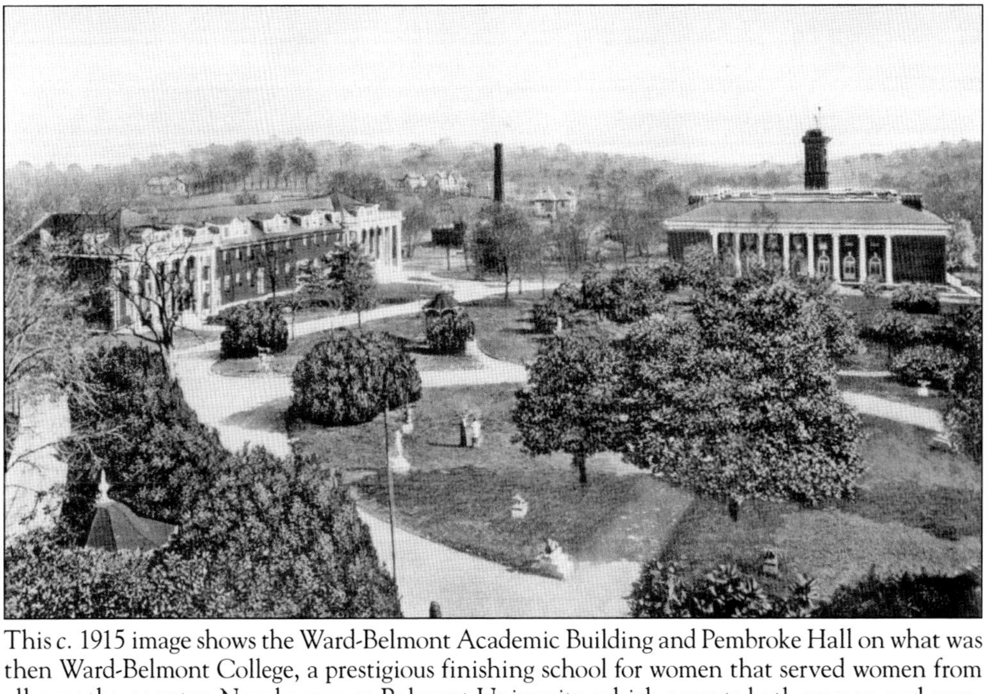

This *c.* 1915 image shows the Ward-Belmont Academic Building and Pembroke Hall on what was then Ward-Belmont College, a prestigious finishing school for women that served women from all over the country. Now known as Belmont University, which accepts both women and men, the college is located on what had been the antebellum estate of Adelicia Acklen. (Courtesy of the author.)

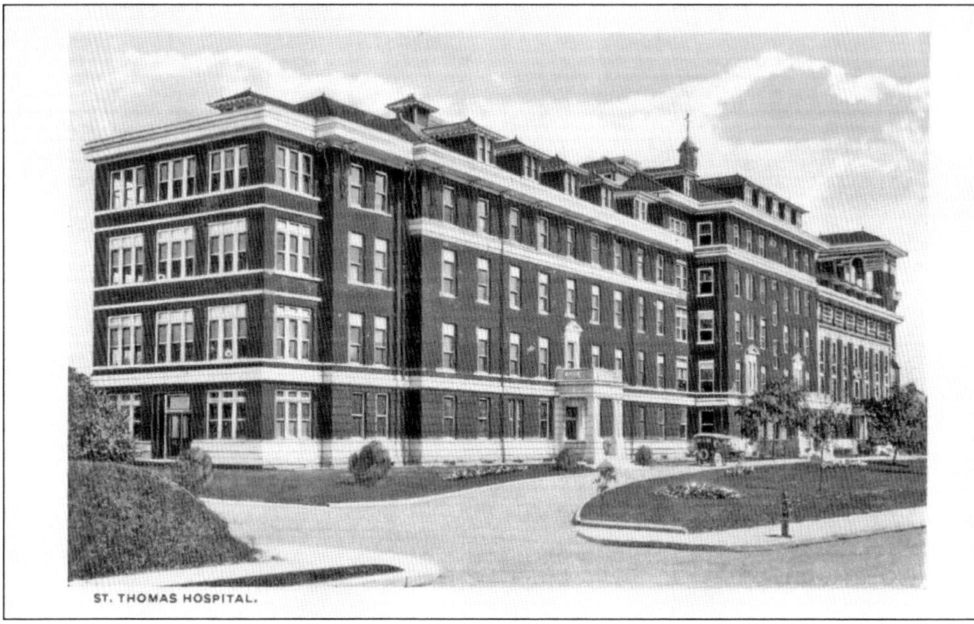


In 1898, Thomas Sebastian Byrne, the Roman Catholic bishop of Nashville, asked the Daughters of Charity to establish a hospital in Nashville. St. Thomas Hospital has served the region, especially the poor and underserved, ever since. This postcard shows the hospital when it was located on Hayes Street at Twentieth Avenue. The hospital moved to Harding Road in 1974. (Courtesy of the author.)

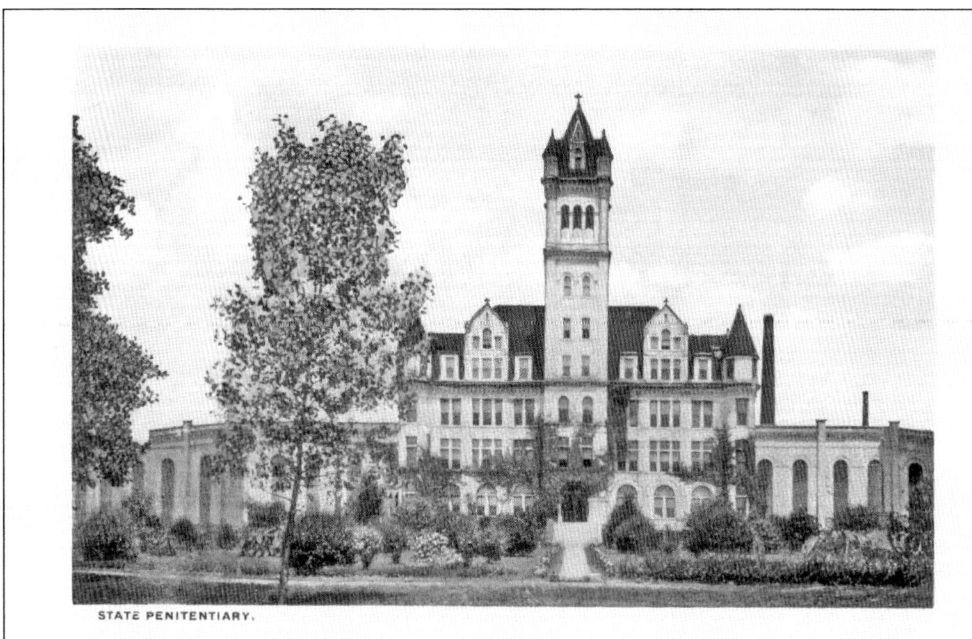


The Tennessee State Penitentiary opened in 1898 as a state-of-the-art facility incorporating the latest philosophies on inmate care. Designed by S. M. Patton of Chattanooga to look like a castle, it continued operating until 1992. This image showing the main entrance may seem familiar, as the prison has been used in several movies and television shows. (Courtesy of the author.)

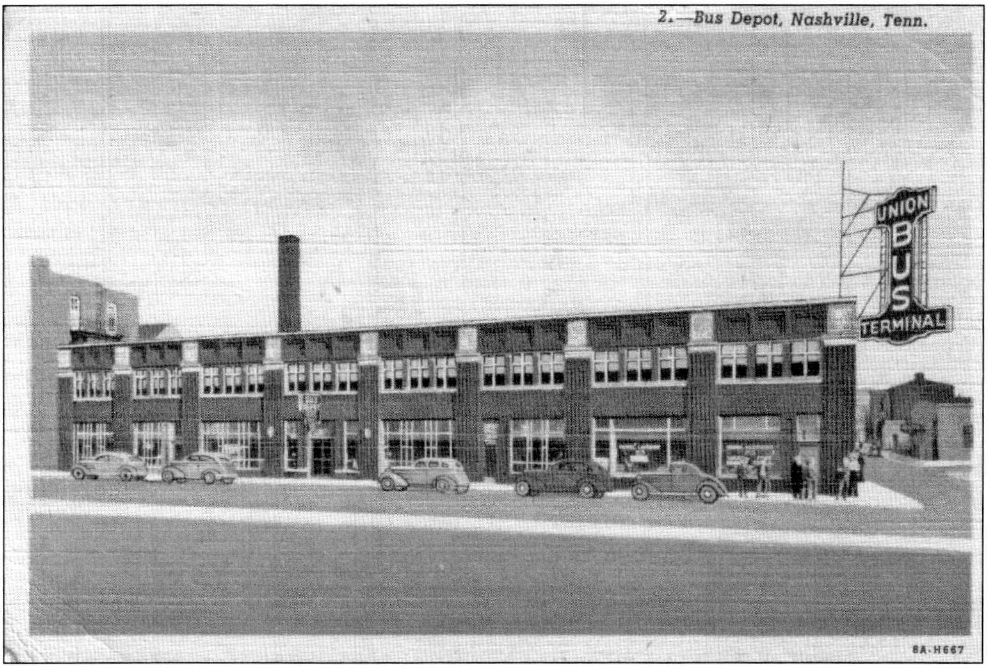


Buses frequented the Dixie Highway to provide transportation to those who did not have their own vehicles. The Union Bus Terminal in Nashville was located at 517 Commerce Street. It was built in the late 1930s and served multiple bus companies. (Courtesy of Jeffrey Lee Durbin.)

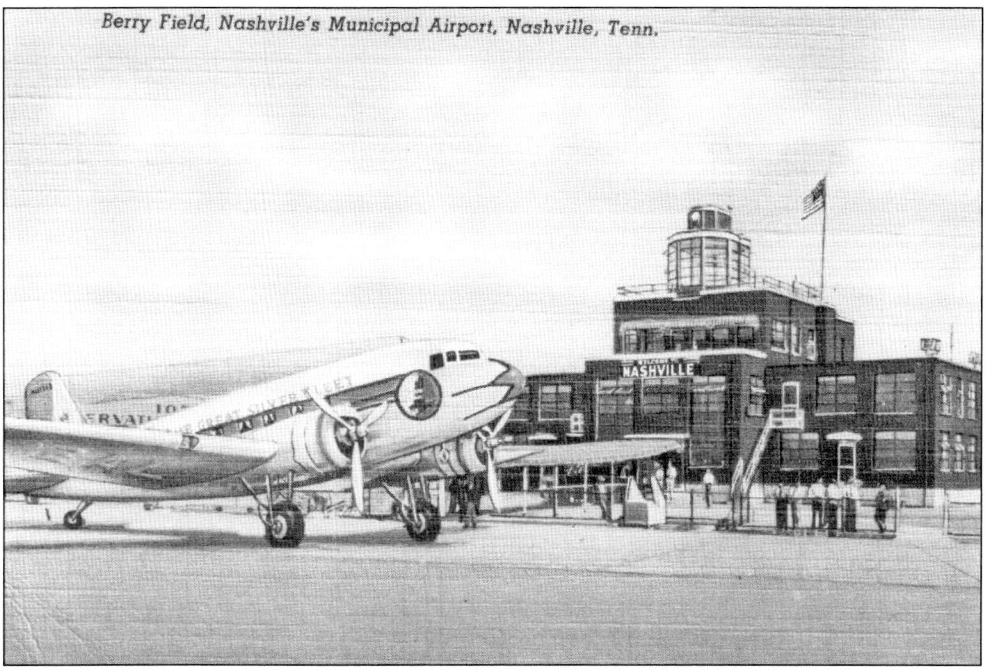


Located on the Dixie Highway, Berry Field offered another mode of transportation. This postcard dates to the 1940s. Berry Field evolved into the Nashville International Airport. Just south of the main terminal, the Tennessee National Guard complex is now called Berry Field. (Courtesy of Jeffrey Lee Durbin.)

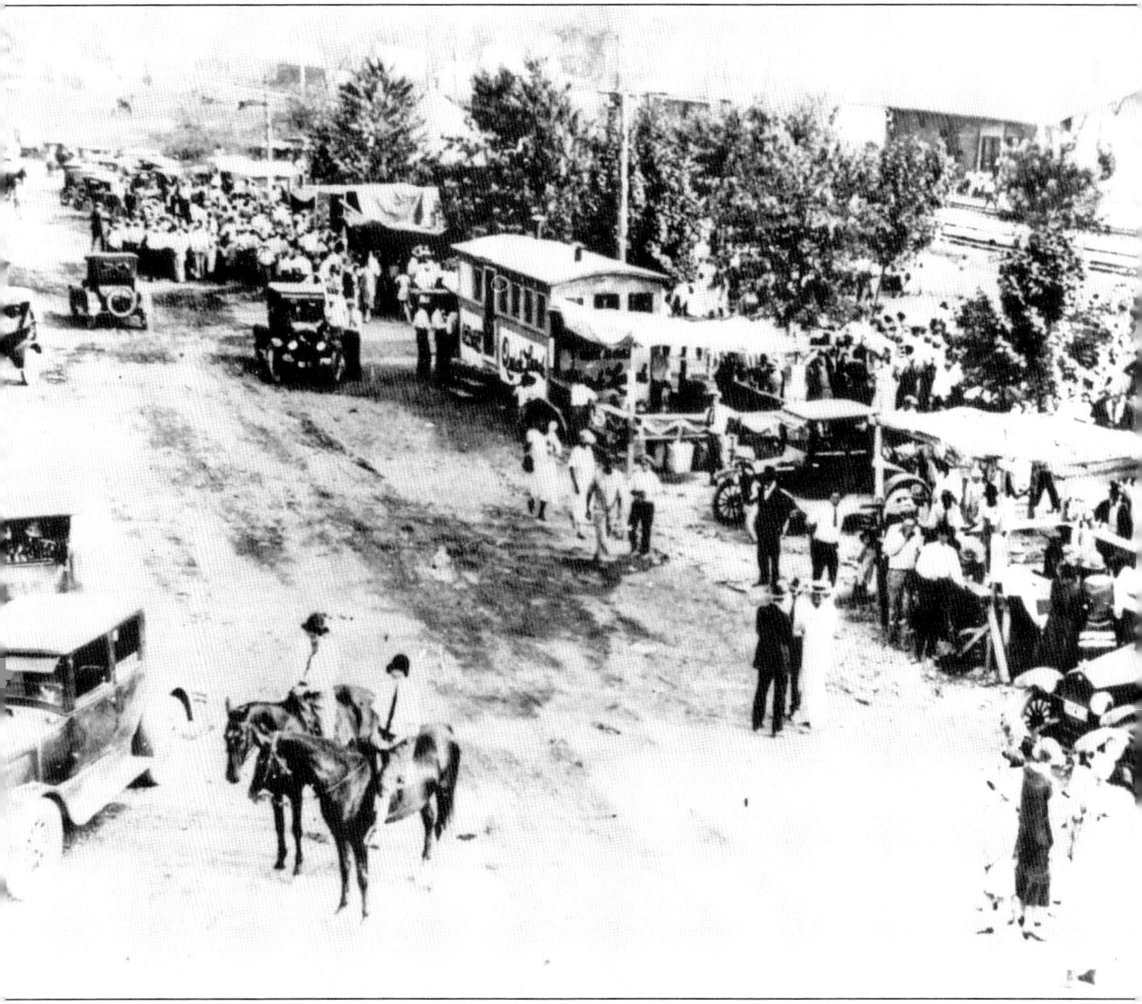

This 1925 image shows the Smyrna Community Fair in Rutherford County. The Nashville and Chattanooga train depot and railroad tracks are visible in the background. There are also cars and horses on the street. These three modes of transportation—car, rail, and horse—coexisted for decades after the automobile became a common site. However, the use of horse and rail transportation declined sharply after the 1920s. Smyrna was originally incorporated in 1869 and then reincorporated in 1915 during the time of the development of the Dixie Highway that provided access to the city. (Courtesy of the Albert Gore Research Center, Middle Tennessee State University.)

The Dixie Highway provided access to Smyrna and LaVergne in Rutherford County. When the federal government mandated that interstate highway systems take on a standardized numbering system, this portion of the route was known as U.S. Route 41. In the 1950s, the original route was bypassed in many sections and expanded, as shown in this 1960s image of U.S. Route 41. (Courtesy of the Albert Gore Research Center, Middle Tennessee State University.)

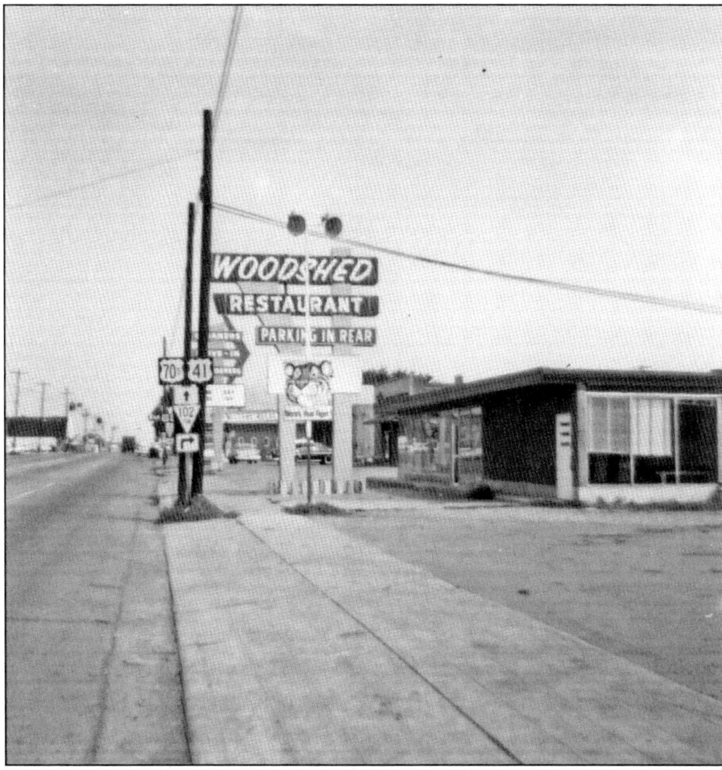


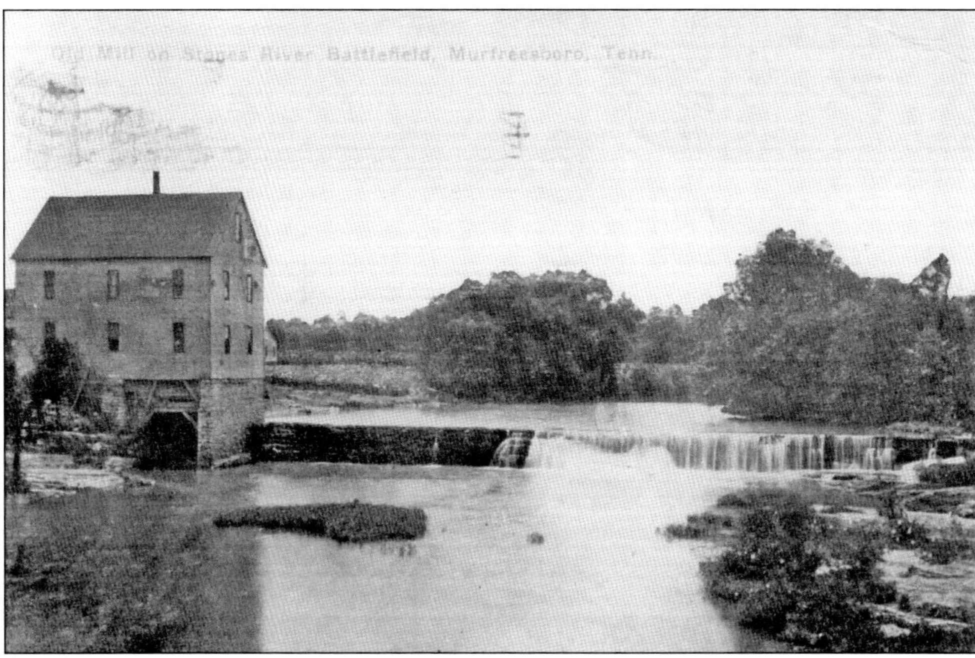


In contrast to the previous image, this idyllic view of the mill on Stones River is what was seen by many early travelers along the Dixie Highway. Best known as the name of an important Civil War battle, the Stones River was a significant economic and natural resource for the area. (Courtesy of the author.)

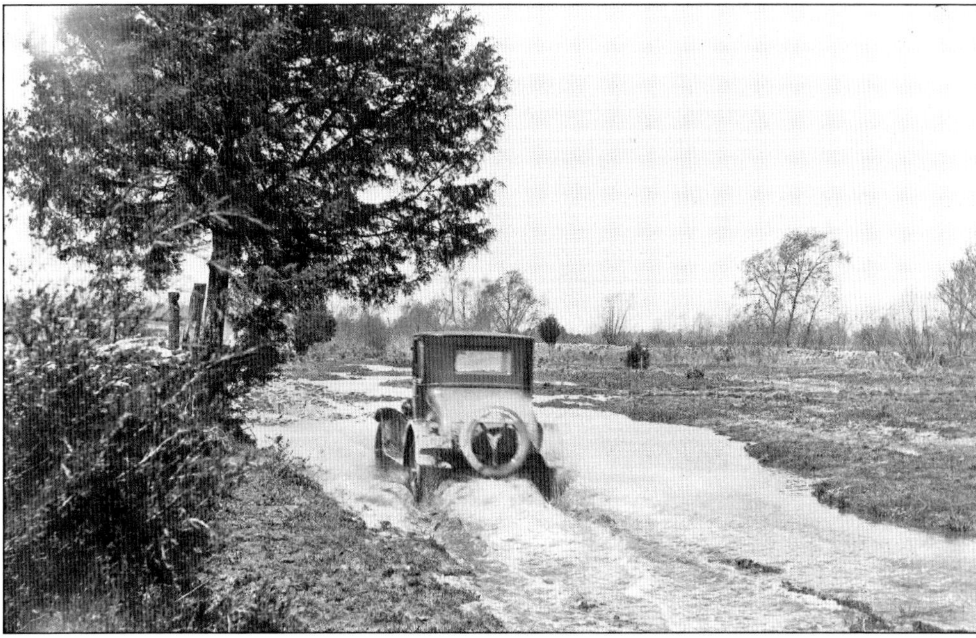

Even with road improvements made during the 1910s and 1920s, flooding following a heavy rain remained a problem on much of the roads throughout the state, as shown in this image of Rutherford County. In *The Dixie Highway* magazine, the travel logs sometimes steered drivers around certain sections during the rainy season. (Courtesy of the Tennessee State Library and Archives.)

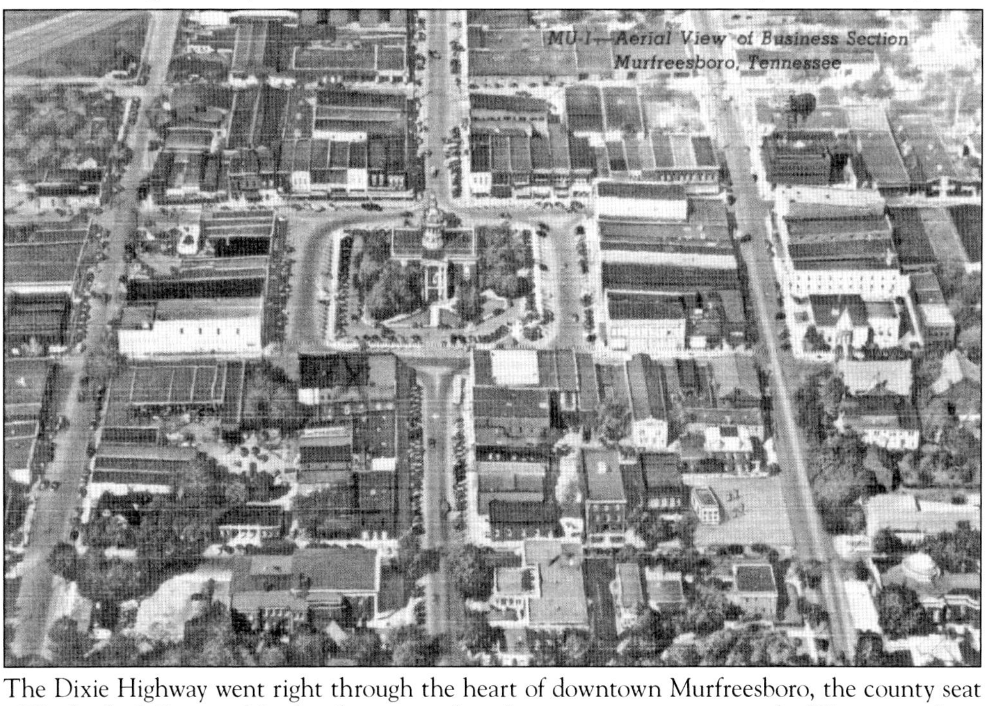


The Dixie Highway went right through the heart of downtown Murfreesboro, the county seat of Rutherford County. Murfreesboro served as the temporary state capital of Tennessee from 1819 to 1826. The courthouse square is visible in the center of this image. (Courtesy of Jeffrey Lee Durbin.)

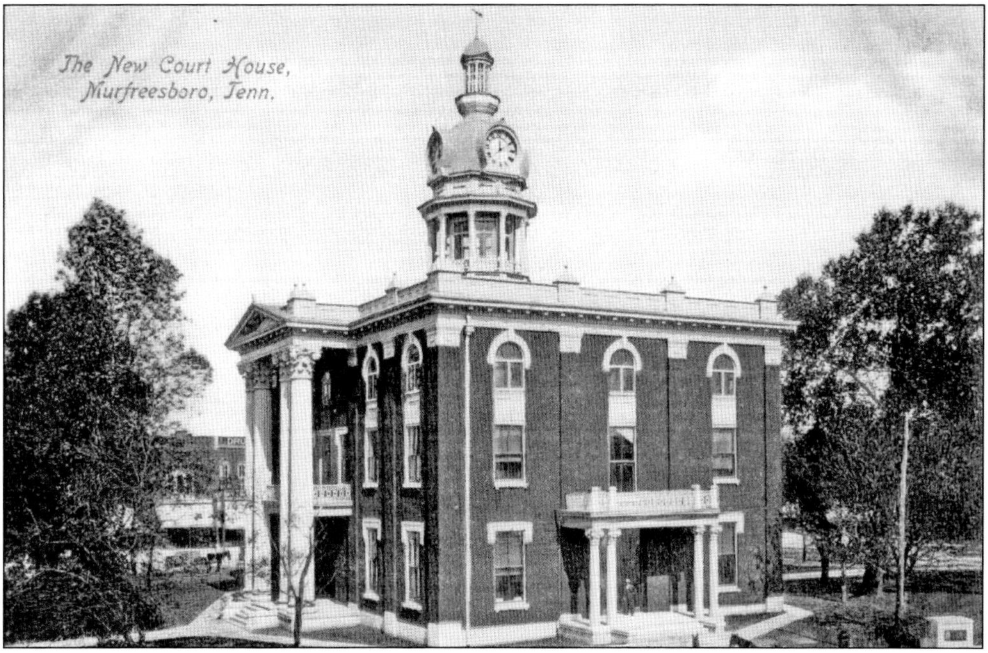


James H. Yeaman designed the Rutherford County Courthouse in Murfreesboro; it was completed in 1859. It is only one of seven antebellum courthouses in the state that still functions as a courthouse. It was occupied by Federal troops during the Civil War, but Confederate general Nathan Bedford Forrest recaptured the courthouse in 1862 in order to rescue prisoners who were about to be hanged. (Courtesy of the author.)

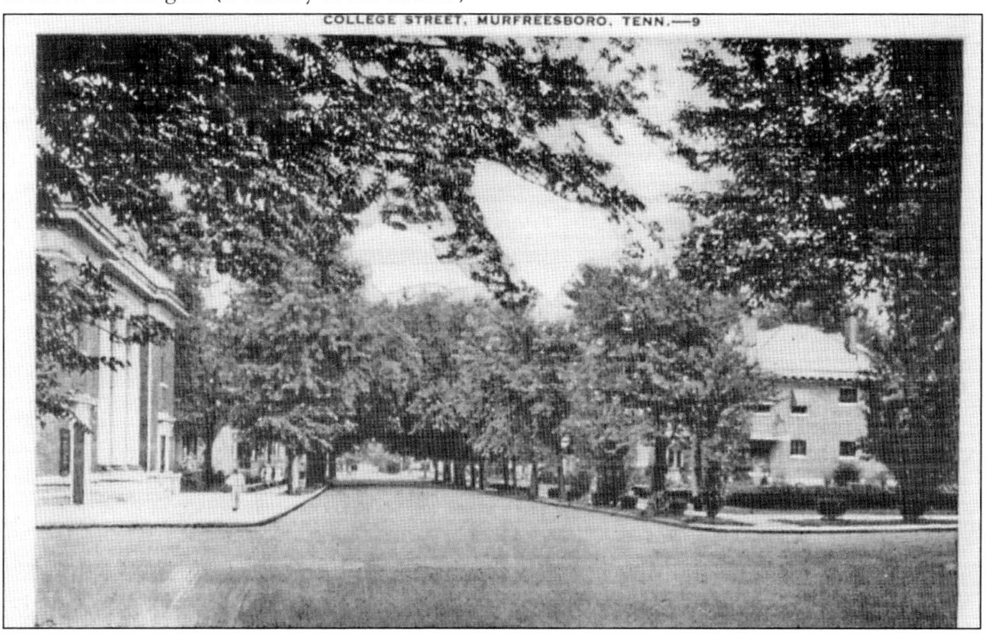


This photograph shows East College Street in downtown Murfreesboro. The photographer is looking east from the Spring Street intersection. The building on the left is the First Presbyterian Church, which is still standing. The house visible on the right has been demolished, however. (Courtesy of the author.)

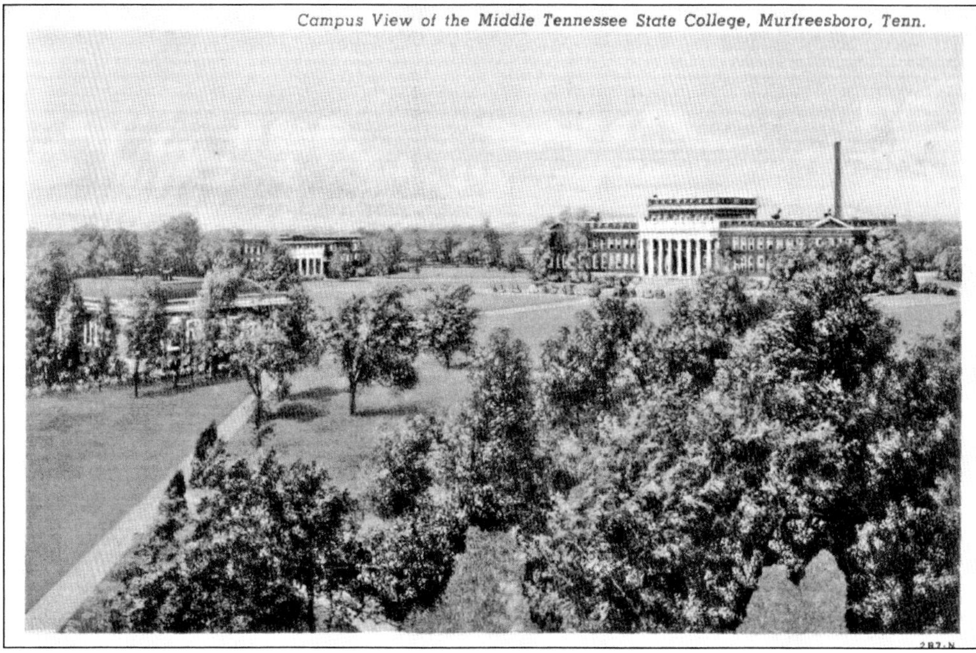


Middle Tennessee State University, as it is known today, traces its roots to 1909, when the General Assembly of Tennessee authorized its creation under the general education bill. It opened in 1911 as the Middle Tennessee Normal School, a school for training teachers. In 1925, it became the Middle Tennessee State Teachers College and began granting bachelor's degrees. The top image shows the administration building at this time. During World War II, the institution's mission was expanded, and it became the Middle Tennessee State College, a name it kept until 1965. The second image shows the school during the 1940s. (Both, courtesy of the author.)

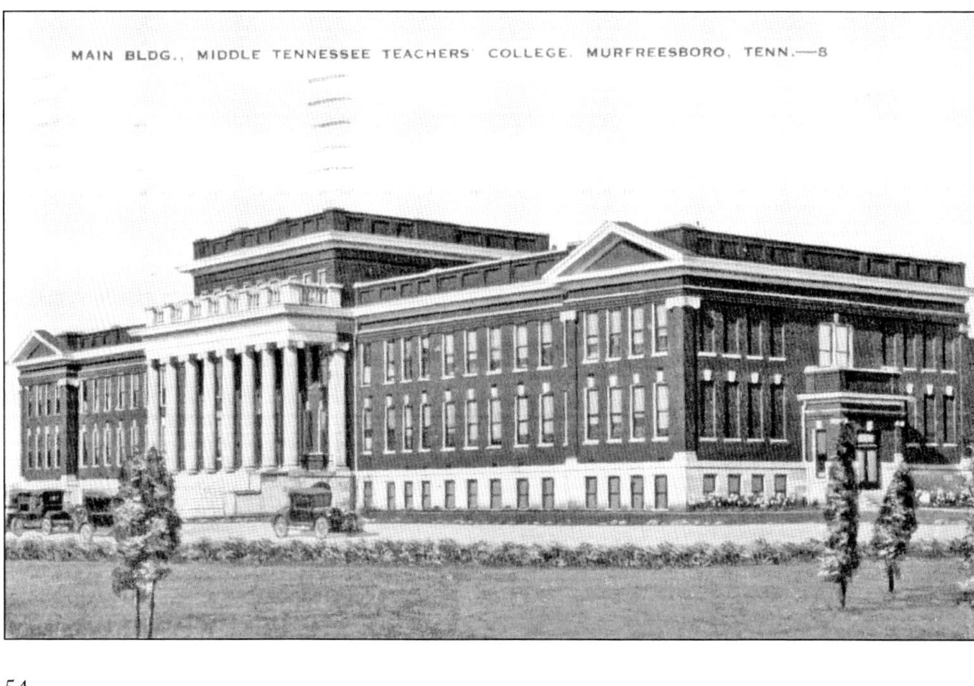

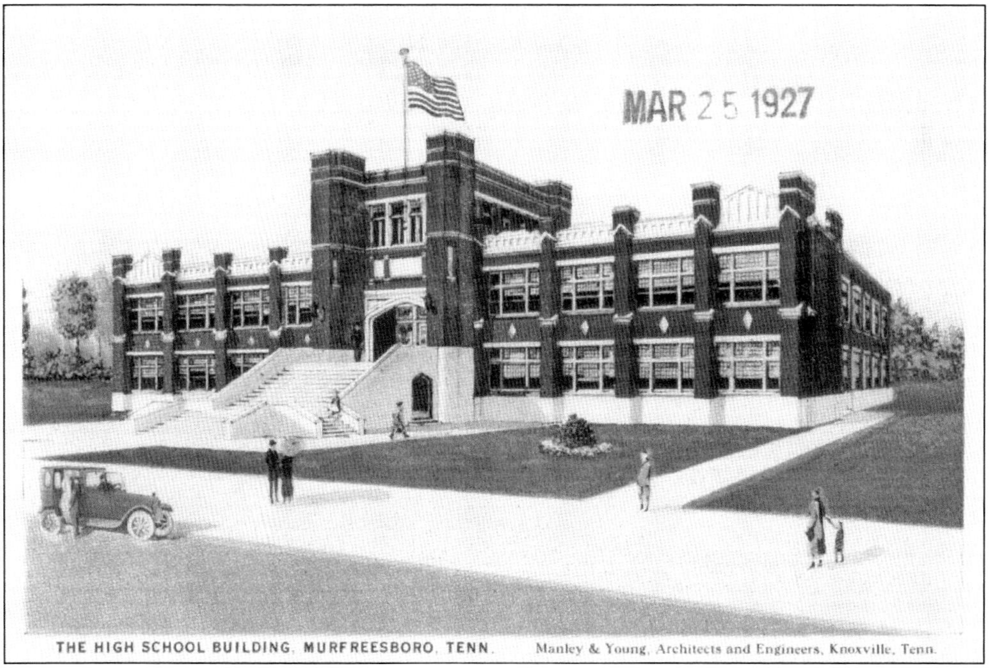


Located on Maple Street, Murfreesboro High School burned in 1944. The high school was then relocated to Main Street. The Knoxville architectural firm Manley and Young designed this building and the nearby African American Bradley School, which was completed in 1917. (Courtesy of Jeffrey Lee Durbin.)

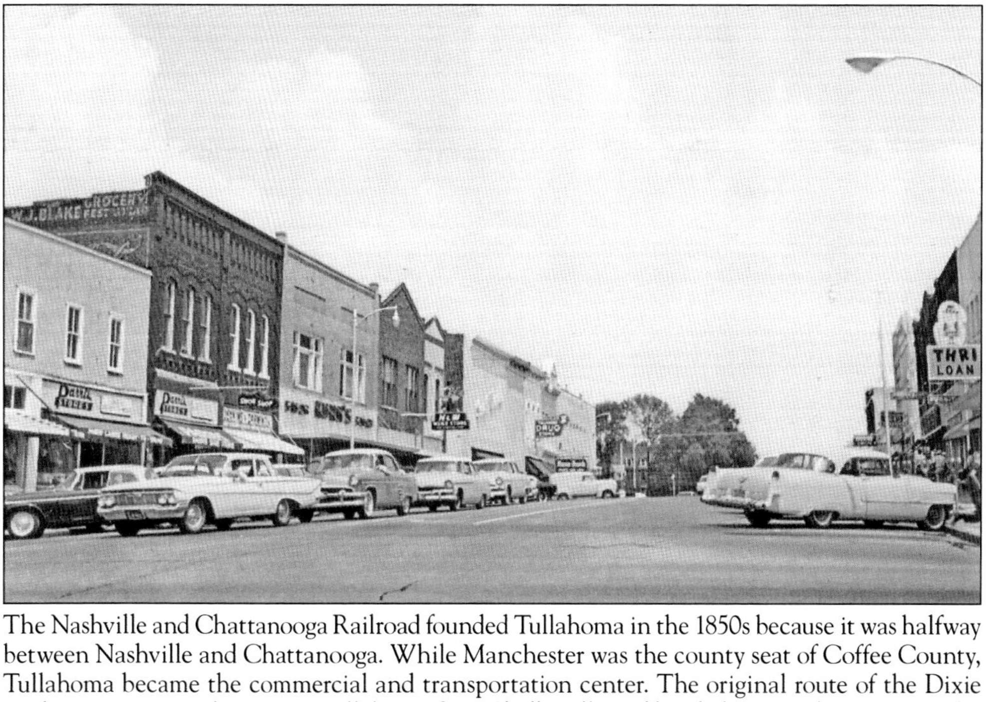


The Nashville and Chattanooga Railroad founded Tullahoma in the 1850s because it was halfway between Nashville and Chattanooga. While Manchester was the county seat of Coffee County, Tullahoma became the commercial and transportation center. The original route of the Dixie Highway came into downtown Tullahoma from Shelbyville and headed to Winchester. Later the U.S. 41 route would lead to Manchester directly from Murfreesboro. (Courtesy of the author.)

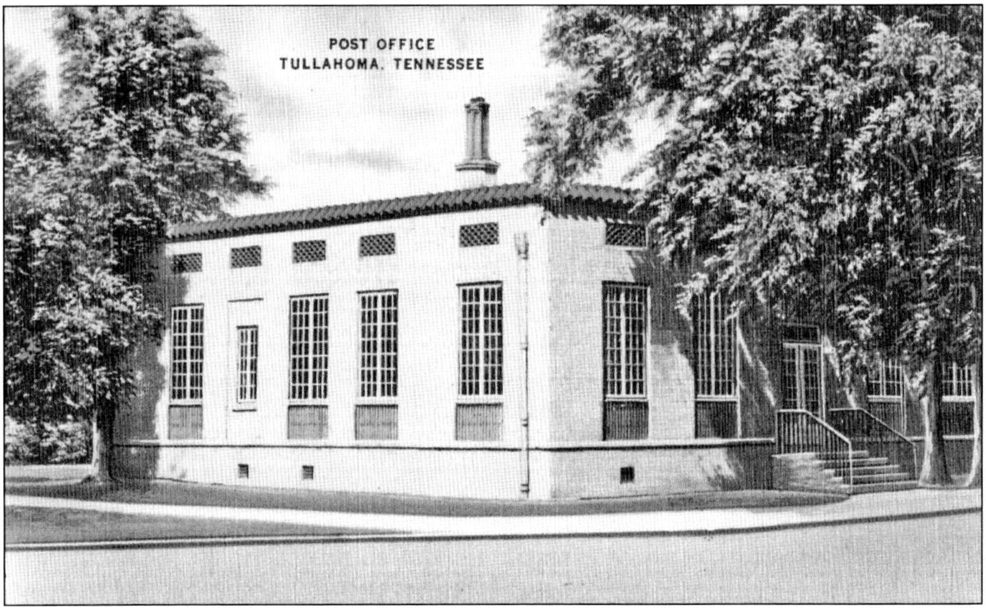


This image shows the old U. S. Post Office in Tullahoma, which opened in 1925. It operated as the post office until 1984, when the federal government built a new facility nearby. The First Christian Church has owned the old post office building ever since. The Dixie Highway provided accessibility and visibility to community landmark buildings such as post offices and courthouses. (Courtesy of the Tennessee State Library and Archives.)

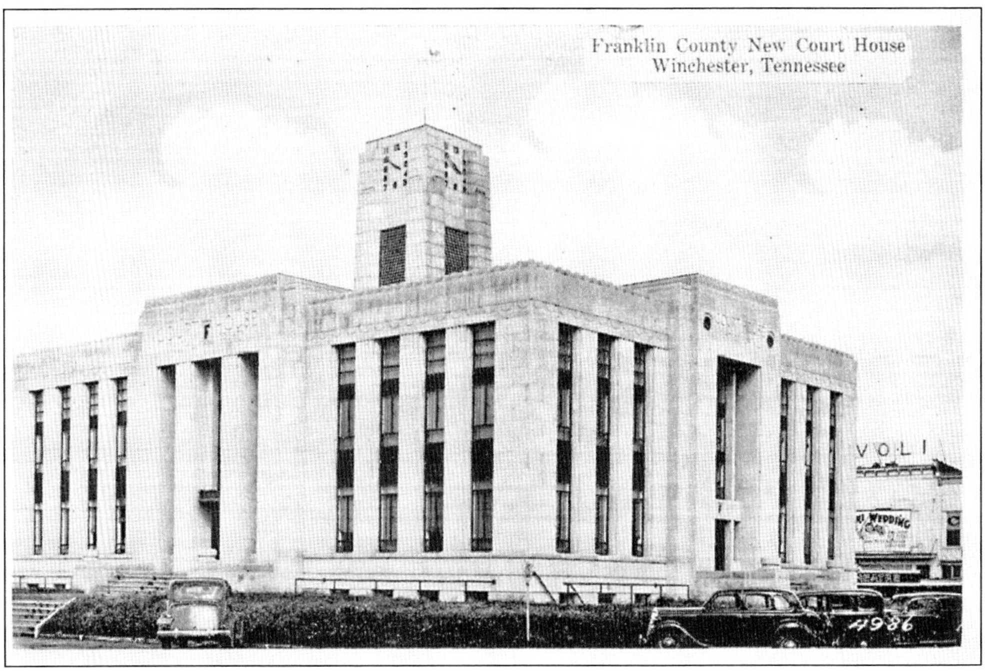


Winchester is the county seat of Franklin County. Nashville architectural firm Marr and Holman designed this building, which was completed in 1937. The county was created in 1807 from Bedford and Warren Counties. The original courthouse was located in this same location. (Courtesy of the author.)

In connecting places, the Dixie Highway offered some spectacular scenery between towns. These 1920s photographs show the portion of the highway between Cowan and Sewanee. Located in Franklin County at the foot of the Cumberland Mountains, Cowan was founded in 1808 but owes its development to when it became a passenger stop on the Nashville and Chattanooga Railroad in 1850s. The historic 1904 depot has been converted into a railroad museum. For the most part, this section of Franklin County is still rural, with agriculture remaining a major industry. (Both, courtesy of the Tennessee State Library and Archives.)

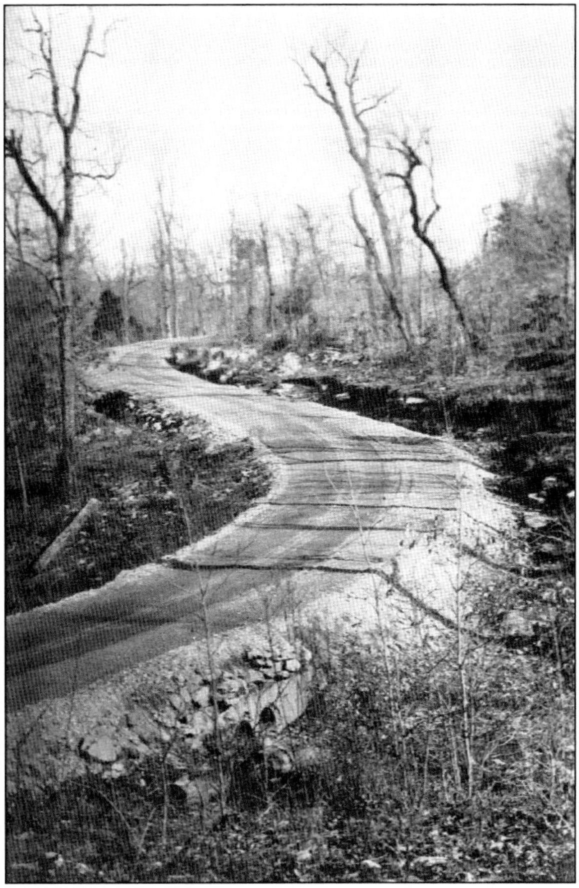

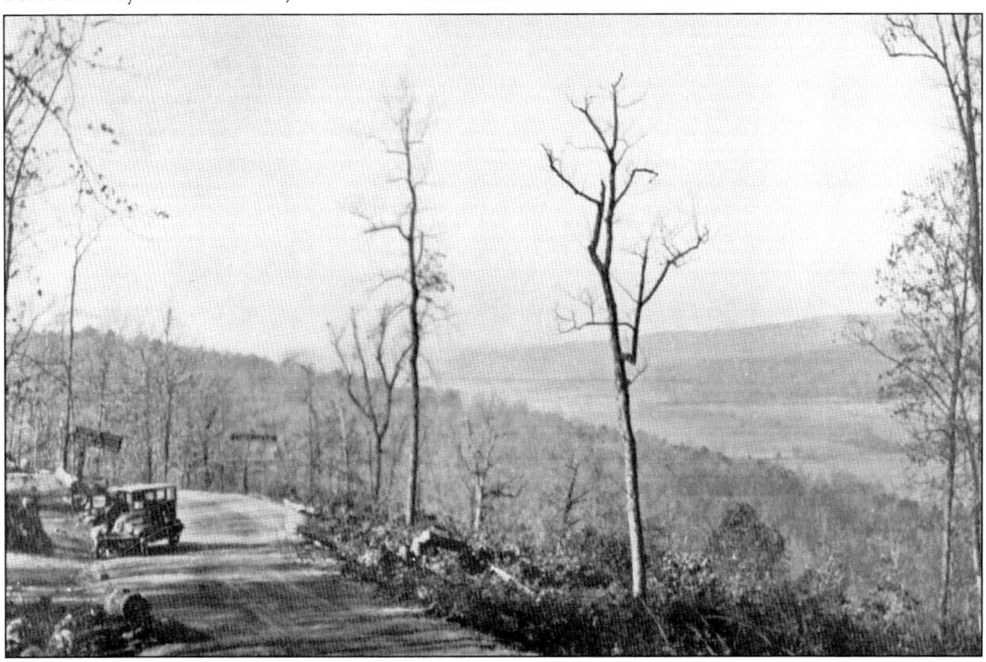

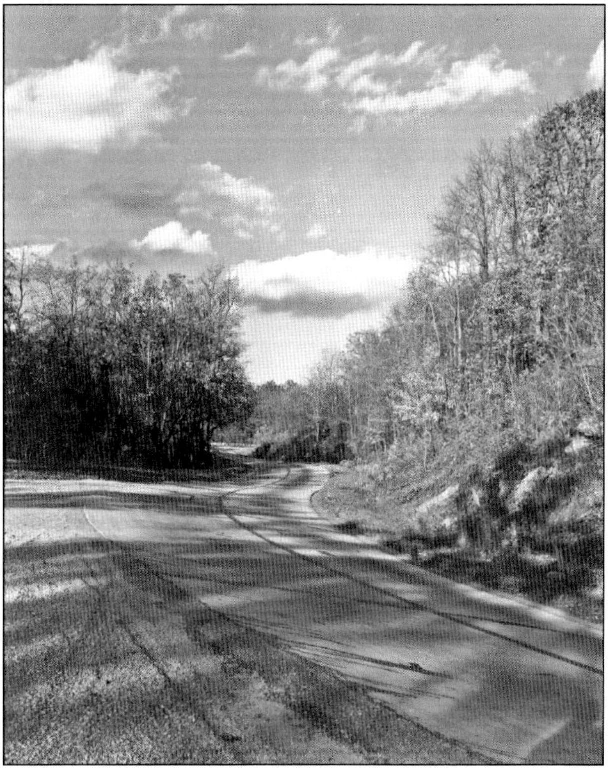

Sewanee is located on the Cumberland Plateau in Franklin County. It is an unincorporated town that is the home to two prestigious academic institutions—the University of the South and St. Andrew's-Sewanee School. Tracing its roots to the 19th century, St. Andrew's is one of the oldest day and boarding schools in the South. (Courtesy of the Tennessee State Library and Archives.)

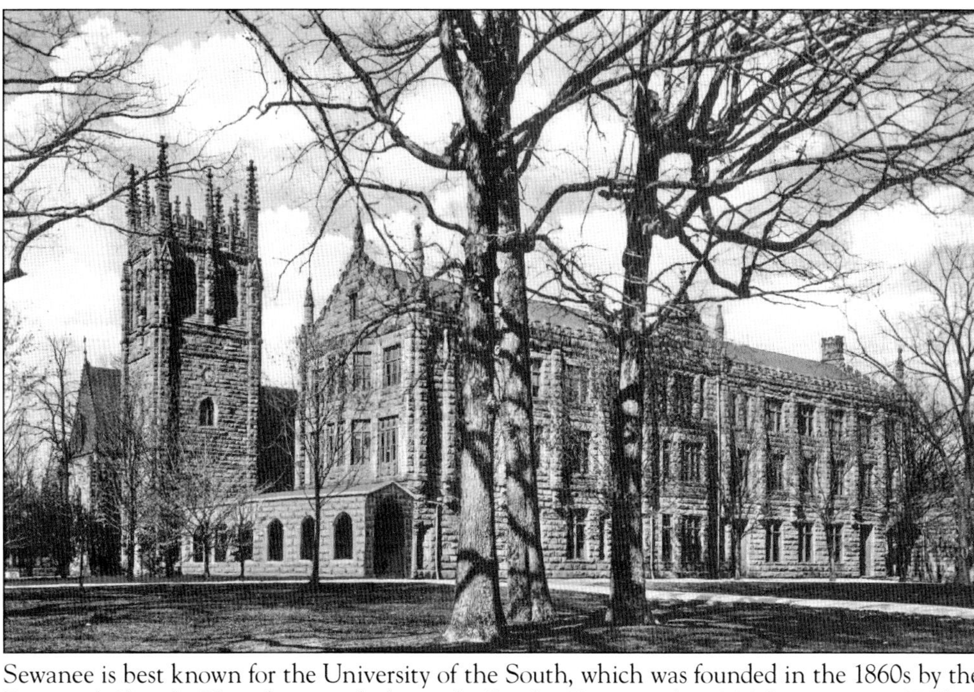

Sewanee is best known for the University of the South, which was founded in the 1860s by the Episcopal Church. This photograph shows the Breslin Tower in the 1886 Convocation Hall on the campus of the university. The Dixie Highway passed right through campus. (Courtesy of the Tennessee State Library and Archives.)

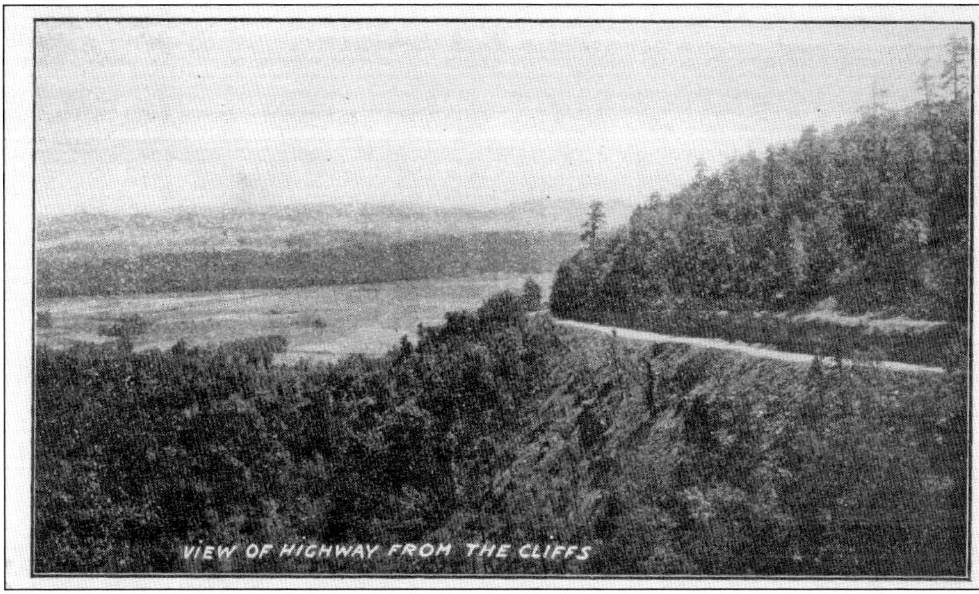


Taken about 20 years apart, these two images show scenic mountain views along the Dixie Highway. Automobile travelers often pulled over to capture these breathtaking vistas. Taking this into consideration, many transportation engineers incorporated scenic overlooks and roadside parks into their planning. People used these areas for picnics, taking a rest from driving, or even having a romantic interlude. The October 1949 photograph below was taken on Cumberland Mountain near Monteagle in Marion County by the Tennessee Department of Conservation. (Above, courtesy of Jeffrey Lee Durbin; below, courtesy of the Tennessee State Library and Archives.)

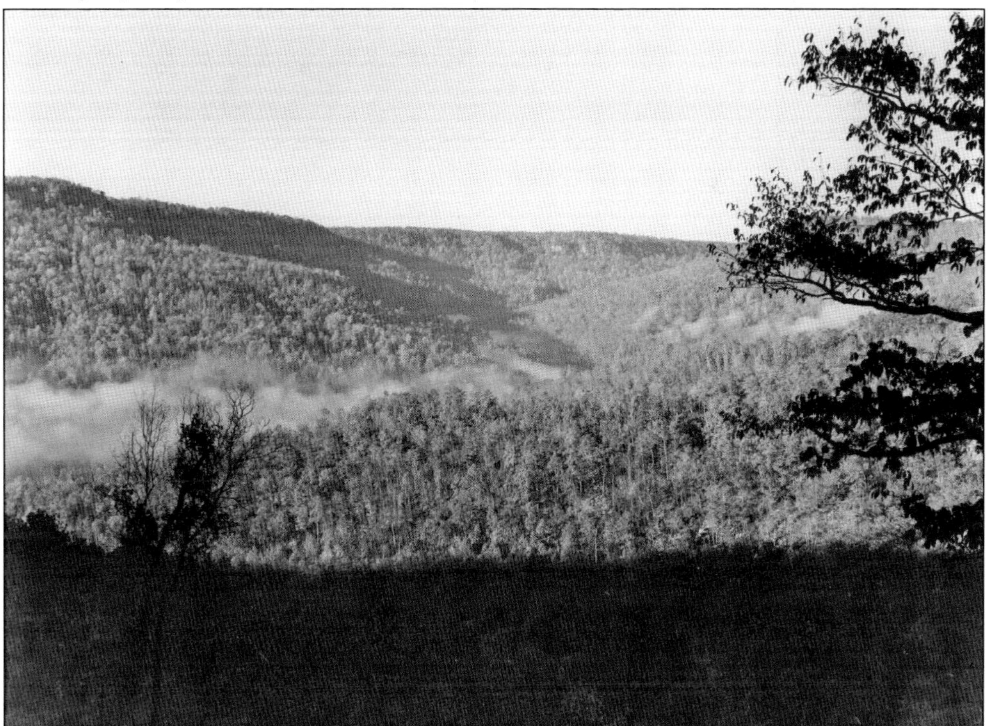

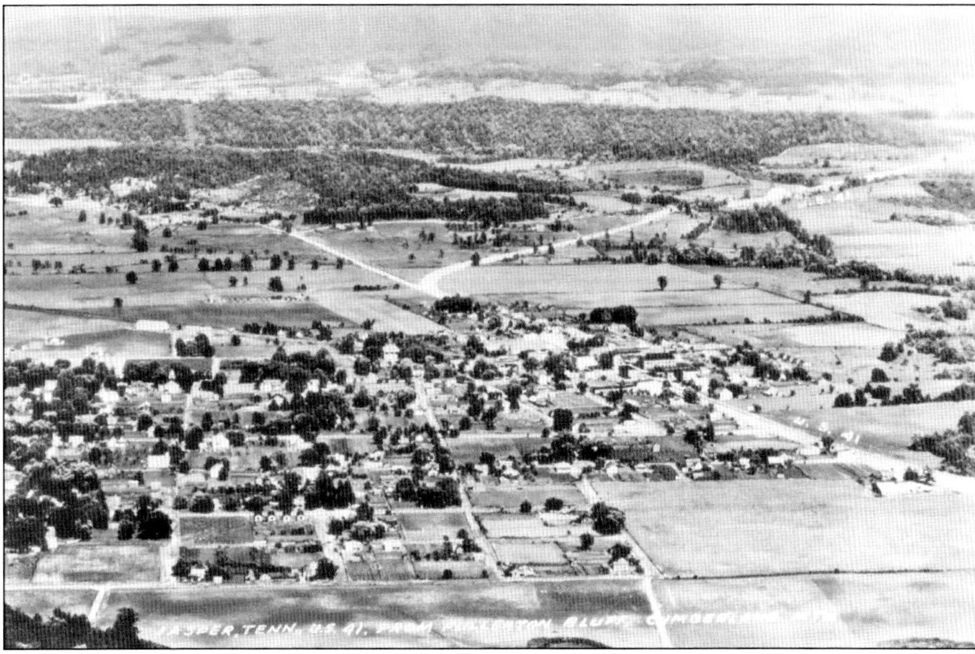


Named for Revolutionary War hero Sgt. William Jasper, the county seat of Marion County is Jasper. Located on the town's courthouse square is a monument honoring Judge Will Cummings, "the pioneer of permanent road building and public improvements in East Tennessee." (Courtesy of Jeffrey Lee Durbin.)

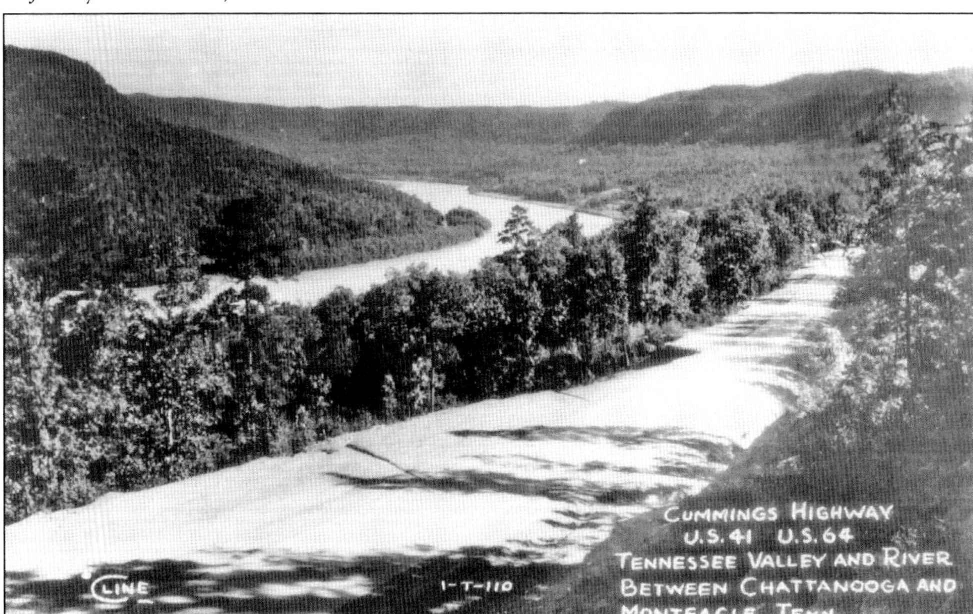


In 1931, the Tennessee legislature issued a joint resolution naming the section of the Dixie Highway from Jasper to Chattanooga the Cummings Highway. Three markers that were placed recognizing Judge Will Cummings's contribution to road building in Marion and Hamilton Counties are found along the route. One of them is located on the courthouse square in Jasper, Marion County. (Courtesy of Jeffrey Lee Durbin.)

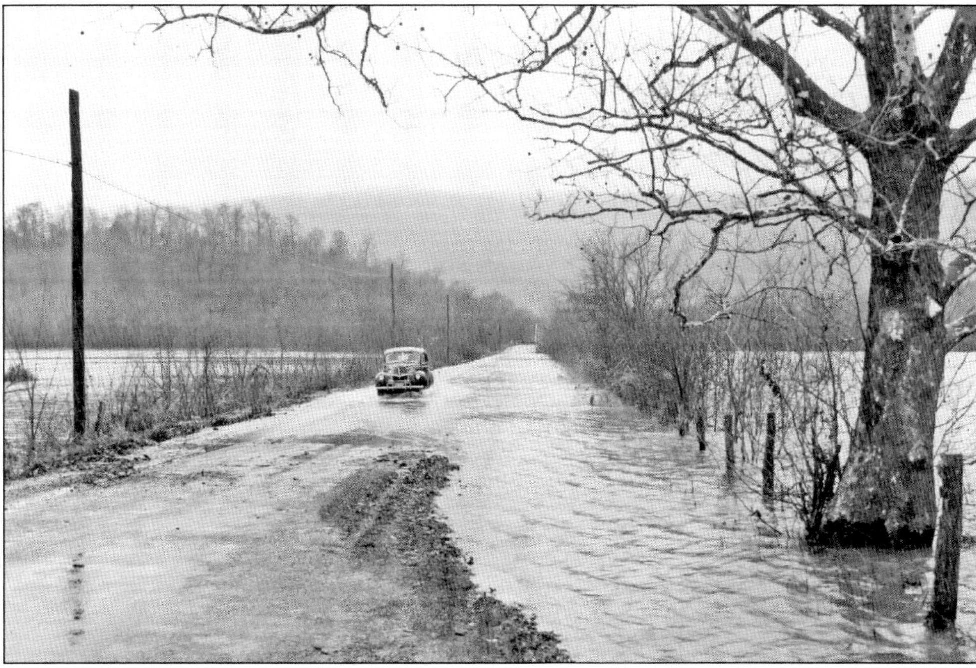

The characteristic straightness and narrowness of the Sequatchie Valley can be seen in this view of the valley. The Dixie Highway ran between Whitwell and Chattanooga over mountains and into the valley. This image shows the valley after the flooding of the Sequatchie Valley. (Courtesy of the Tennessee State Library and Archives.)

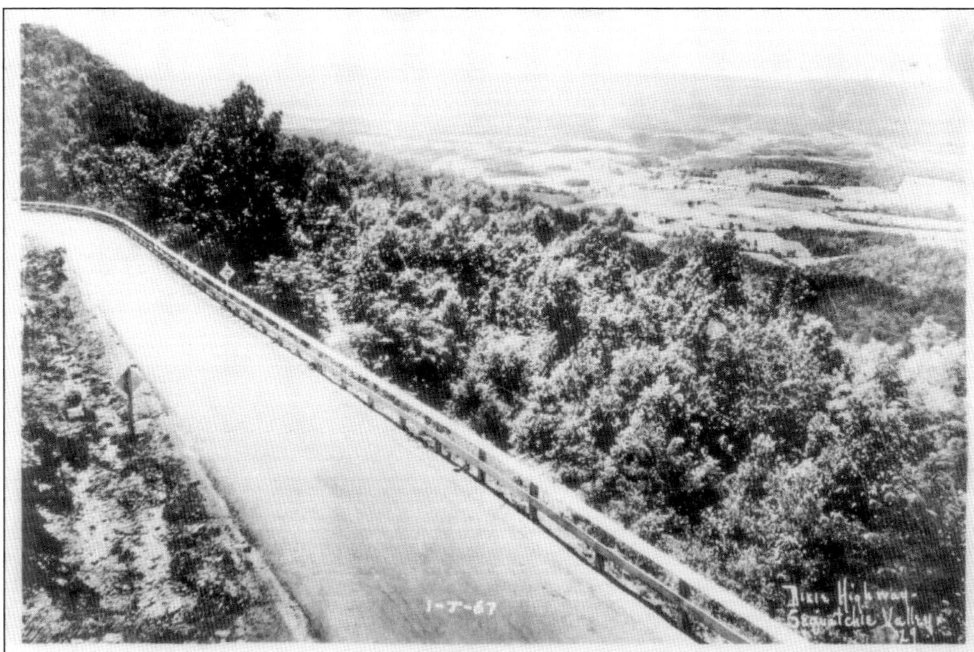


This postcard shows the Dixie Highway overlooking the spectacular Sequatchie Valley, which runs from the mountainous portion of the Cumberland Plateau known as the Crab Orchard Mountains to central Alabama, south of the Tennessee River. (Courtesy of Jeffrey Lee Durbin.)

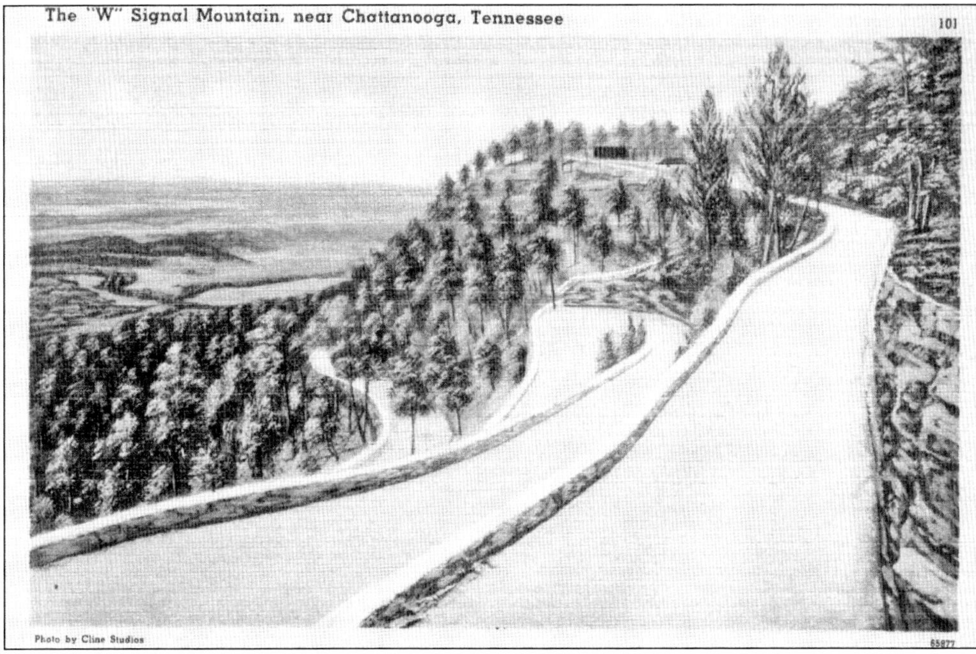


The town of Signal Mountain, Tennessee, is located along Walden's Ridge. The State of Tennessee granted its charter in 1919. Charles E. James, president of the Signal Mountain Land Development Company and one of the founding members of the Dixie Highway Association, began developing the area and was elected as Signal Mountain's first mayor. (Courtesy of Jeffrey Lee Durbin.)

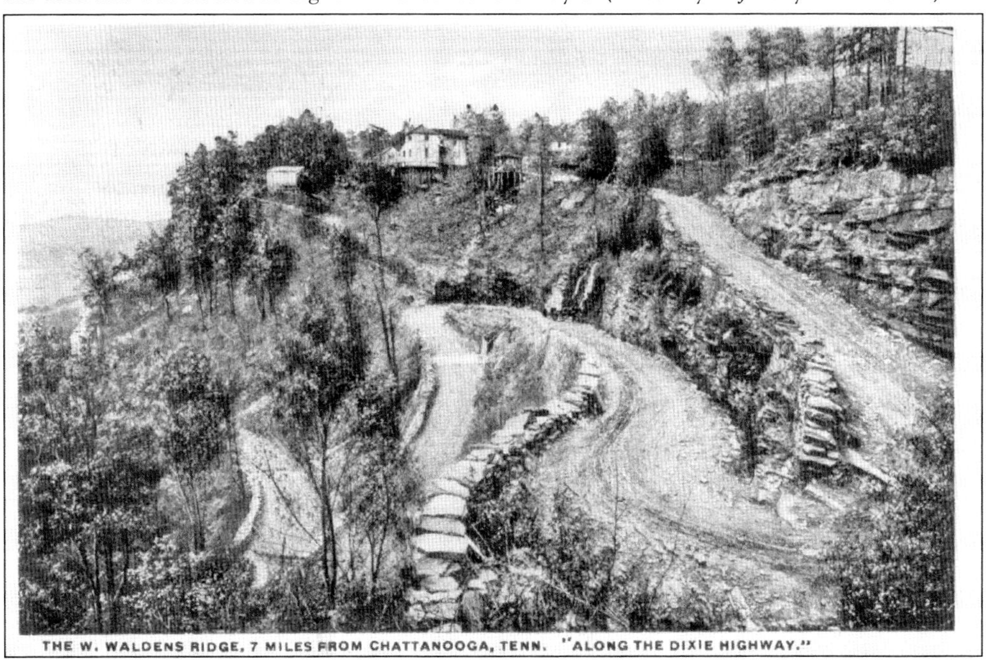


This image provides some sense of how difficult completing the highway was in Marion County. At 3,048 feet, Walden's Ridge is the highest point on the Dixie Highway and is sometimes referred to as Hinch Mountain. The ridge runs along the eastern edge of the Cumberland Plateau. (Courtesy of Jeffrey Lee Durbin.)

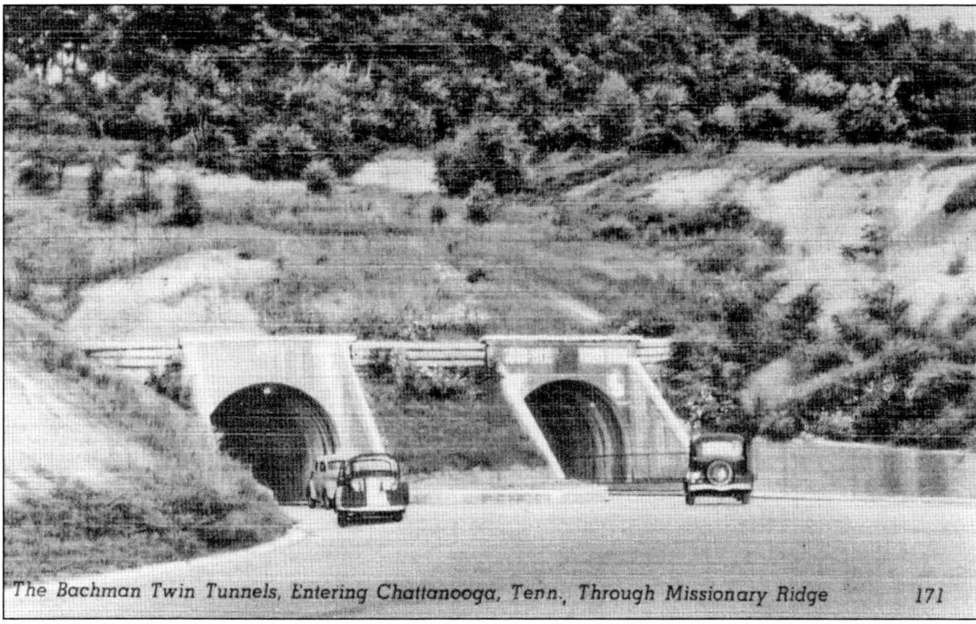


Known as the Bachman Tubes or the Twin Tunnels, this pair of single-lane tubes takes travelers on Ringgold Road/U.S. 41-76 from Chattanooga through Missionary Ridge to the adjacent Tennessee town of East Ridge. A feat of engineering, each tunnel is 1,034.8 feet long. They are named for Nathan L. Bachman, who was Chattanooga's city attorney, circuit court judge, associate judge of the Tennessee Supreme Court, and U.S. senator. Judge Will Cummings played an important role in getting these 1929 tunnels constructed. (Above, courtesy of the author; below, courtesy of the Chattanooga–Hamilton County Bicentennial Library.)

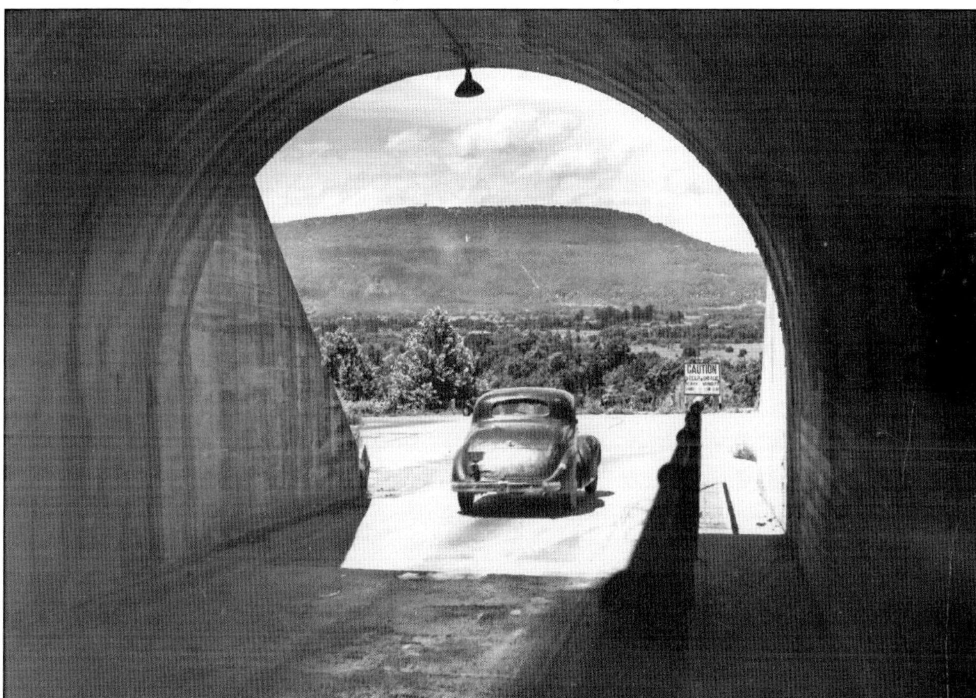

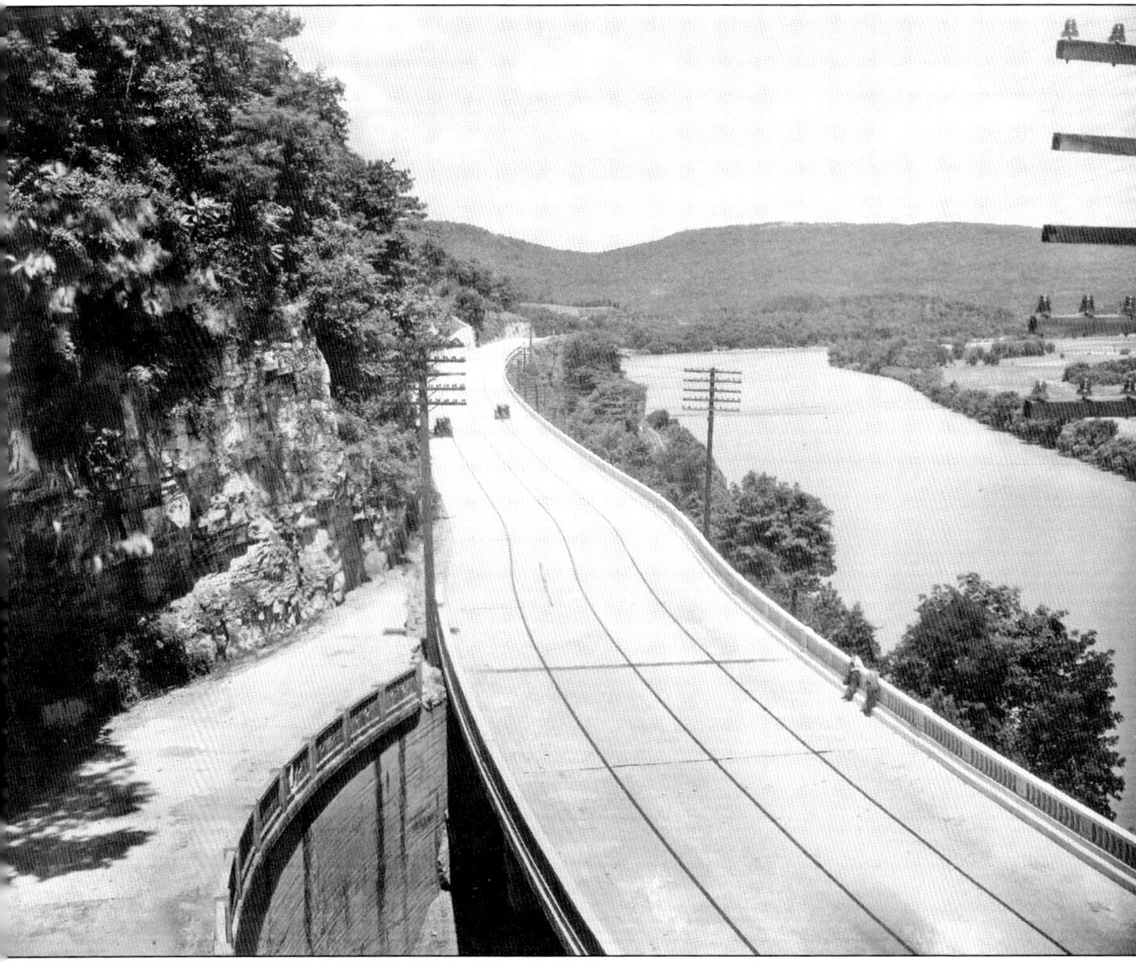

Although the initial development of the Dixie Highway occurred between 1915 and 1927, the highway's route continued to change over time. After the national standardized numbering system was adopted in 1925, the original route of the Dixie Highway was changed in several sections from Springfield to Chattanooga, oftentimes creating a more direct route from north to south through the state. In addition, as road construction methods, technologies, materials, and processes improved, sections were bypassed to meet new safety standards and to further straighten out the route. This photograph clearly shows a bypassed portion of the road near Chattanooga that utilized modern building techniques. The Tennessee River and agricultural fields are visible to the right of the photograph. (Courtesy of the Chattanooga-Hamilton County Bicentennial Library.)

# *Four*

# SERVICING THE PUBLIC

The promoters of the Dixie Highway saw the potential for the highway to bring economic prosperity to the region, and citizens capitalized on the highway by starting businesses along the route. These businesses served not only the local communities but also the tourists who were traveling through or stopping for a visit. Entrepreneurs constructed gas stations, overnight accommodations, restaurants, automobile showrooms, stores, and other roadside buildings and attractions. In addition to the obviously automobile-related ventures that dotted the highway, industrialists and governments desired the improved access offered by the highway and constructed new factories, public buildings, and even military facilities to take advantage of the road.

Whereas early curbside and shed filling stations were located in the central business district, house-type stations usually were built nearer the residential sections of town. In order to blend in with the neighborhood, these stations of the 1920s were built with a domestic appearance. Later stations were standardized and modern in appearance, with canopies, multiple bays, and larger parking lots.

As touring the country became popular, the need for overnight accommodations rose. Hotels were in cities, but these were usually expensive and required a certain level of decorum. New motorists did not keep tight schedules or necessarily clean appearances due to the new freedom that car travel provided and the problems associated with the car and muddy roads. These rustic travelers began camping out along the highways, living a gypsy-like existence. Soon property owners began to resent the campers, not all of whom were always respectful of private property. To solve this problem, some owners began to charge for camping or offered rented rooms. Some cities opened municipal camps to encourage tourism.

Many entrepreneurs saw opportunities for commercial success growing out of the rising demand for tourist homes and auto camps. They provided cabins and other facilities for the road-weary motorist. In order to fulfill the changing needs of automobile travelers, many cabin camps, cottage courts, motor courts, motor inns, and highway hotels developed over the 20th century, as did other businesses included in this chapter.

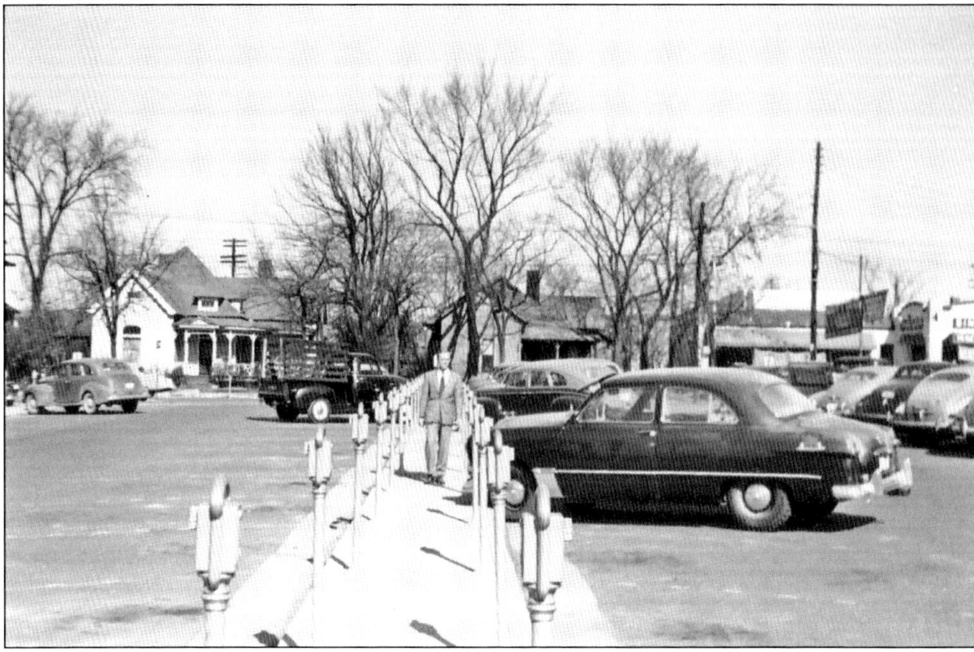

This photograph shows how the automobile changed the character of residential neighborhoods. In the foreground there is a parking lot with meters, and in the background is a Sinclair gas station that resembles a house, making it fit in better with the surrounding residential community. (Courtesy Tennessee State Library and Archives.)

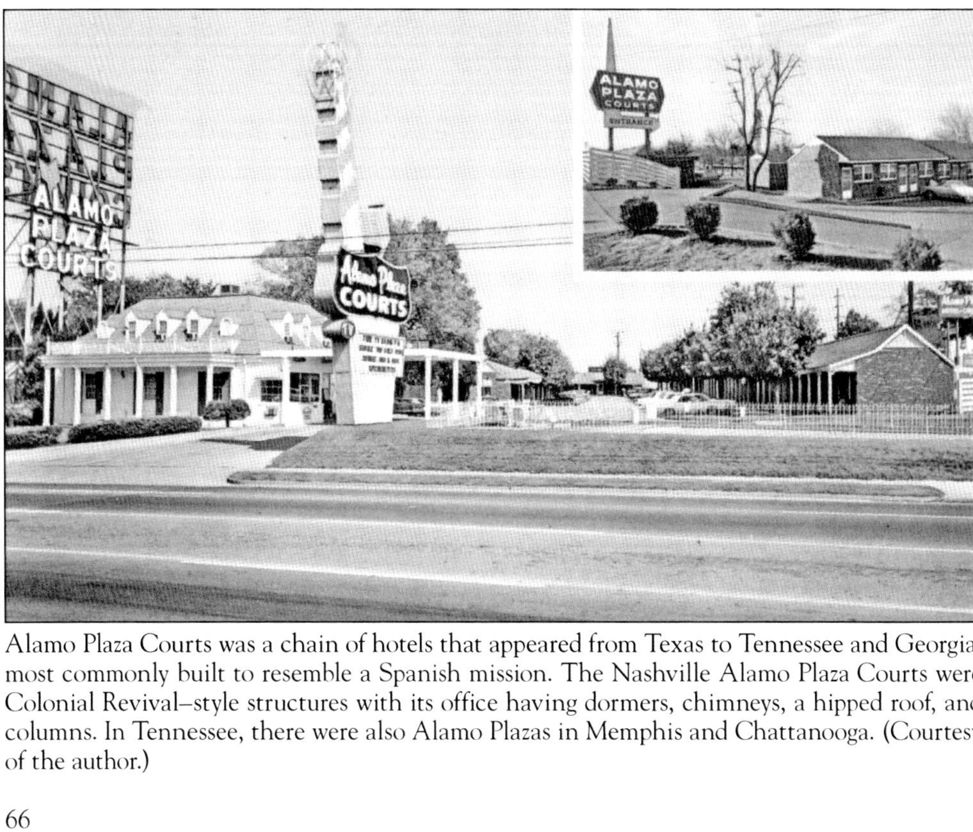


Alamo Plaza Courts was a chain of hotels that appeared from Texas to Tennessee and Georgia, most commonly built to resemble a Spanish mission. The Nashville Alamo Plaza Courts were Colonial Revival–style structures with its office having dormers, chimneys, a hipped roof, and columns. In Tennessee, there were also Alamo Plazas in Memphis and Chattanooga. (Courtesy of the author.)

This 1951 photograph demonstrates how buildings were used as advertisements, a predecessor to the modern billboard. These advertisements were designed big enough to catch the attention of the driving public. This sign is marketing the regional Goo-Goo Cluster candies at the intersection of Fourth and Cedar (now Charlotte) Streets in Nashville. (Courtesy of the Tennessee State Library and Archives.)

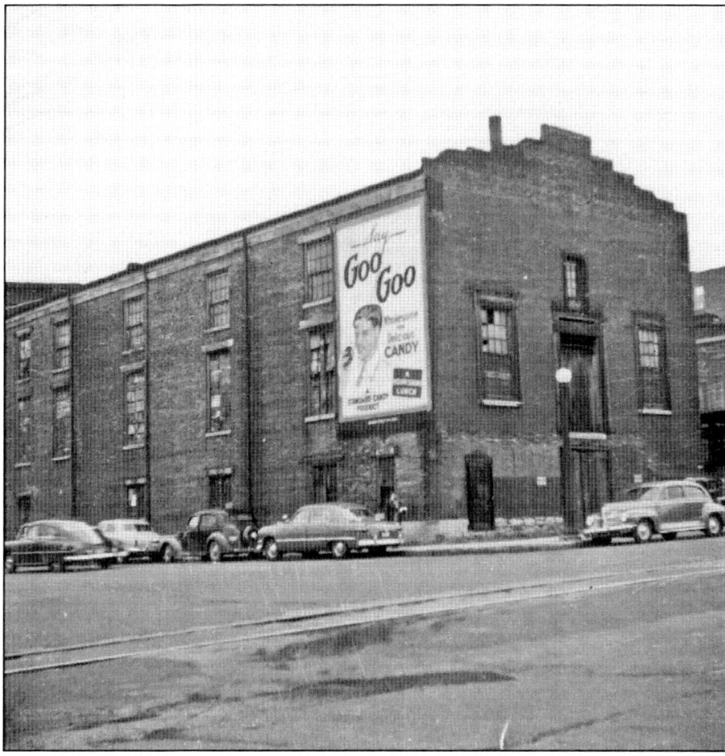


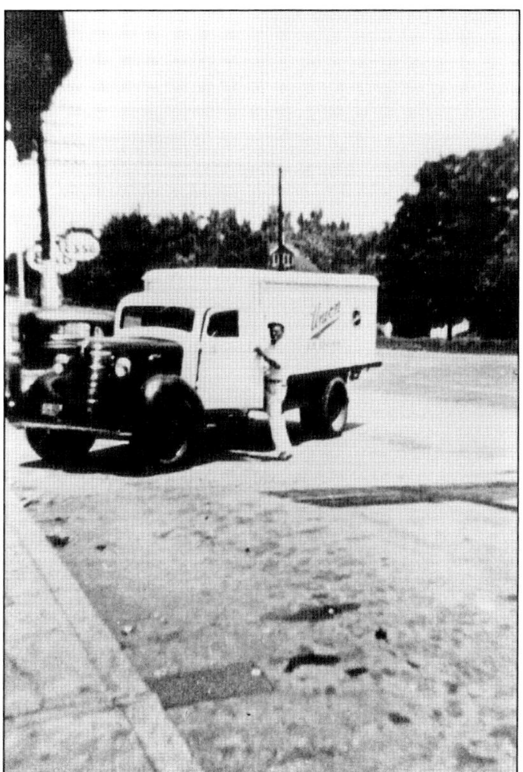

The highway offered more employment opportunities than just running a roadside business. The driver of this Union Ice Cream truck made his living off the good roads, delivering to stores and gas stations. Pictured in the 1930s or 1940s, the delivery man is bringing his frozen treats to an Esso gas station in Nashville. (Courtesy of the Tennessee State Library and Archives.)

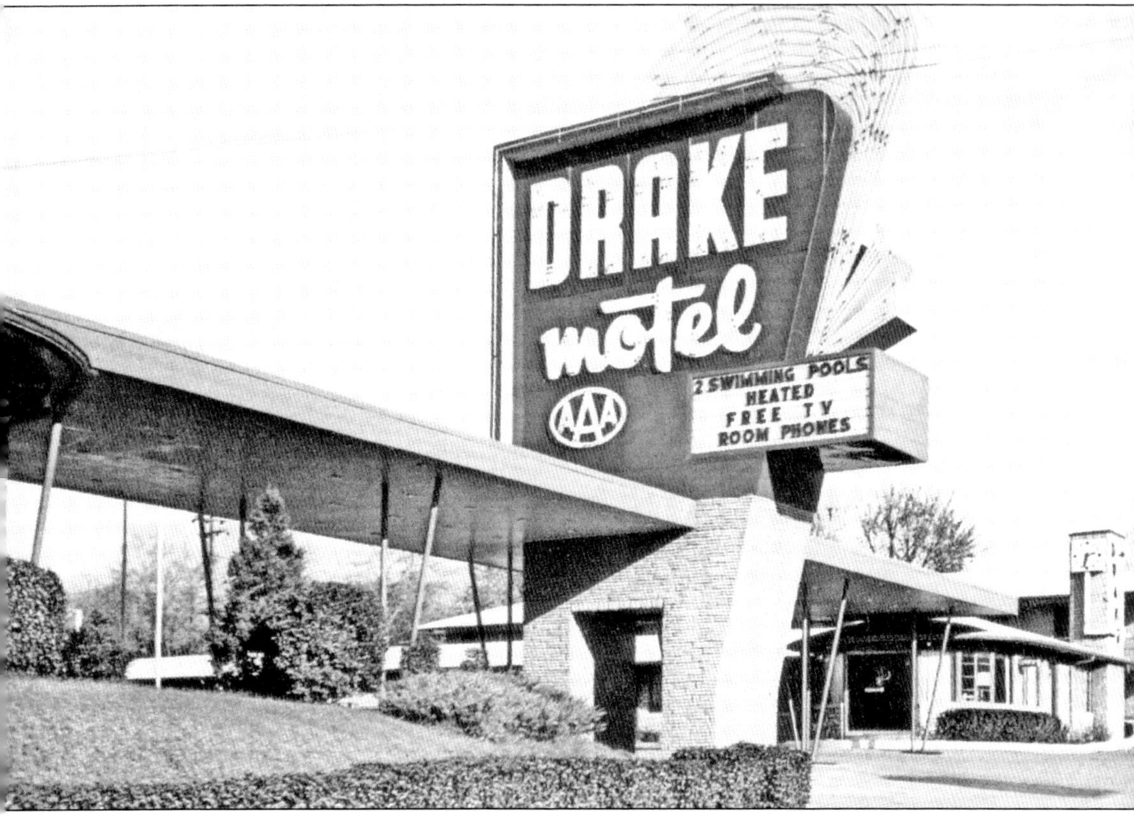


The Drake Hotel Courts still operates just south of downtown Nashville on Murfreesboro Road as transitional housing. When it was built, it was advertised as the "South's newest and finest," as well as having two heated swimming pools, free television, and telephones in the rooms. These amenities marked the Drake Hotel as a modern place to stay. The hotel also offered discounts to members of the American Automobile Association, as designated by the large AAA on its sign. A second Drake Hotel Courts and Restaurant operated on Broad Street in downtown Chattanooga, also along the route of the Dixie Highway on U.S. Route 41. (Courtesy of Jeffrey Lee Durbin.)

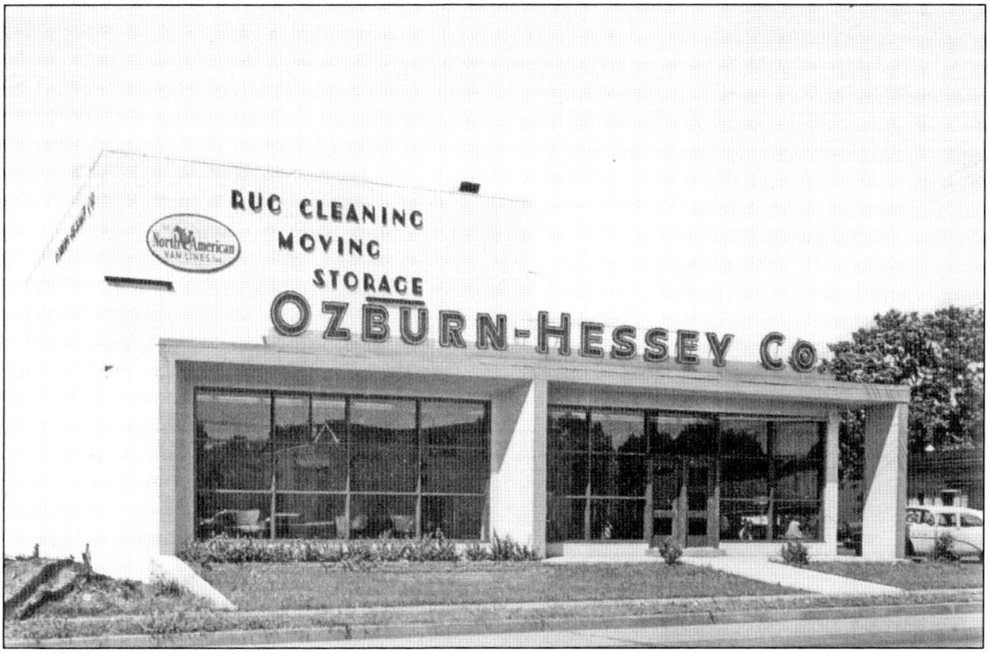


Still in business at its original location on Murfreesboro Road in Nashville, the Ozburn-Hessey Company started in a prominent location to take advantage of the traffic that passed by. The company offered rug cleaning, storage, and moving services. (Courtesy of Jeffrey Lee Durbin.)

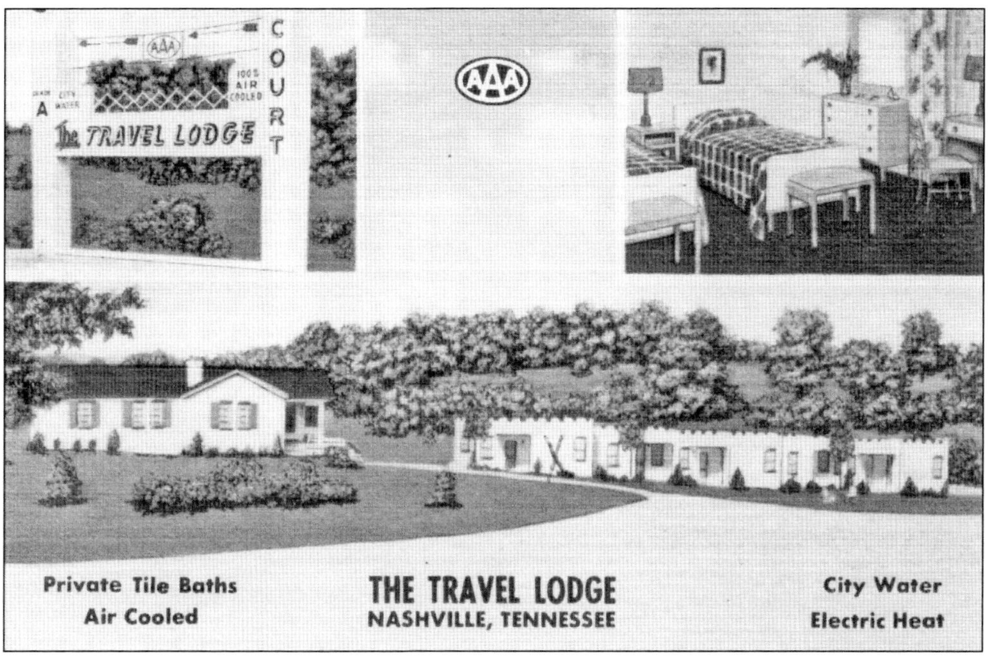


Another overnight accommodation that remains in operation as apartments is the Travel Lodge, also on Murfreesboro Road 9 miles south of downtown Nashville. The marketing for it read, "attractive restful furnishings in buildings of masonry" and "resting in picturesque valley away from traffic noise." The historic signage was replaced around 2003. (Courtesy of the author.)

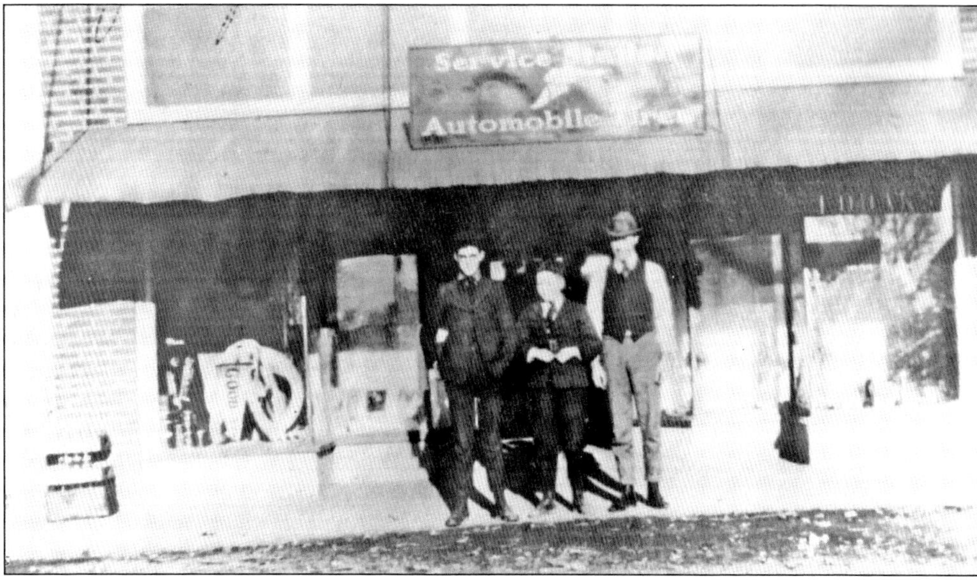


This 1919 photograph shows, from left to right, Joe Edwards, John Lowery, and Batey Grisham standing in front of a service station in downtown Smyrna. The signage indicates that they repaired automobiles and sold tires. A Goodyear pennant is visible in the window. (Courtesy of the Albert Gore Research Center, Middle Tennessee State University.)

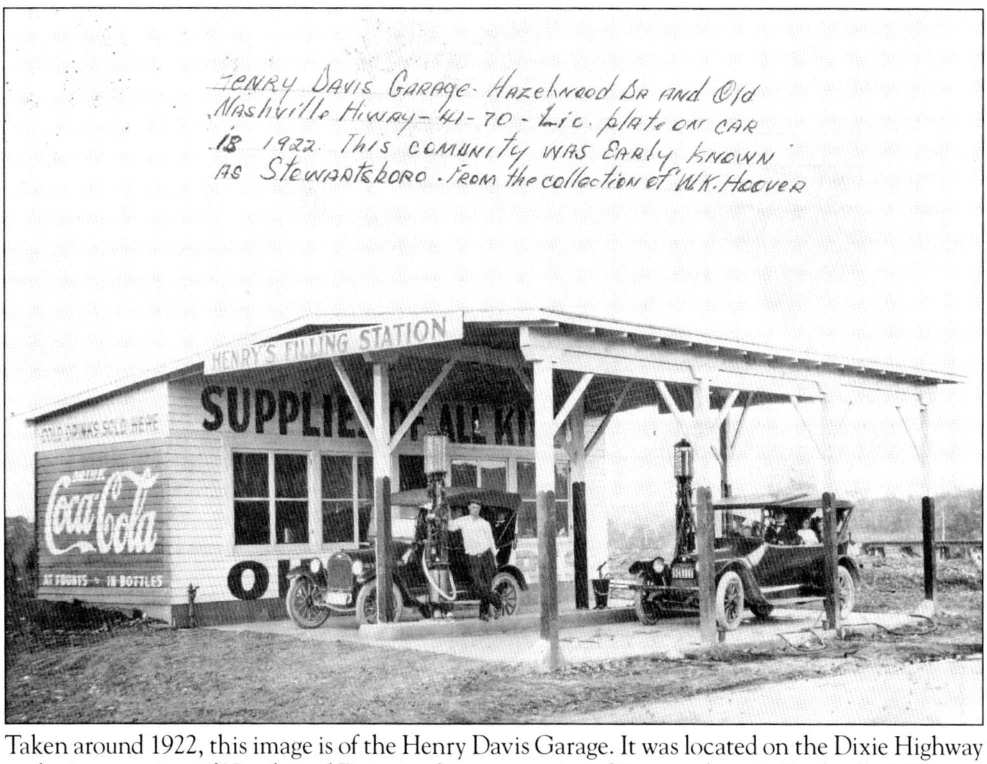


Taken around 1922, this image is of the Henry Davis Garage. It was located on the Dixie Highway at the intersection of Hazelwood Drive in the community of Stewartsboro in Rutherford County. Along with its painted Coca-Cola sign, its advertisement reads, "Supplies of all kinds." (Courtesy of the Albert Gore Research Center, Middle Tennessee State University.)

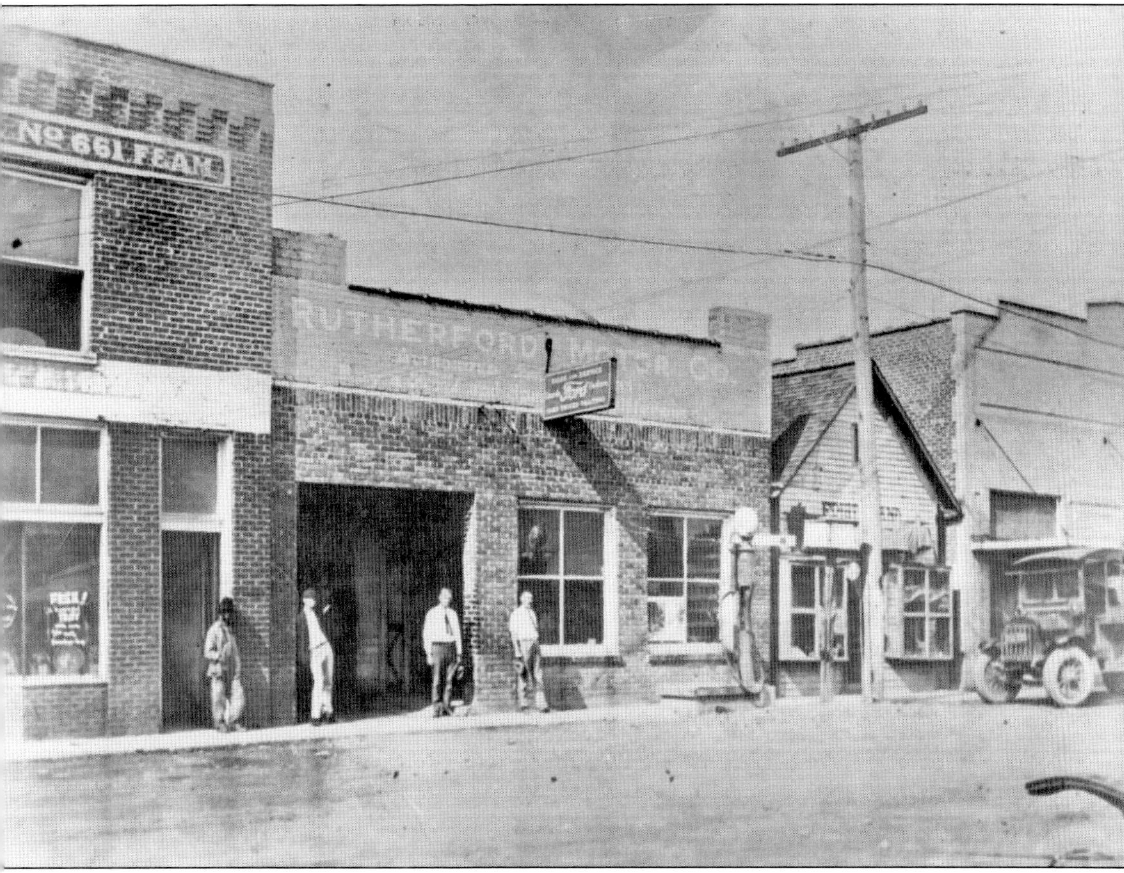


The Rutherford Motor Company, established on November 1, 1922, was located in an attached commercial building in downtown Smyrna. This 1924 image shows the business as an authorized Ford dealer with gas pumps on the curb, as was often the case with early stations. Smyrna residents Jim Harris, Rary Quarrells, and B. S. Flowers are standing out front. To the left of the Rutherford Motor Company is a two-story building. The first floor housed some type of commercial establishment, and the second floor housed the Lodge No. 661 of the Free and Accepted Masons (abbreviated as F&AM on the front facade). There still exists a Sam Davis Lodge No. 661 of the F&AM that dates its first bylaws to 1911. (Courtesy of the Albert Gore Research Center, Middle Tennessee State University.)

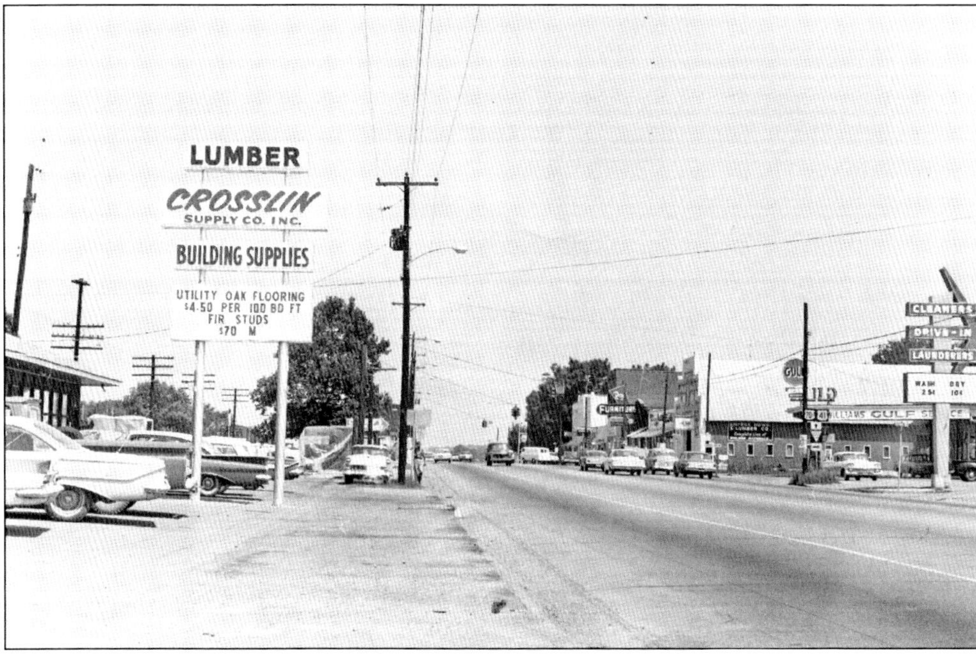


This image of U.S. Route 41/70 in Rutherford County shows the roadside development that included lumber companies, a Gulf station, furniture store, and dry cleaners. The signage for the cleaners advertises their drive-through window, which provided an added convenience for the driving customer. (Courtesy of the Albert Gore Research Center, Middle Tennessee State University.)

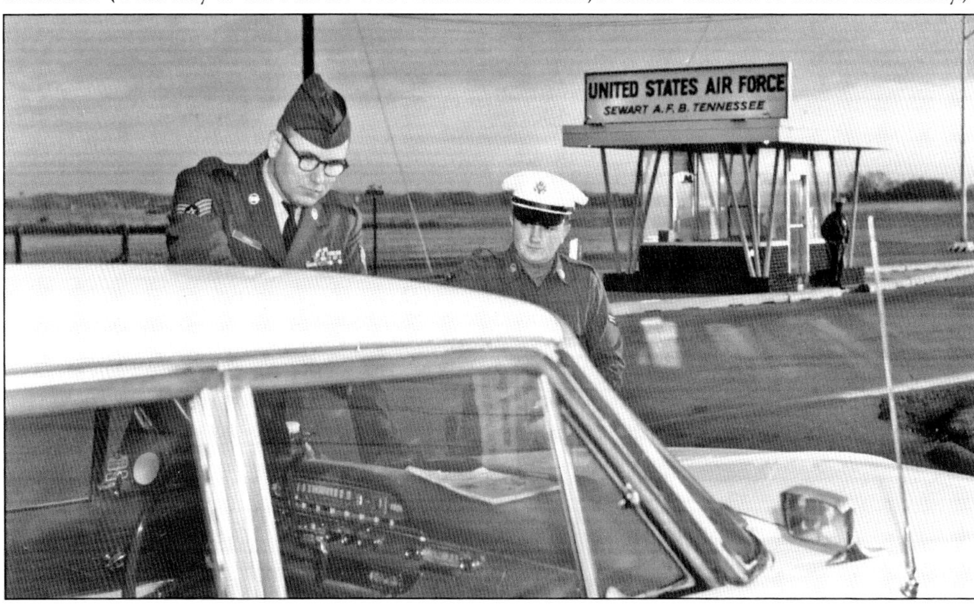


From its early days, promoters touted the Dixie Highway as a "national necessity" to assist with the war effort during World War I. The military connection continued as the federal government located several facilities along the Dixie Highway in Tennessee, including National Guard armories in Murfreesboro and Shelbyville, Stewart Air Force Base in Smyrna (shown in this image), and the Arnold Engineering Development Center in Tullahoma. (Courtesy of the Albert Gore Research Center, Middle Tennessee State University.)

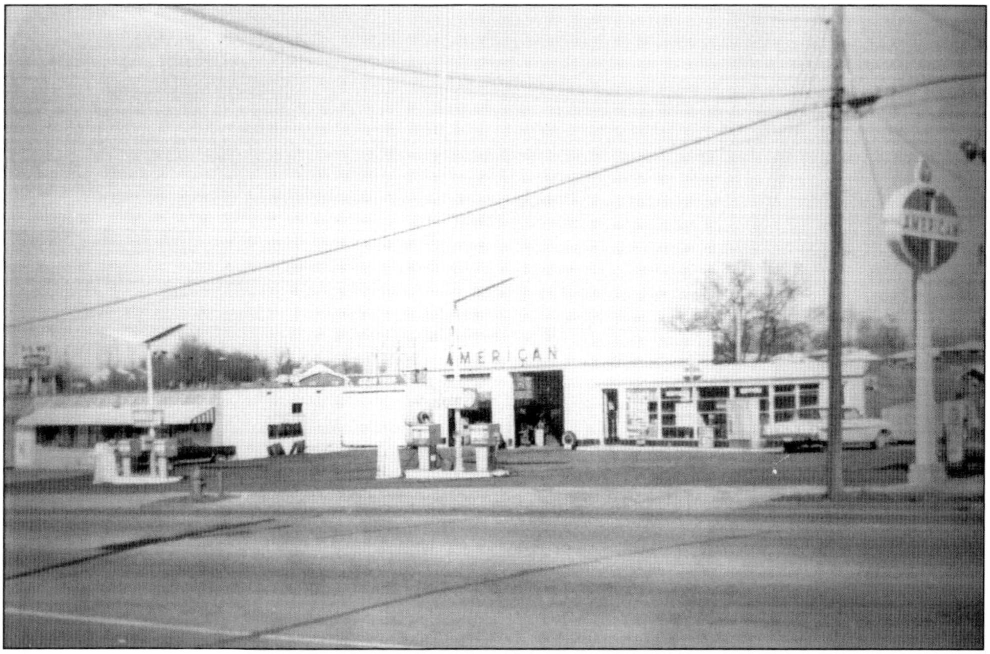

This photograph shows a more modern service station in Rutherford County. Its high service bays accommodated most vehicles, and its glass office sold motor oil, tires, car batteries, and other accessories. (Courtesy of the Albert Gore Research Center, Middle Tennessee State University.)

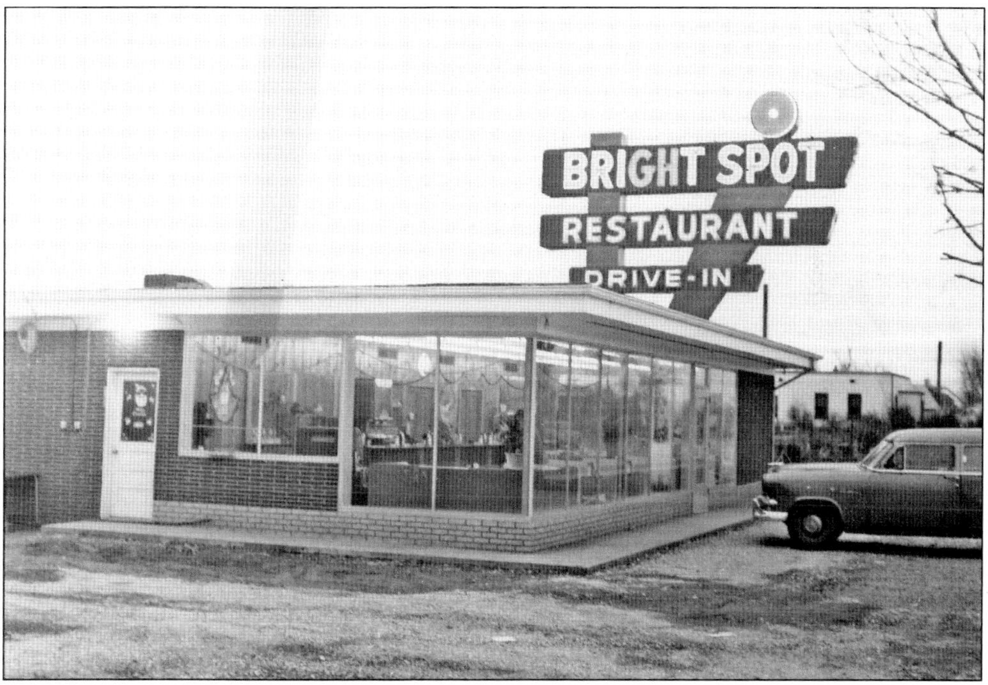

Located in Smyrna, the Bright Spot Restaurant offered its customers sit-down dining. For people who were in a hurry, the restaurant offered drive-through service. (Courtesy of the Albert Gore Research Center, Middle Tennessee State University.)

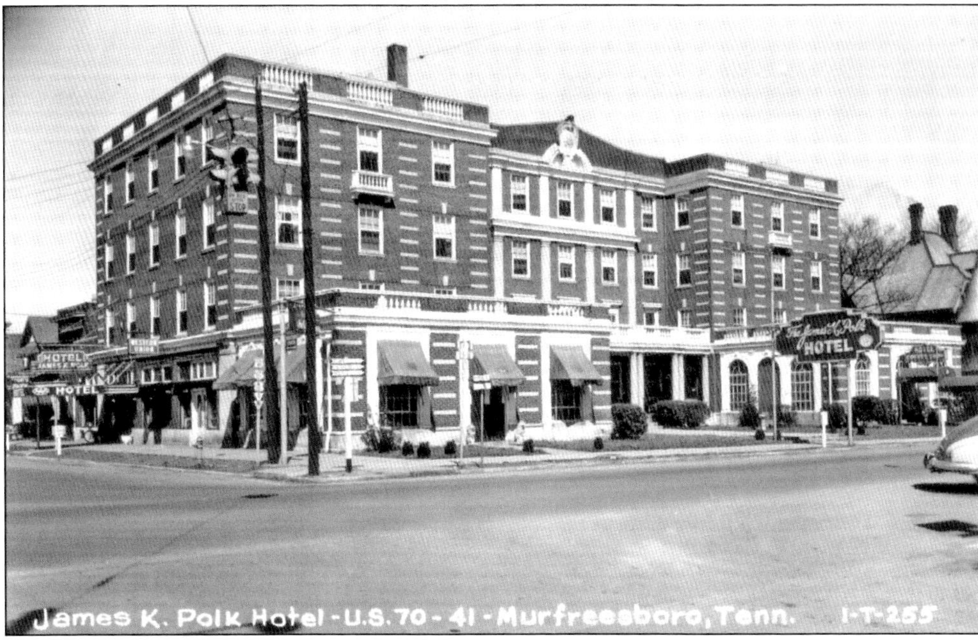

The James K. Polk Hotel was located in downtown Murfreesboro, just off the courthouse square on Main Street. The hotel was named after the 11th president of the United States, whose wife, Sarah Childress Polk, was from Murfreesboro. (Courtesy of Jeffrey Lee Durbin.)

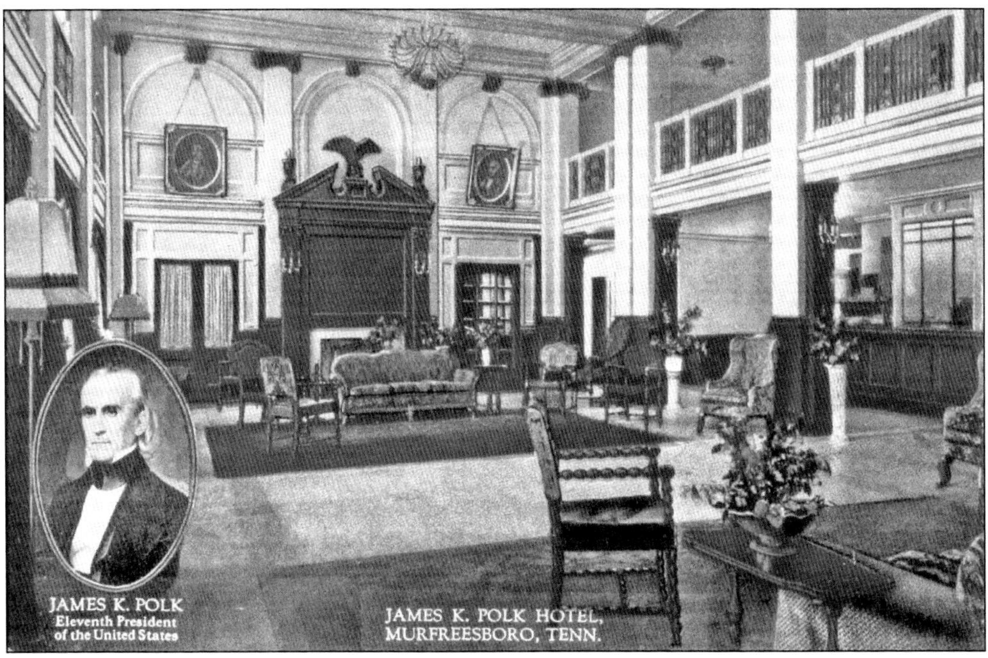

Although designed in an extremely traditional style of architecture, the James K. Polk Hotel in Murfreesboro advertised itself as "A strictly modern hotel, including every room with bath, circulating ice water and ceiling fan. All rooms luxuriously furnished, and a homelike atmosphere throughout." The hotel was torn down around 1980 for the construction of a bank. (Courtesy of Jeffrey Lee Durbin.)

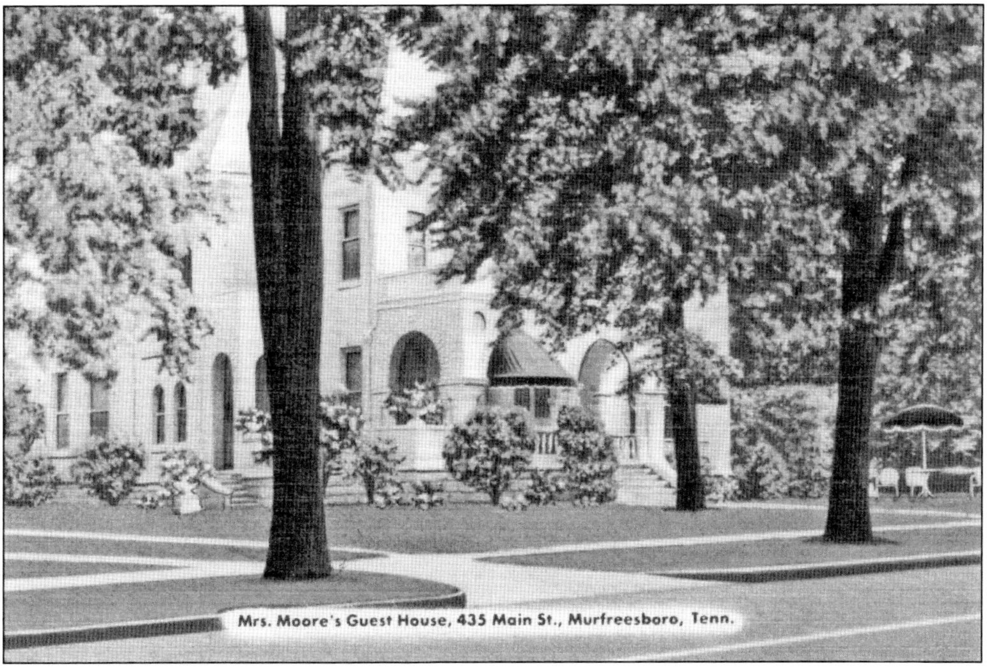


Most recently known as Clardy's Guest house, a bed-and-breakfast inn that also provided rooms for rent, Moore's Guest House on Main Street in downtown Murfreesboro offered guests room and board both on a short-term and a long-term basis. (Courtesy of Jeffrey Lee Durbin.)

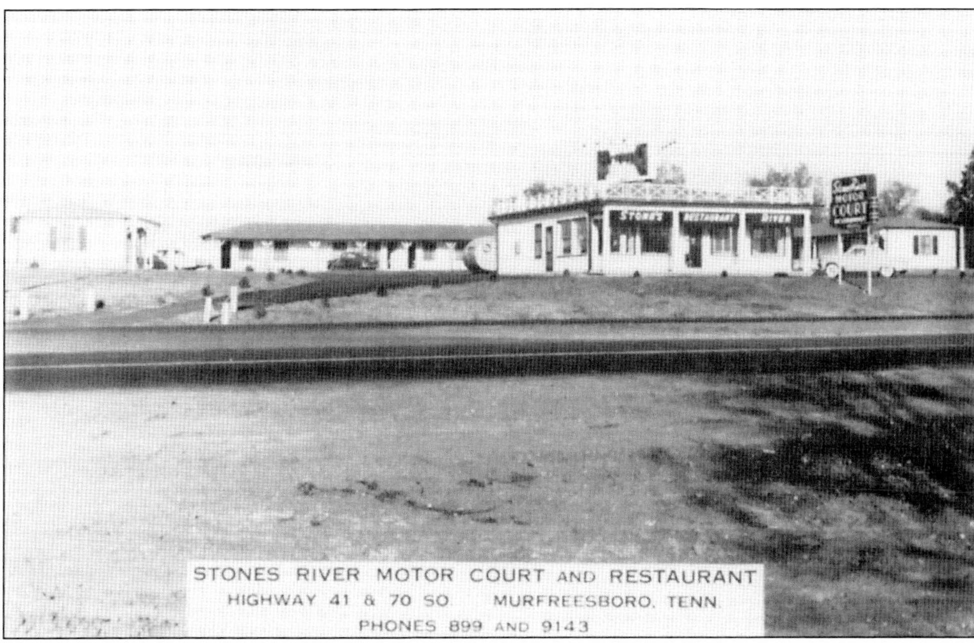


The Stones River Motor Court and Restaurant was located in Murfreesboro near the Stones River battlefield. Its advertised rates were $4 and up, and its restaurant served "fine cuisine." This motor court had multiple buildings that are recognizable as an early form of a motel-type accommodation. (Courtesy of Jeffrey Lee Durbin.)

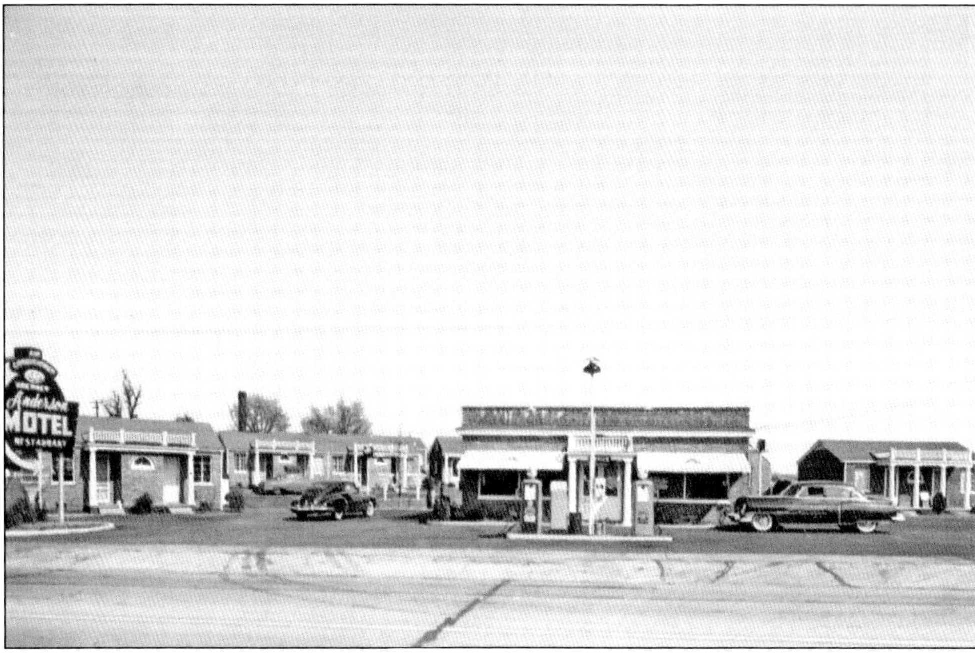


The Anderson Motel and Restaurant in Murfreesboro also offered the traveler gasoline with its pumps right in front of the office along U.S. Route 41. The Colonial Revival–style duplex cottages had semi-elliptical windows, columns, and roof balustrades. The restaurant served pork chops, fried chicken, and steaks. (Courtesy of Jeffrey Lee Durbin.)

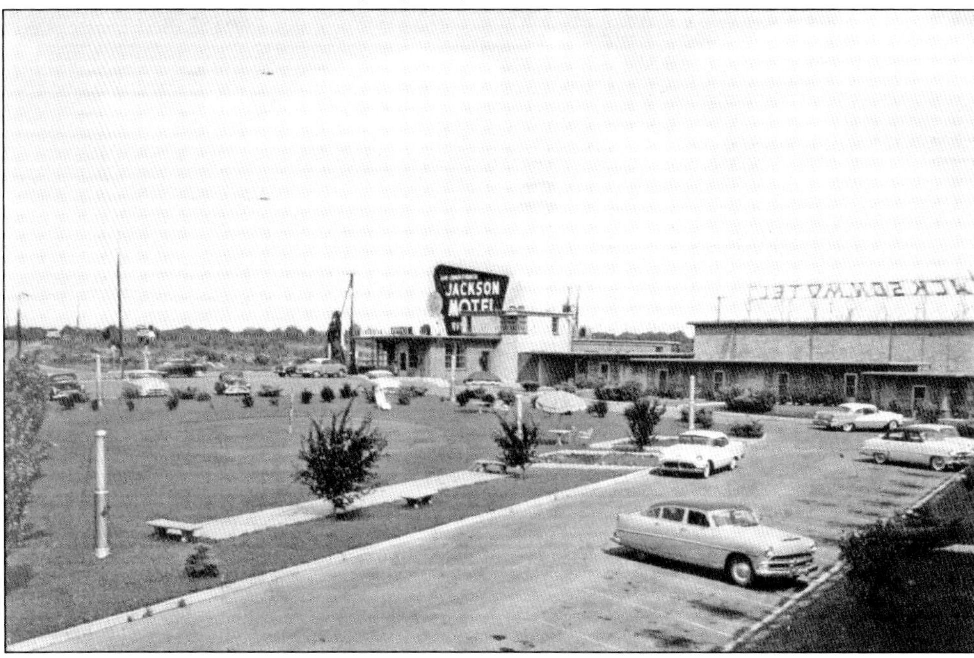


Although postdating the heyday of the Dixie Highway, the Jackson Motel still operates at the edge of downtown Murfreesboro and retains much of its early signage. It catered to its guests with a putting green, shuffleboard, convention rooms, and a restaurant. It called itself "the Waldorf of motels." (Courtesy of Jeffrey Lee Durbin.)

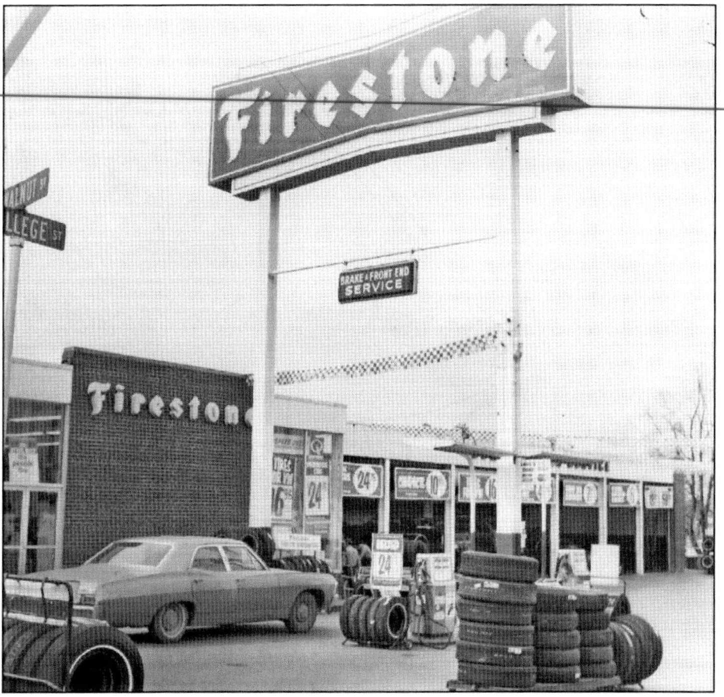


The Firestone Complete Auto Care on West College Street in Murfreesboro remains in operation. This business illustrates that a portion of downtown Murfreesboro was home to many automobile-related businesses. Just a few blocks to the west, the town's "gasoline alley" was home to at least 14 businesses catering to the automobile in the 1930s. (Courtesy of the Albert Gore Research Center, Middle Tennessee State University.)

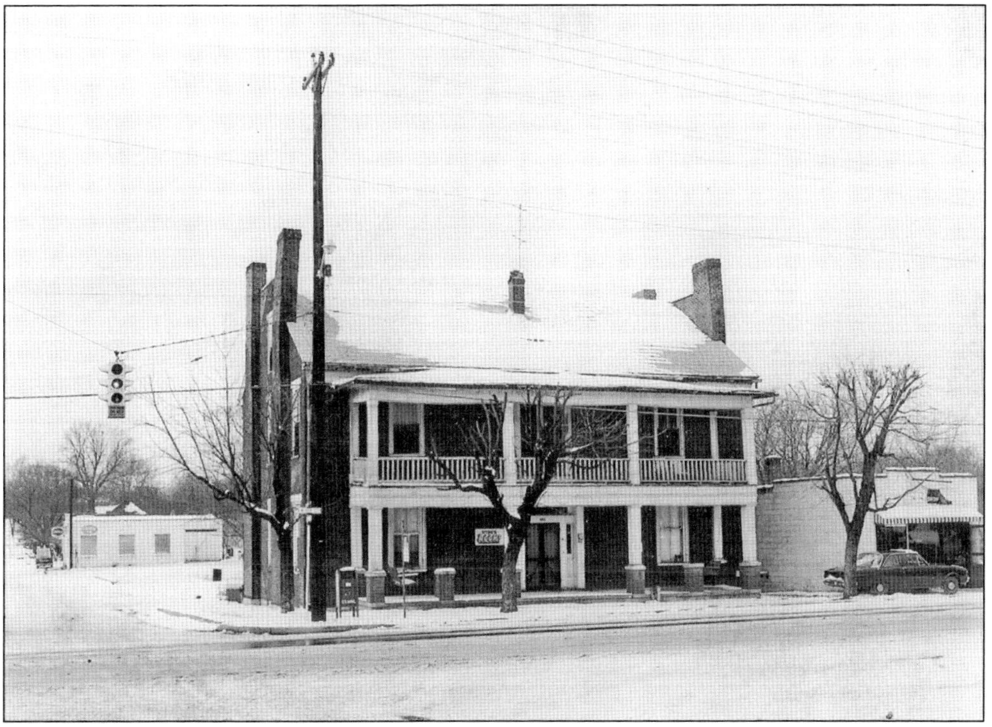

The Black House was a tourist home in Shelbyville on what is now U.S. Route 231. It was run by a local family before there were motor courts and motels. This image of the house was taken in the 1950s, and the building was torn down in the late 1960s or early 1970s as the street was widened. (Courtesy of Jane Townes.)

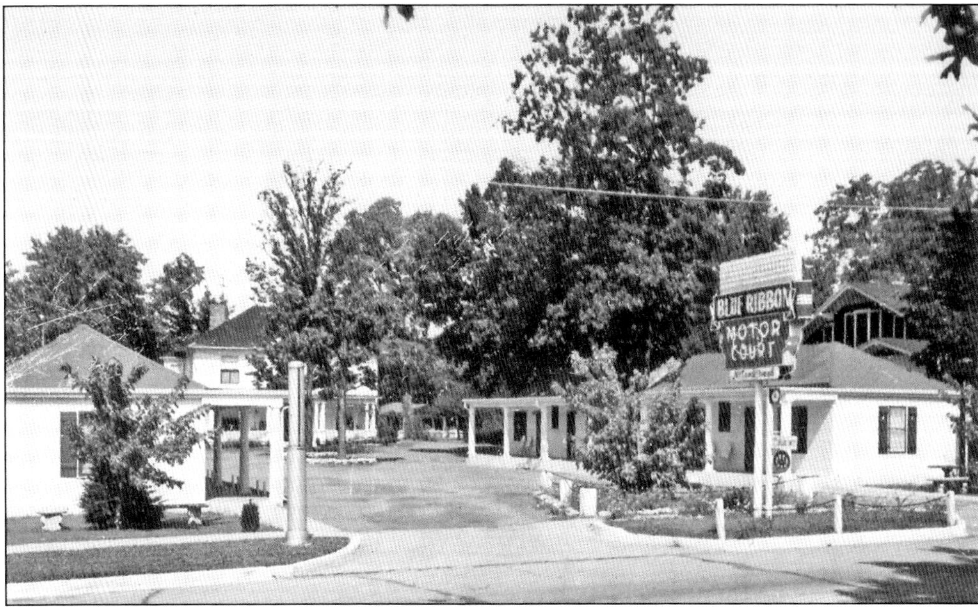


These two postcards show different styles of overnight accommodations—the earlier classical Blue Ribbon Motor Court and the later modern Magnolia Motel. As hosts of one of the best known equestrian events in the country, the Tennessee Walking Horse National Celebration, Shelbyville witnessed an increased need for lodging. The Dixie Highway enabled visitors, trainers, and owners to attend these events, and even if they did not place, they could stay in the Blue Ribbon Motor Court and eat at its Saddle Restaurant. The brainchild of Henry Davis of Wartrace, Tennessee, the Tennessee Walking Horse National Celebration began in 1939 as a way to annually celebrate Bedford County's greatest asset—its walking horses. The event is held around Labor Day every year and has grown to feature 2,000 horses during 11 days of the celebration. (Both, courtesy of the author.)

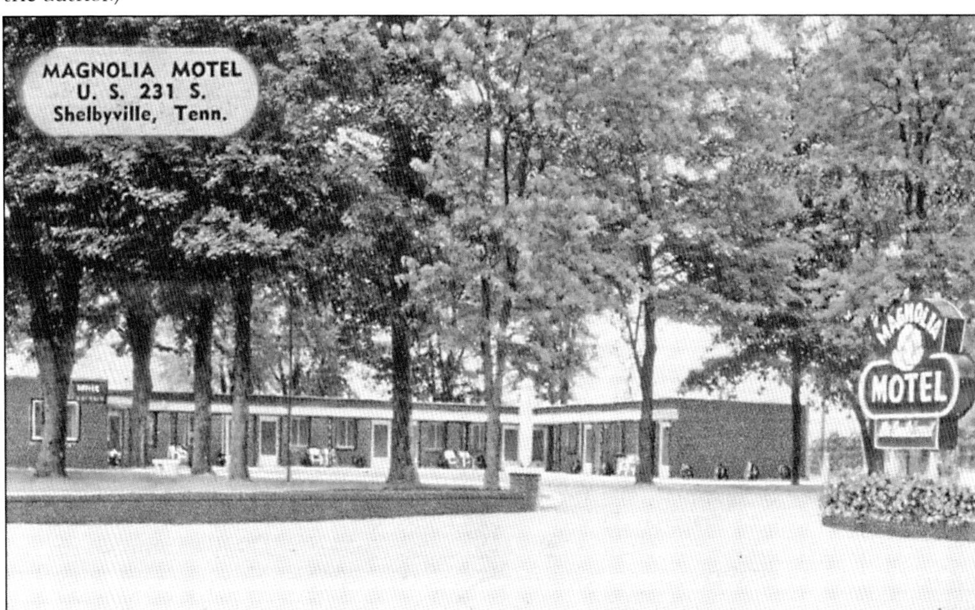

From the turn of the 20th century, Tullahoma became home to sports equipment manufacturing. This photograph shows women sewing covers on baseballs at home. The Dixie Highway allowed for the Tullahoma manufacturers to ship their products outside the region via trucks. (Courtesy of the Tennessee State Library and Archives.)

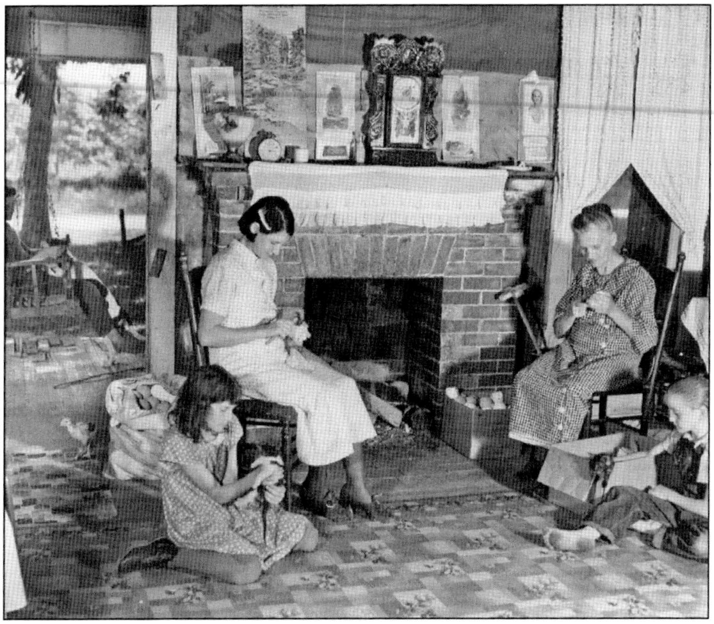

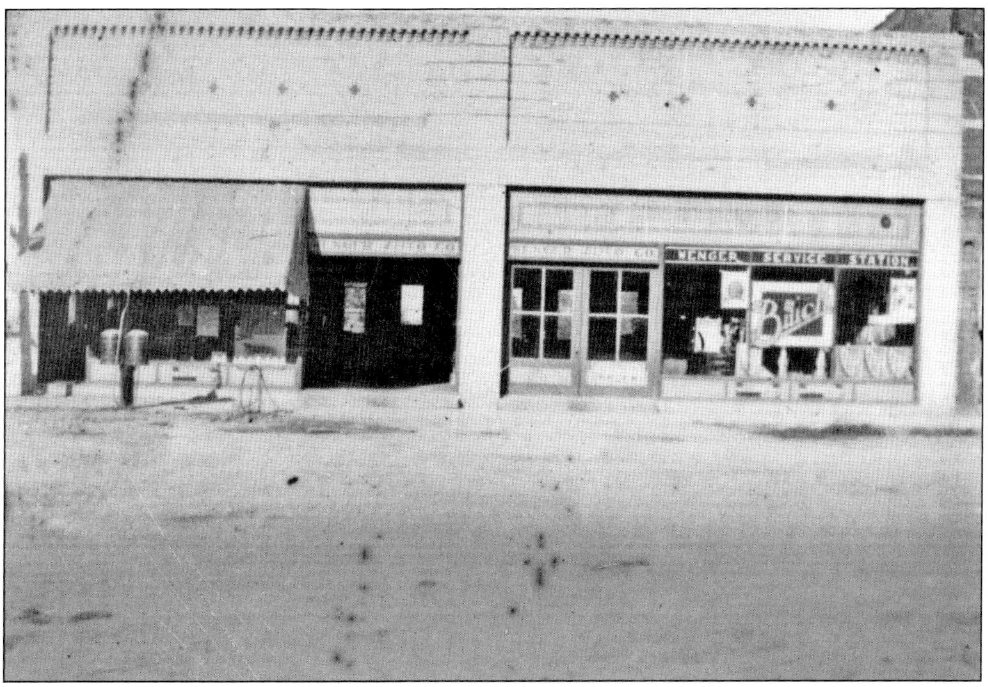


The Wenger Auto Company and Service Station was located on the east side of the square in Winchester. An automobile dealership, this business sold and repaired cars. The photograph was taken in 1916. (Courtesy of the Tennessee State Library and Archives.)

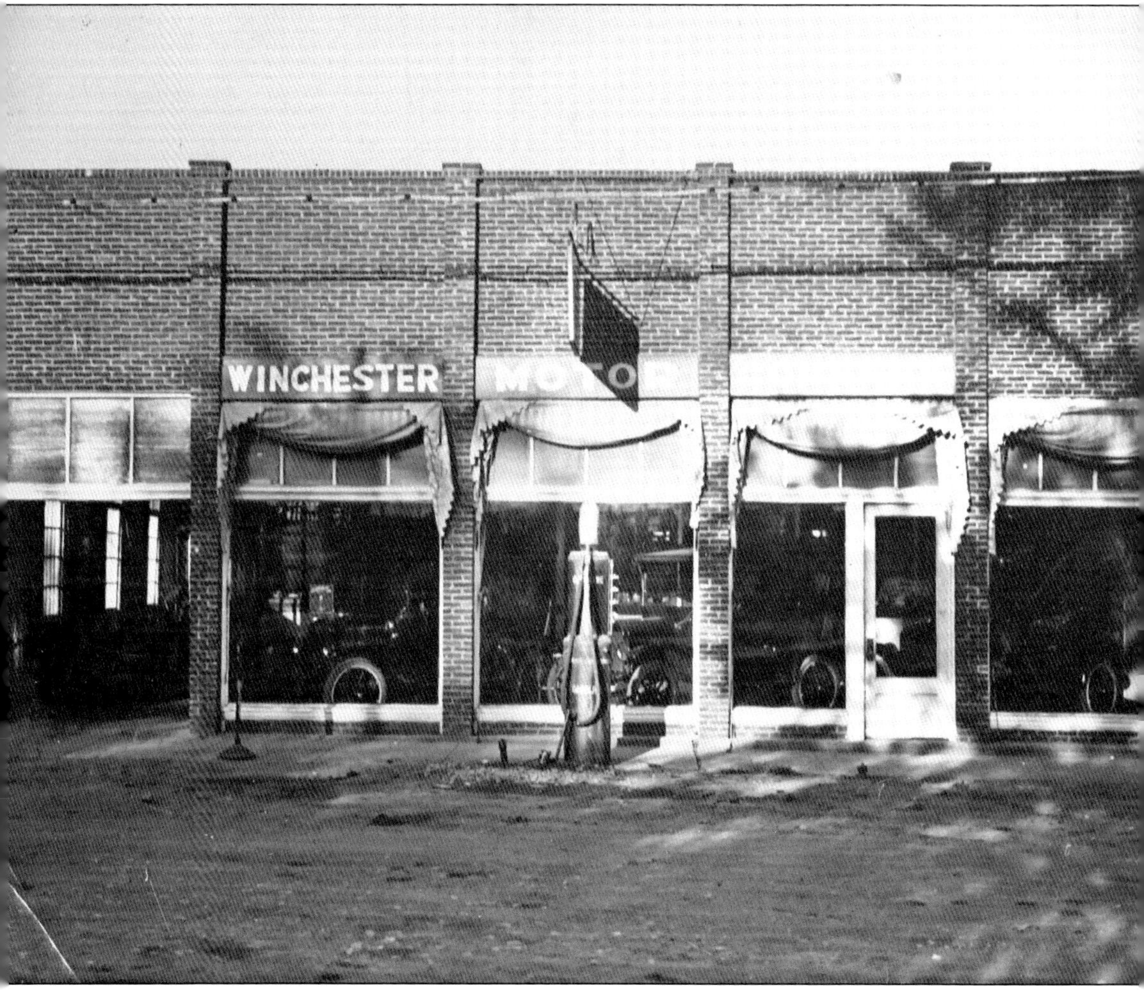


This c. 1925 photograph shows gasoline pumps in front of the automobile dealership Winchester Motor Company. As more and more people owned cars and traffic increased, the curbside pumps disappeared. Dedicated filling and service stations took their place, offering a safer place off the roadway for people to fill their tanks. Visible in this photograph are the interior automobile showroom with multiple cars on display and the service bay with a large opening that was used to bring cars in and out. The form of this building is very much like the modern dealership with the main entrance, showroom, and service area. (Courtesy of the Tennessee State Library and Archives.)

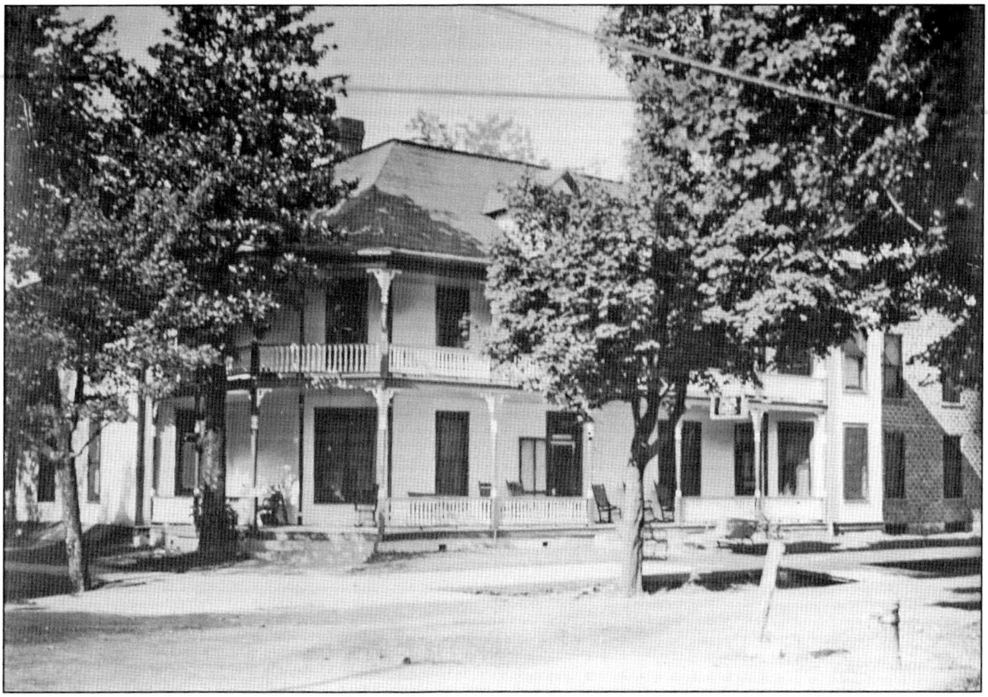

This photograph from around 1917 shows the Fuller Hotel in Winchester. Though built to accommodate railroad travelers at the turn of the century, the Fuller Hotel in Winchester served the people who drove to town too. It was a 19th-century style of hotel that contrasted greatly with the individual cabins found at the tourists' courts a decade later. (Courtesy of the Tennessee State Library and Archives.)

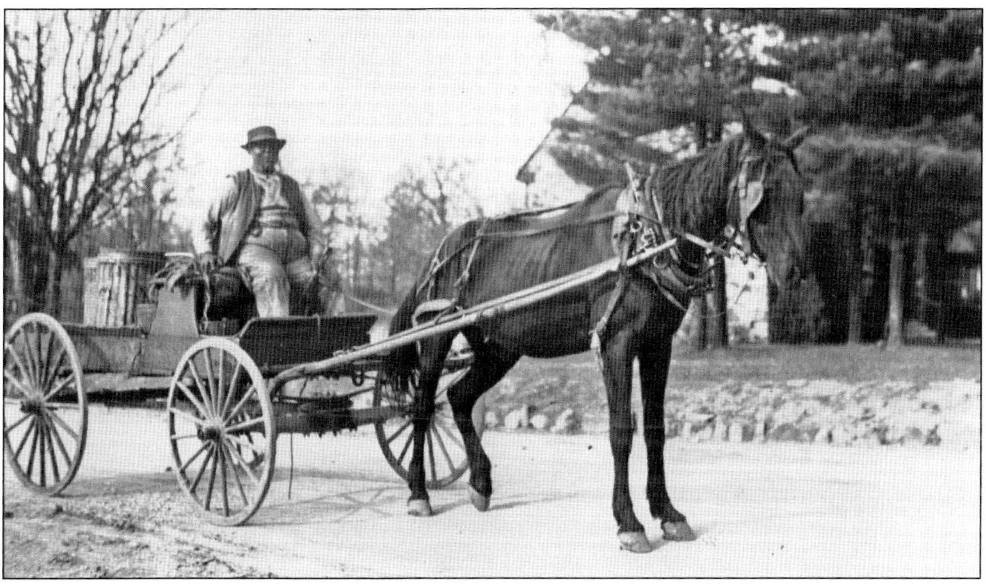

Although the Dixie Highway's birth can be linked to the rise in the use of the automobile, people and institutions continued using horsepower throughout the 1920s and 1930s. This 1920s photograph shows University of the South trash collector Cal Phillips driving a horse and wagon. (Courtesy of the Tennessee State Library and Archives.)

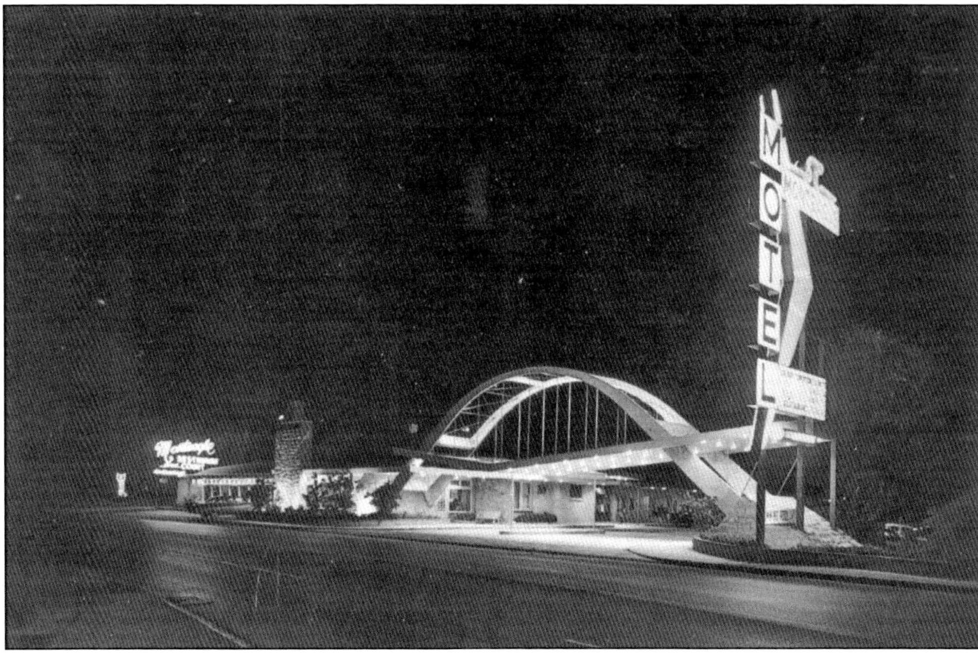


This view of the Monteagle Restaurant and Motor Court shows the lengths that business owners went to in order to attract the car-traveling public. Not only was the signage bold and bright, but the architecture also was fresh and on the cutting edge. (Courtesy of Jeffrey Lee Durbin.)

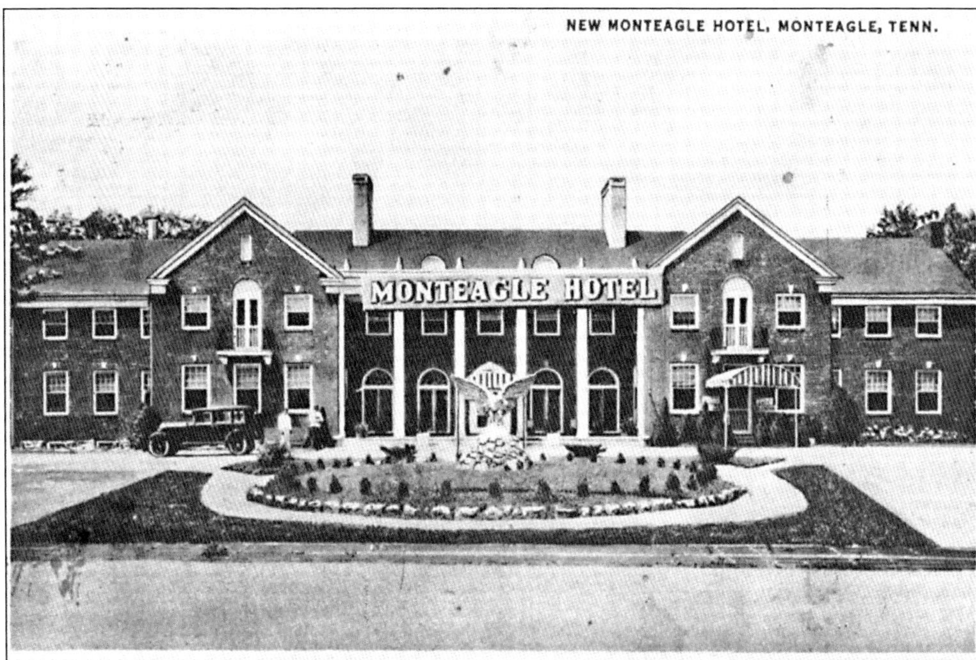


The Colonial Revival–style Monteagle Hotel, as shown in this 1938 image, attracted travelers seeking an upscale, traditional place that feels like home. Postcards from the 1930s show that even after the numbering system came about, people used the named roads, as one of the hotel reads "on U.S. 41 and Dixie Highway." (Courtesy of the Tennessee State Library and Archives.)

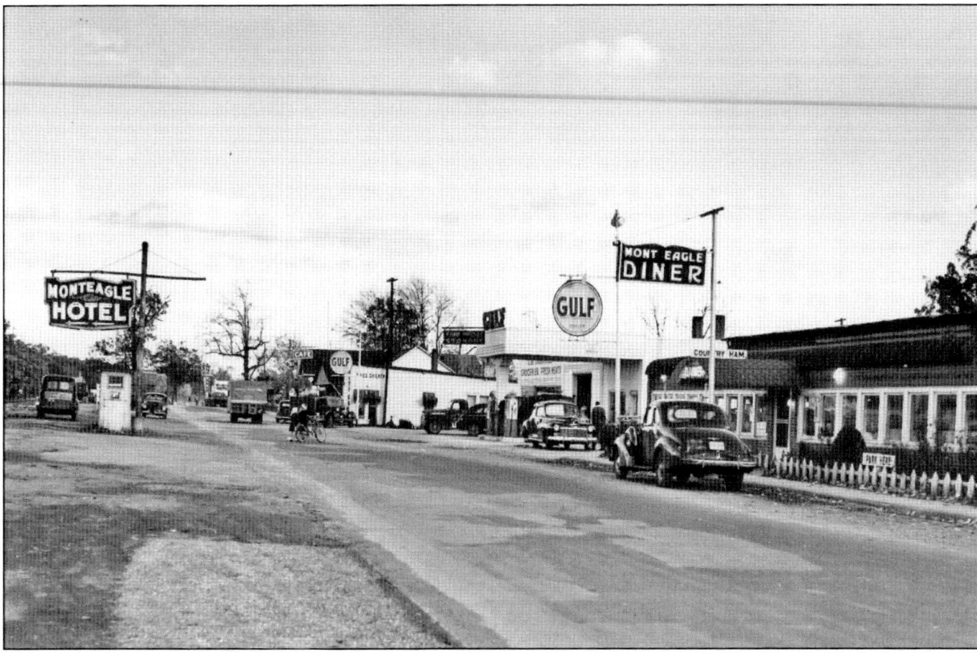


This 1947 view of Monteagle illustrates how the early automobile highways developed into transportation corridors that catered to the traveling public. On the left of the photograph is the Monteagle Hotel, while on the right are the Monteagle Diner, a Gulf gas station, and another café. (Courtesy of the Tennessee State Library and Archives.)

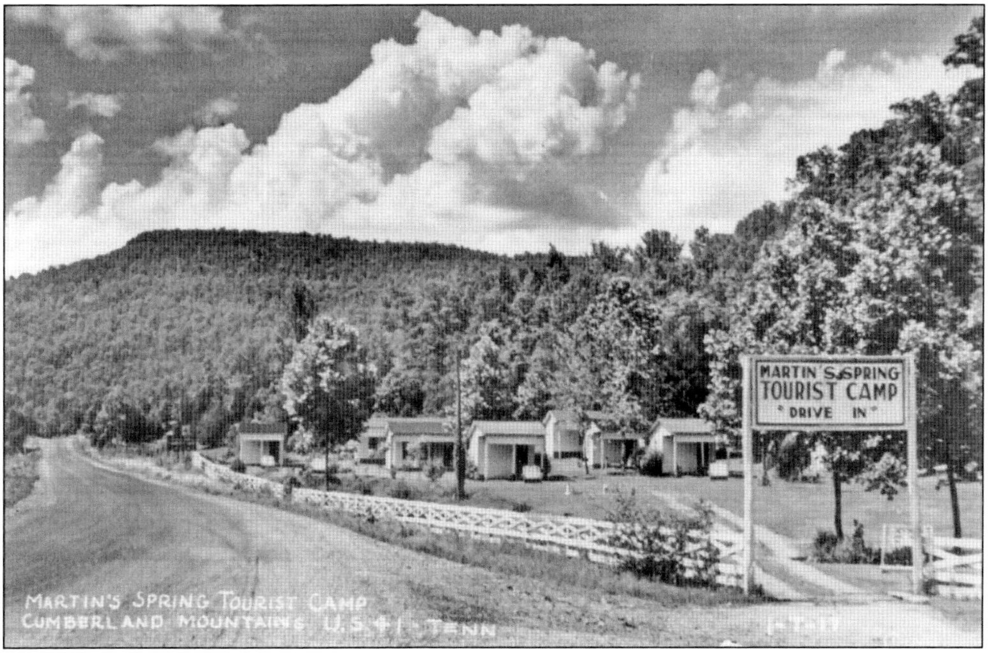


The Martin Springs Tourist Camp was located north of Jasper on the Dixie Highway and advertised home-cooked meals, modern cottages, and a gift shop. Guests stayed in individual cabins and could drive their cars right in the camp. Martin Springs purportedly flowed 6,500 gallons per hour from a cavern in the Cumberland Mountains. (Courtesy of Jeffrey Lee Durbin.)

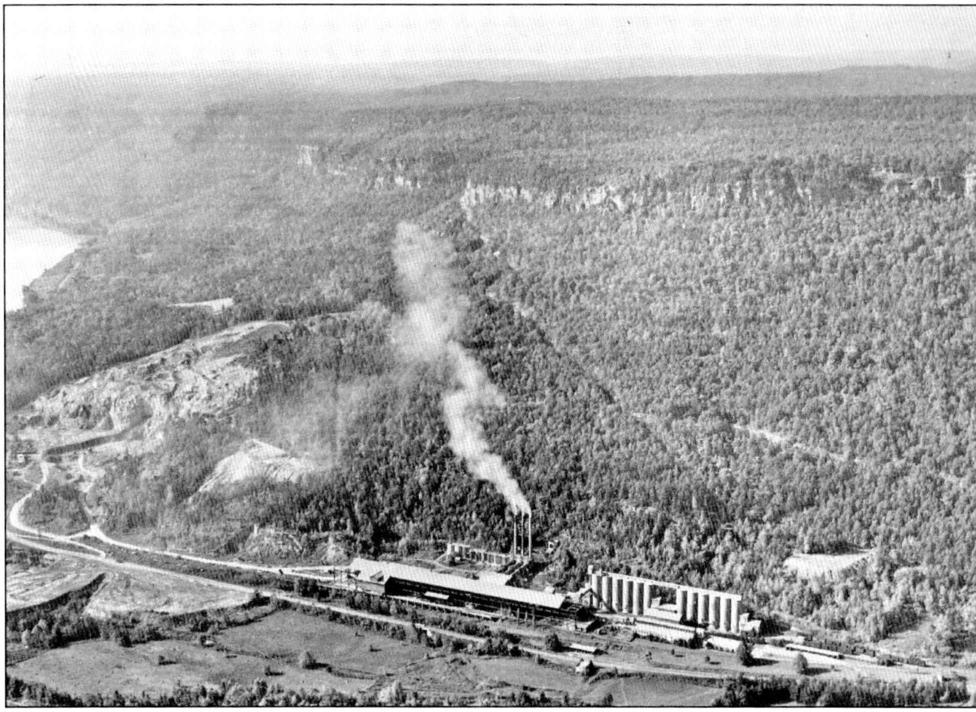

Access to cement was a necessity with all the building and improving of roads associated with the Dixie Highway. The Signal Mountain Portland Cement Company, and several others in the area, fulfilled that need. Founded in 1920 and located on Signal Mountain, this company is one of a few that still remains from the era of the development of the Dixie Highway. The top photograph is an aerial view of the company, and the image below shows the limestone mine at the company. Both photographs were taken in 1939. (Both, courtesy of the Tennessee State Library and Archives.)

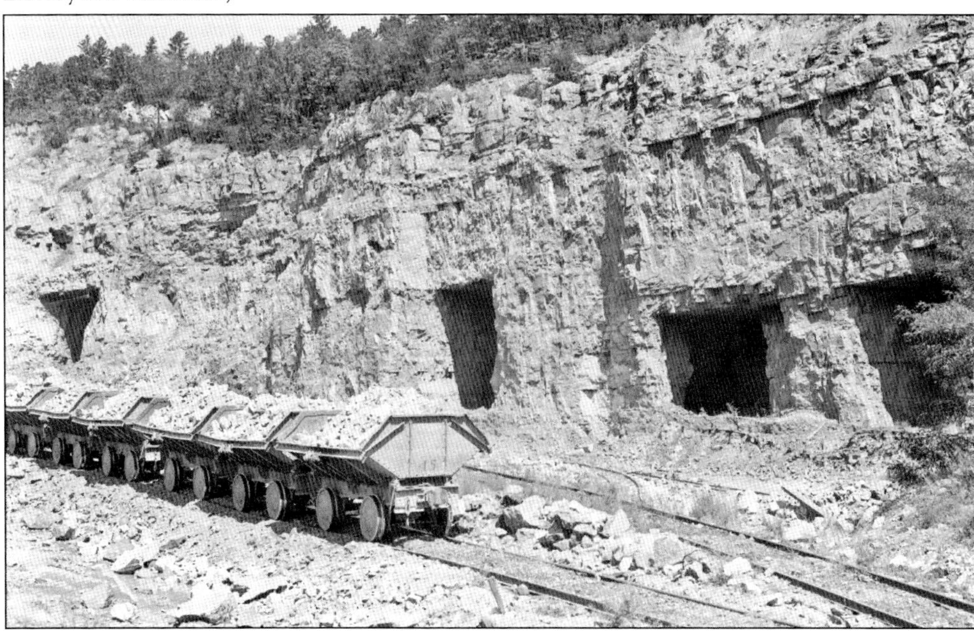

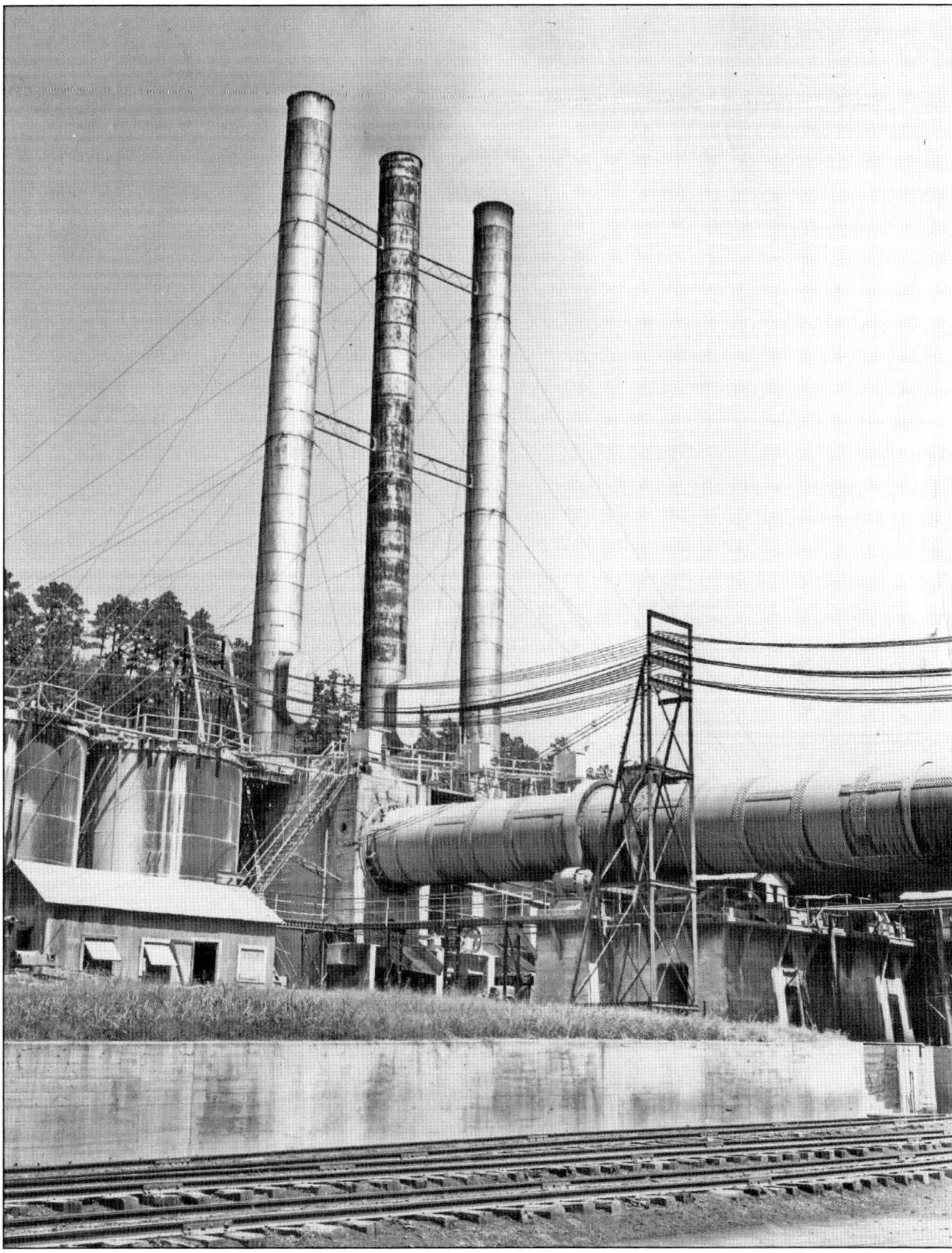

The May 1924 issue of *The Dixie Highway* magazine advertised that the Signal Mountain Portland Cement Company was "being used in highway construction in Tennessee, Georgia, North Carolina, South Carolina, Florida, and Kentucky." The Dixie Highway Association minutes recorded that after locating along the Dixie Highway, the cement company promised to complete the road in front of their plant. Unfortunately, the company did not fulfill their obligation, and Tennessee's highway department paved the highway. The cement kilns of the Signal Mountain Portland Cement Company are depicted in this 1939 photograph. A fine powder, Portland cement is the basic ingredient of concrete. About 85 percent of the mass of cement is lime and silica. (Courtesy of the Tennessee State Library and Archives.)

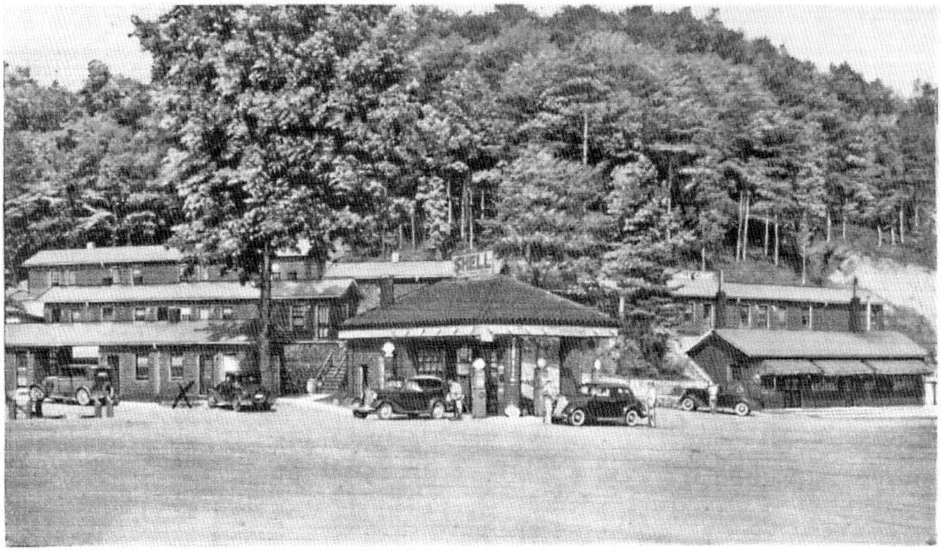



GLENDALE TOURIST COURT
2 MILES NORTH OF CHATTANOOGA ON TENNESSEE NO. 27 AND U. S. NO. 37, AT FOOT OF SCENIC SIGNAL MOUNTAIN. 20 NEW MODERN BRICK COTTAGES. ALL HOTEL ACCOMMODATIONS AT CAMP PRICES. CAFE, SERVICE STATION.

Located just north of Chattanooga at the foot of Signal Mountain, the Glendale Tourist Courts have been apartments since the 1970s. J. H. Haston built the courts, filling station, and café around 1925. The craftsman-style buildings were designed to fit into the steep terrain with rows of attached cottages. (Courtesy of the author.)

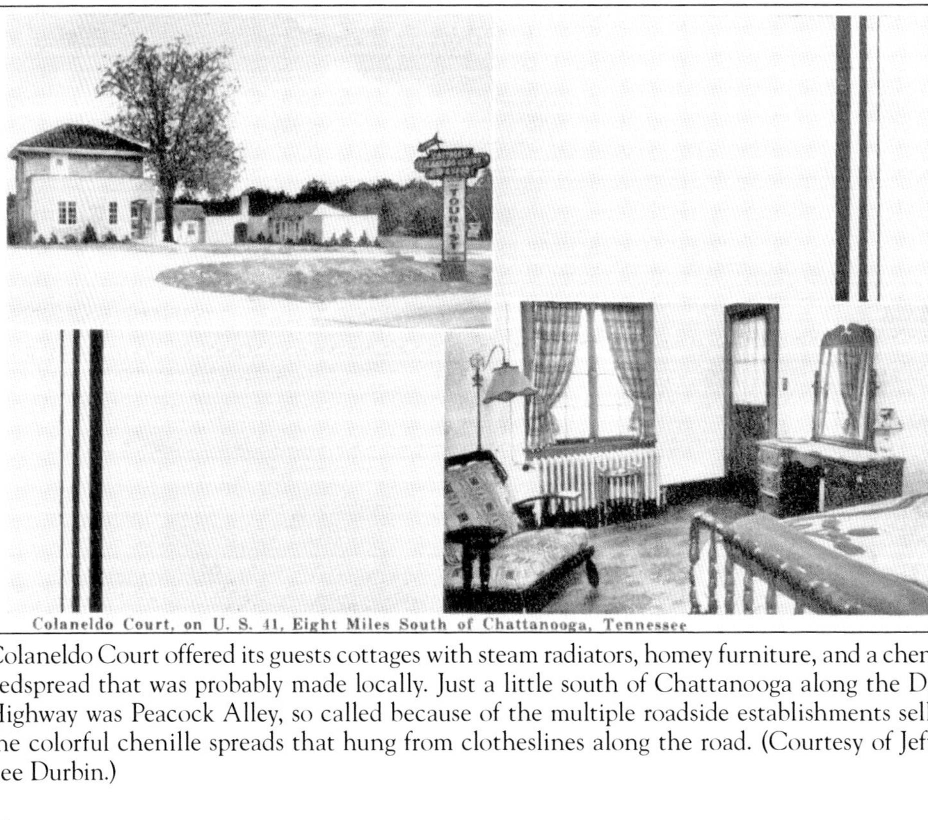



Colaneldo Court, on U. S. 41, Eight Miles South of Chattanooga, Tennessee

Colaneldo Court offered its guests cottages with steam radiators, homey furniture, and a chenille bedspread that was probably made locally. Just a little south of Chattanooga along the Dixie Highway was Peacock Alley, so called because of the multiple roadside establishments selling the colorful chenille spreads that hung from clotheslines along the road. (Courtesy of Jeffrey Lee Durbin.)

# Holmes Tilt-Bed Carrier

produced around 1916

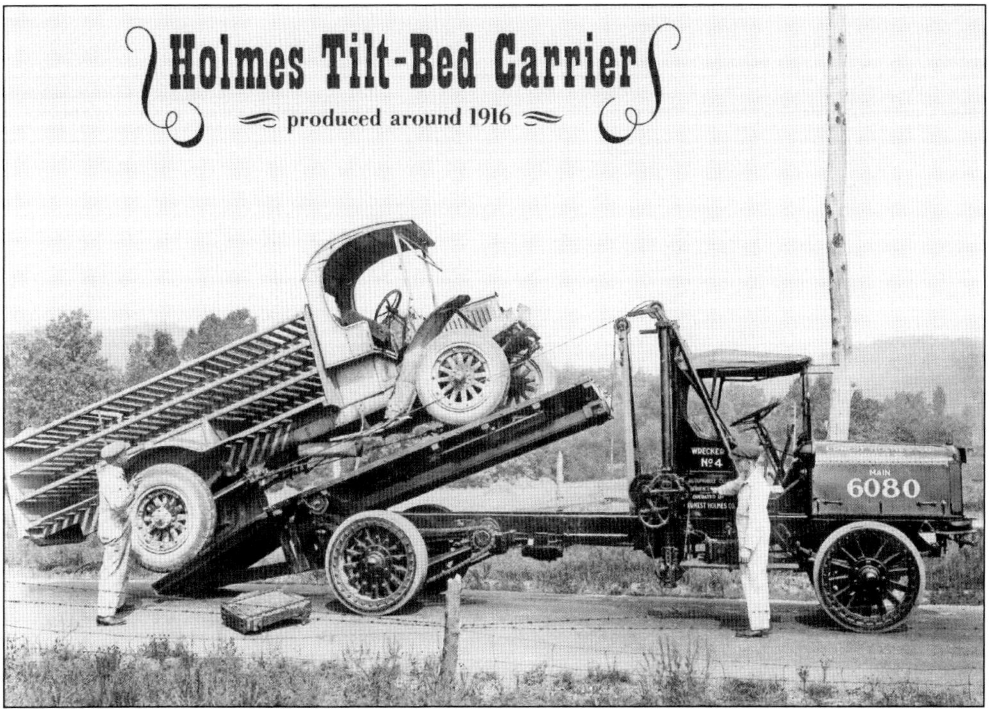


Ernest Holmes Sr. of Chattanooga is credited with the founding of the towing industry in 1916 after pulling a friend's car with equipment hooked to the frame of a 1913 Cadillac. The Ernest Holmes Company manufactured automobile wreckers and towing equipment. This photograph from around the 1920s shows a tilt-bed carrier with two unidentified men at the time the company was located along the Dixie Highway. Taken in the 1940s or 1950s, the image below shows four unidentified men at the Ernest Holmes Company, which had relocated to East Forty-third Street in Chattanooga. The company remained in the family until the 1970s. (Both, courtesy of Chattanooga–Hamilton County Bicentennial Library.)

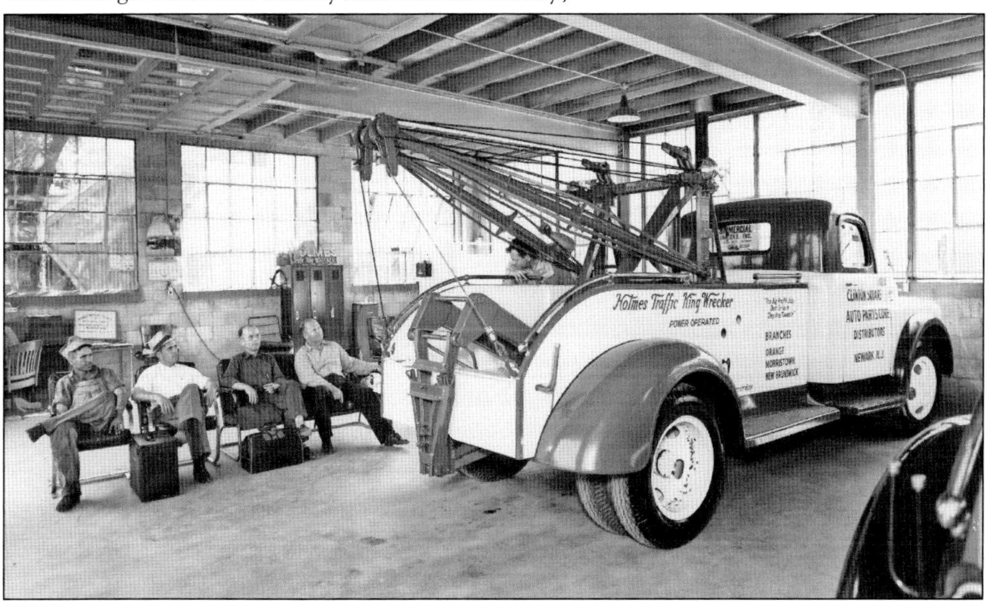

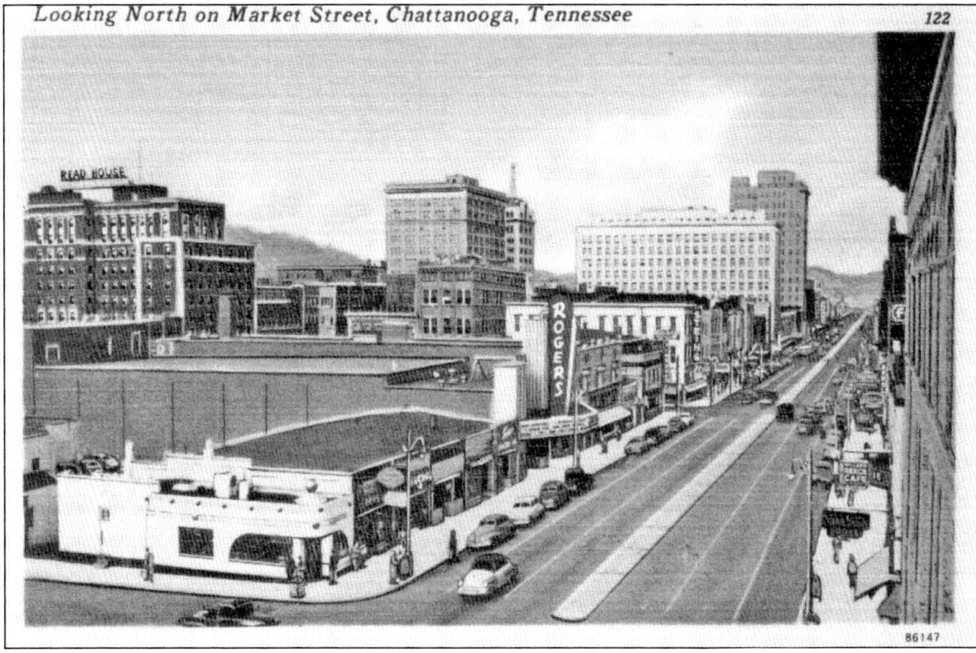


This image of Market Street shows the Read House Hotel, left, the Rogers Theater, center, and multiple stores and cafés. The reverse of the postcard reads, "The City is known as the 'Dynamo of Dixie' because of the great hydroelectric power development in its vicinity." (Courtesy of Jeffrey Lee Durbin.)

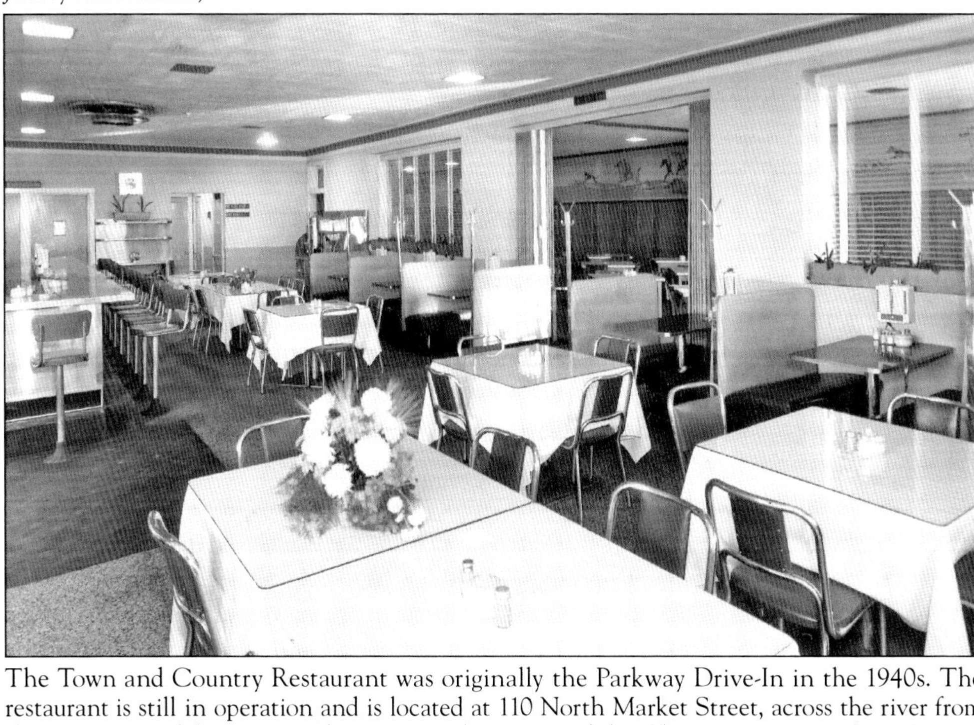

The Town and Country Restaurant was originally the Parkway Drive-In in the 1940s. The restaurant is still in operation and is located at 110 North Market Street, across the river from the main part of downtown Chattanooga. (Courtesy of the Chattanooga–Hamilton County Bicentennial Library.)

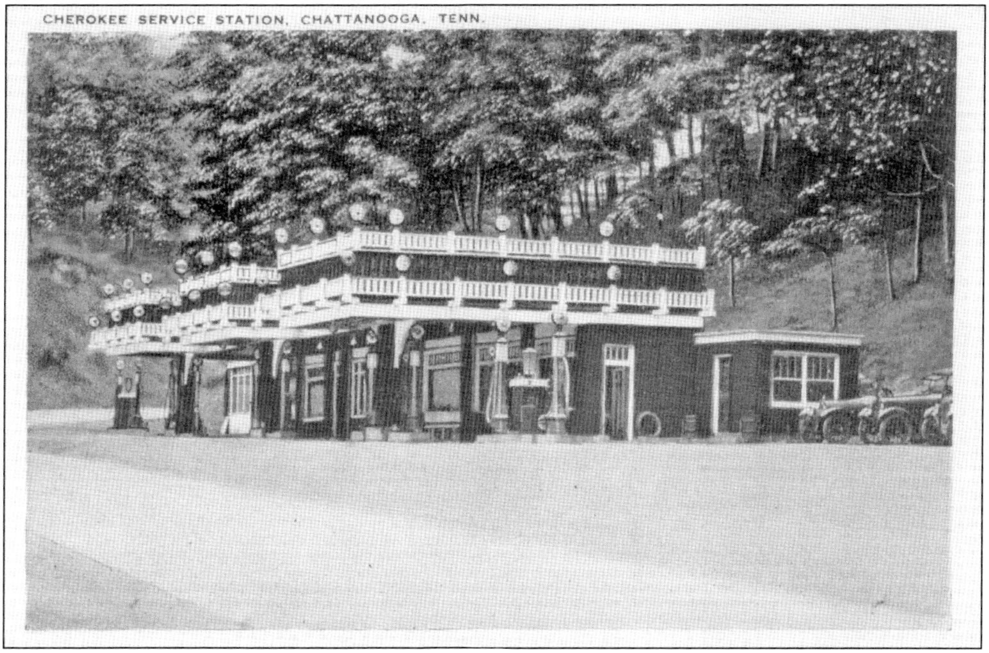


The Cherokee Service Station was advertised as "the South's largest and most beautiful filling station, located at the tunnel on the Dixie Highway" on the postcard. It carried "nine different brands of gasoline and 17 different brands and grades of motor oils." With both men's and women's restrooms and a lunch room, the station was always open and welcomed tourists. (Courtesy of the author.)

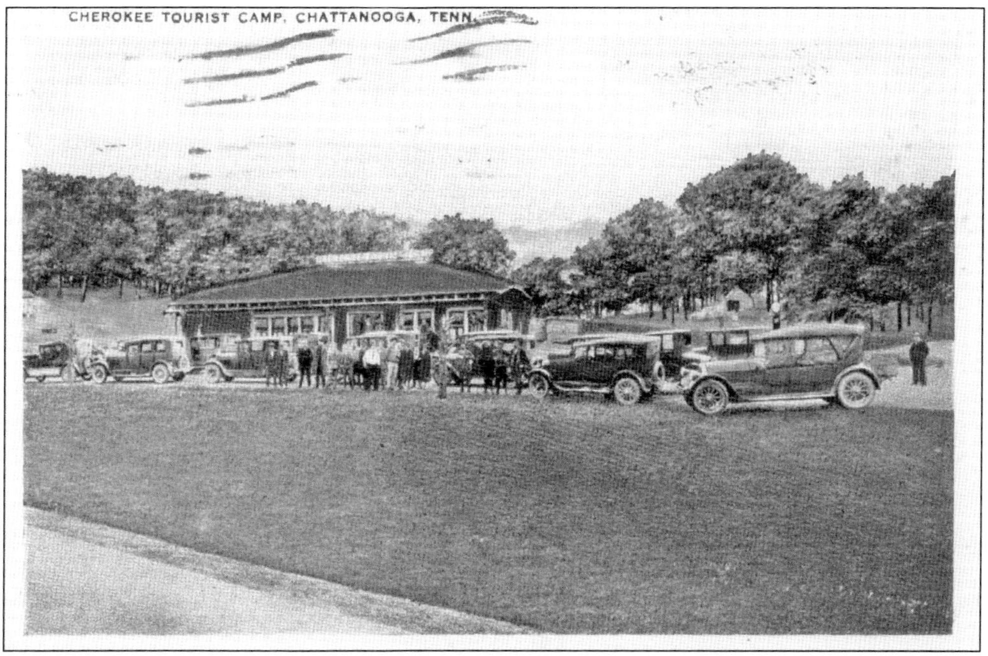


On this postcard from around 1930, the Cherokee Tourist Camp directed its guests to the "Dixie Highway, numbers 27 and 29," showing the continued use of the name after the implementation of the numbering system. This business had a grocery store, lunchroom, showers, baths, restrooms, and completely furnished cottages. It was modern throughout. (Courtesy of the author.)

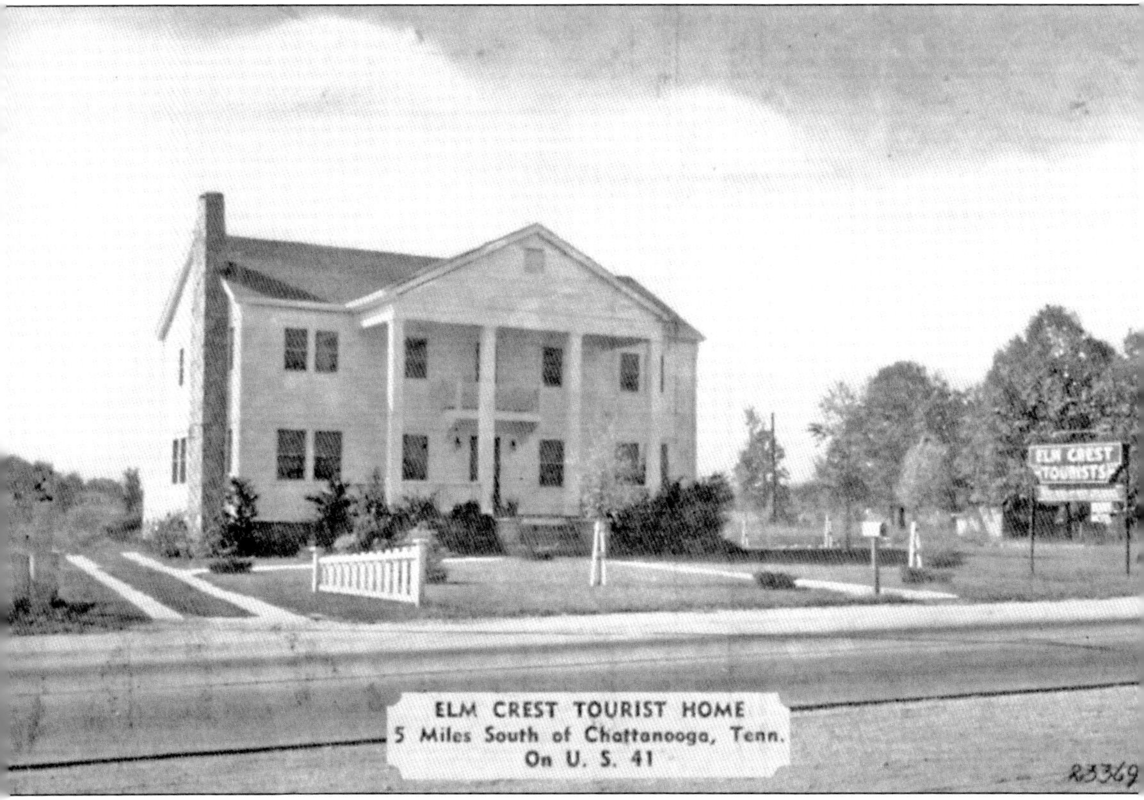


The Elm Crest Tourist Home, with its large sign that read "Tourists," captured the attention of passersby. Managed by Ruth T. Murphy, this tourist home advertised itself as "an approved motel" with "stoker heat, garages, Beautyrest mattresses, and popular prices." Oftentimes property owners like Murphy first opened their houses as overnight accommodations, then as business grew, they built cabins or cottages to serve more people. The advertised garages are not clearly visible in this photograph, but there are cabins to the right of the photograph. The Elm Crest Tourist Court was located on U.S. Route 41, five miles south of Chattanooga. (Courtesy of the author.)

# *Five*

# Seeing the Sites

People not only used the Dixie Highway for business, they also used the road for pleasure. Whether people were going on a Sunday drive, heading out to the movies, or going on vacation, the Dixie Highway provided access to other towns, a variety of tourist attractions, and many beautiful spots. The highway brought city life closer to rural areas and the countryside closer to the city. As more and more people bought cars and had some disposable income, automobile touring and vacationing gained popularity.

People increasingly traveled roads such as the Dixie Highway for leisure. Some of the main tourist destinations in Tennessee developed along the highway, which provided easy access for people from inside and outside of the state. People headed to Sulphur Springs in Rutherford County and Martin Springs in Marion County for relaxation, fun, and outdoor recreation. The developers of Rock City and Ruby Falls at Lookout Mountain created family-friendly attractions and marketed them all over the country with painted barns, large billboards, and brochures. The Parthenon, the Hermitage, and the Brainerd School appealed to the history- and culture-loving tourists. The capital of Tennessee, Nashville, was the hub of business, politics, and entertainment for the state. Country music, presidential history, religious publishing, the Civil War, and educational institutions drew people from all over the South to the city. Another popular form of entertainment, Civil War-related tourism along the Dixie Highway, is described in the next chapter.

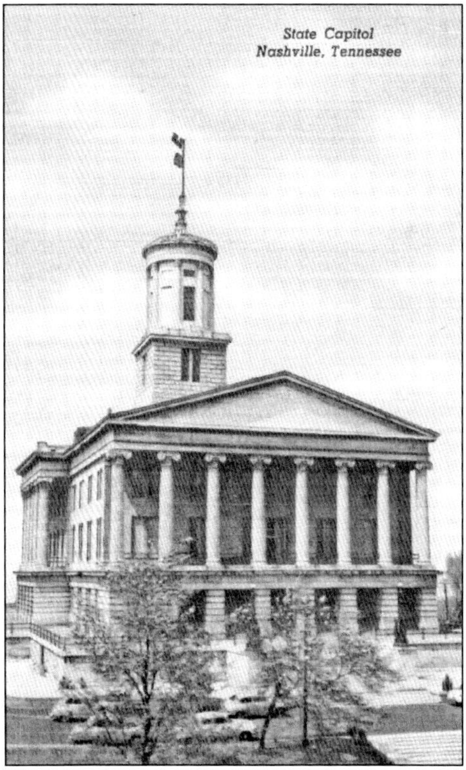


As the capital city, Nashville attracted visitors from around the state for business, politics, education, and fun. Some people specifically came to see the Greek Revival–style statehouse designed by noted architect William Strickland (1788–1854), who is buried in a crypt inside the building. Strickland also designed the nearby Egyptian Revival–style First Presbyterian Church (now Downtown Presbyterian Church). Both are National Historic Landmarks. (Courtesy of the author.)

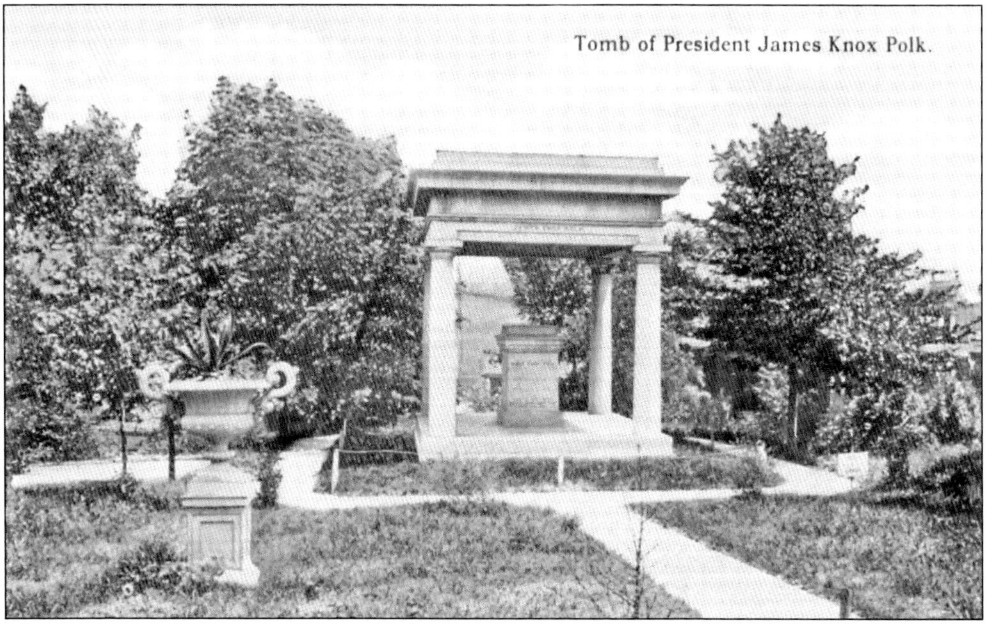


The tomb of James K. Polk (1795–1849), governor of Tennessee and 11th president of the United States, and his wife, Sarah Childress Polk, is located on the grounds of the Tennessee State Capitol. It was originally located at his home on Polk Place in Nashville. The tomb was moved to the capitol in 1901 when the house was demolished. His family home in Columbia, Tennessee, is still standing. (Courtesy of the author.)

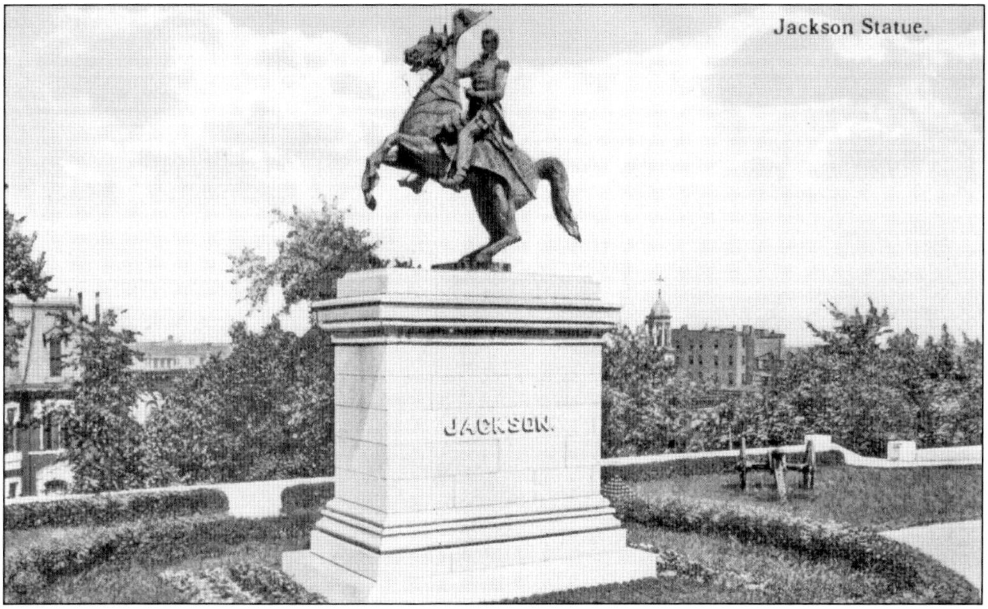


On the grounds on the Tennessee State Capitol is a statue of Andrew Jackson, the seventh president of the United States and a military hero. The American sculptor Clark Mills depicted Jackson riding a rearing horse and tipping his hat during the Battle of New Orleans. It was one of three identical statues cast for Nashville, New Orleans, and Washington, D.C. Nashville dedicated its statue in 1897 as part of its centennial celebration. (Courtesy of the author.)

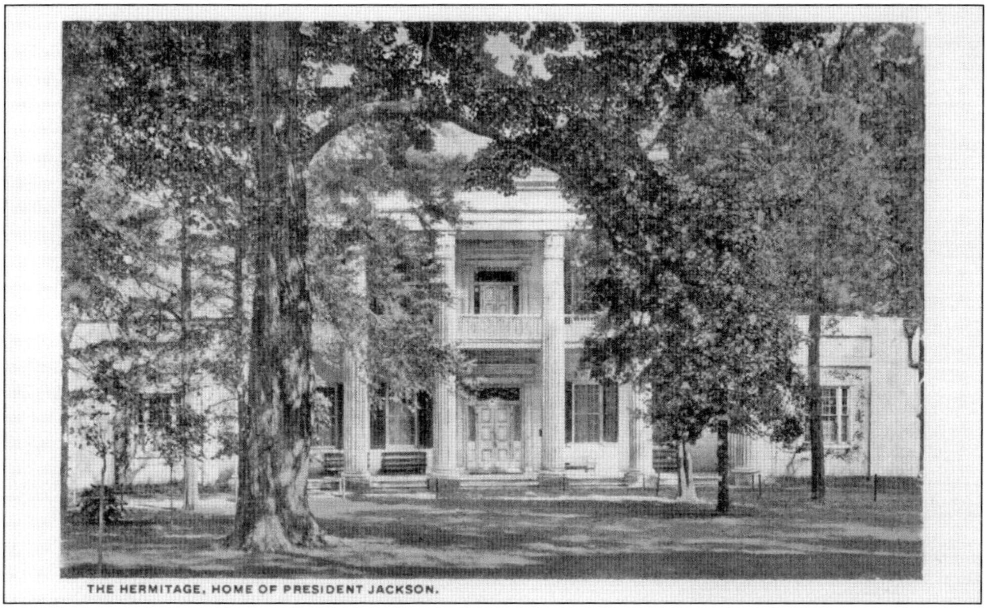


The Hermitage, the home of Pres. Andrew Jackson (1767–1845) and his wife, Rachel Donelson Jackson (1767–1828), is located 12 miles east of Nashville. The Ladies Hermitage Association and the State of Tennessee led the preservation of the house and grounds. It has been open as a historic house museum since 1889 and includes more than 1,000 acres, 32 historic buildings, gardens, and archaeological sites. The main house was built between 1819 and 1821. (Courtesy of the author.)

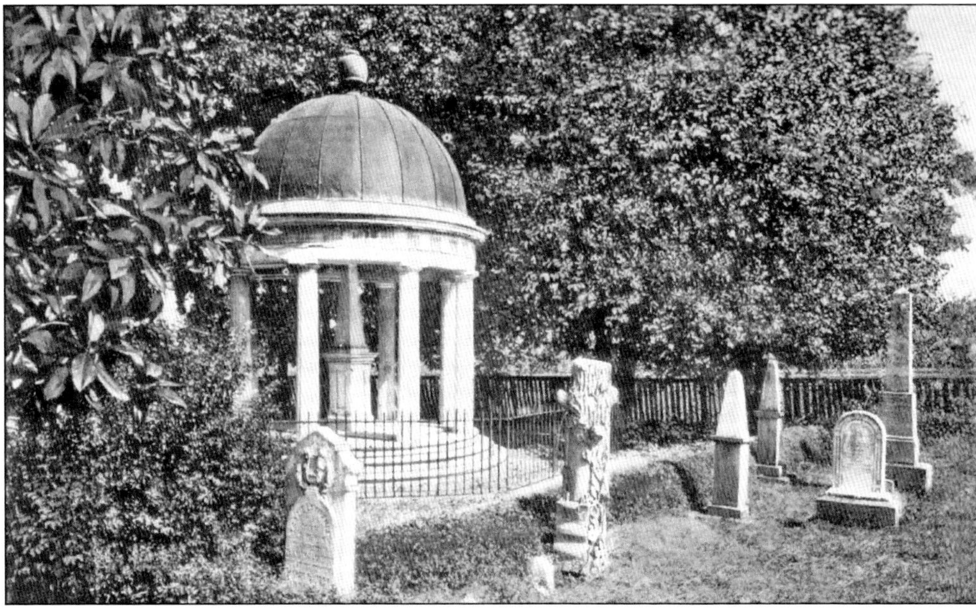

The seventh president of the United States, Andrew Jackson, and his wife, Rachel Donelson Jackson, are buried in this tomb on the grounds of the Hermitage in a corner of the gardens. In 1831, Jackson commissioned architect David Morrison to design the tomb in the form of a Grecian monument after the death of his beloved Rachel. Other family members are buried nearby. (Courtesy of the author.)

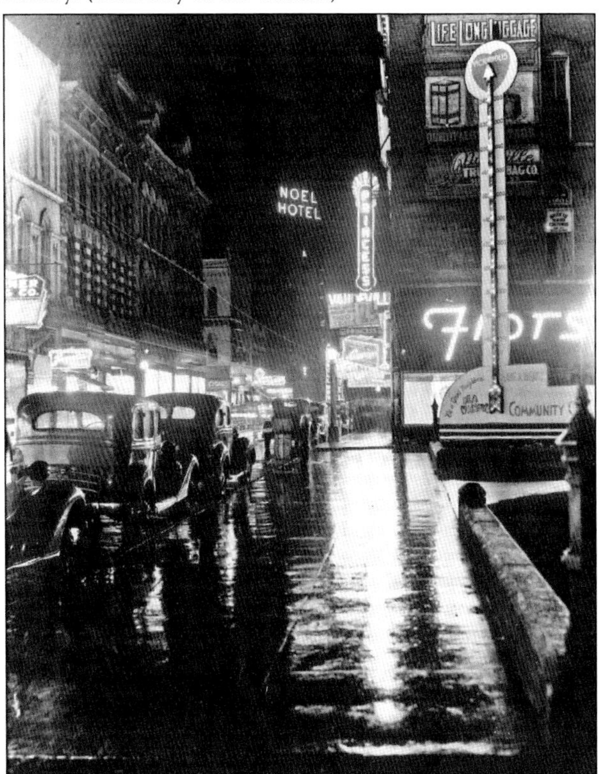


Taken in 1937, this photograph by Robert Wallace gives a sense of what the downtown Nashville nightlife looked like during the 1930s on Church Street between Fourth and Fifth Avenues. The Princess Theater featuring vaudeville is visible on the right. (Courtesy of the Tennessee State Library and Archives.)

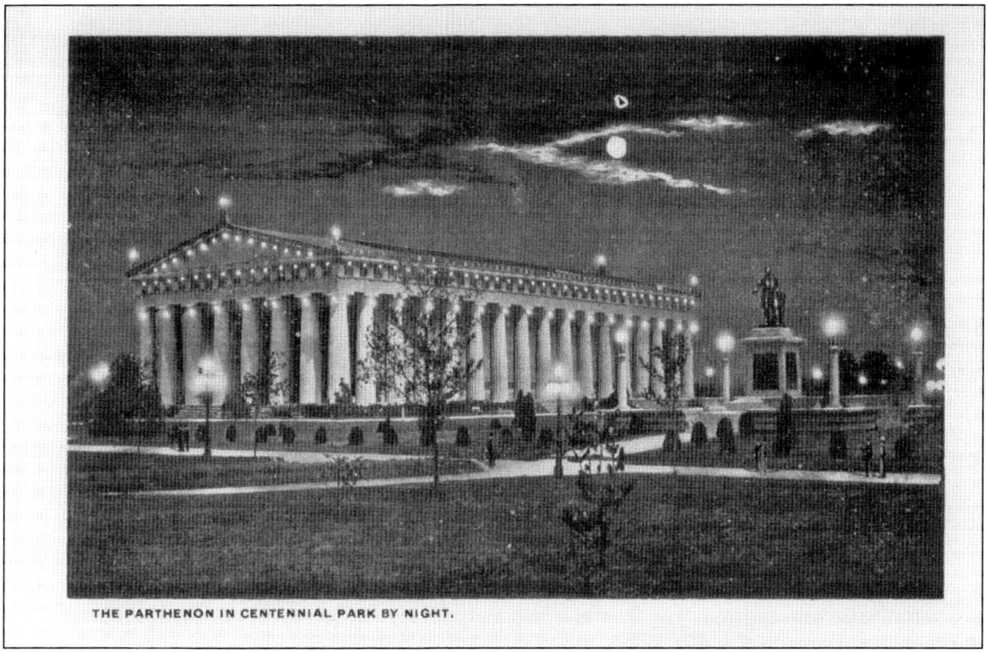


In 1897, Nashville hosted the Tennessee Centennial Exposition in honor of the state's 100th birthday (one year late). The exposition had almost two million visitors. As a focal point to the centennial exposition, the City of Nashville constructed a plaster, wood, and brick replica of the Greek Parthenon as the Fine Arts Building. The Parthenon was the perfect symbol for the up-and-coming new South city of Nashville; its nickname was and still is "the Athens of the South." The temporary Parthenon remained in the middle of the empty Centennial Park until 1915, when the city hired local architect Russell Hart to build a more permanent and faithful replica. Following the donation of more than 60 paintings by James Cowan to the city in the late 1920s, the Parthenon became an art museum that opened to the public in 1931. (Both, courtesy of the author.)

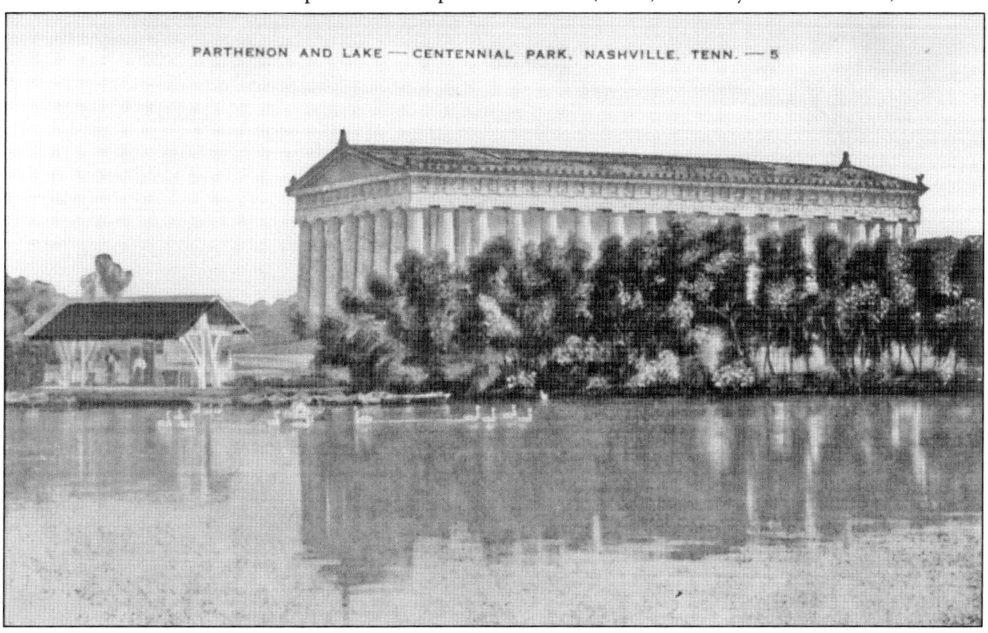

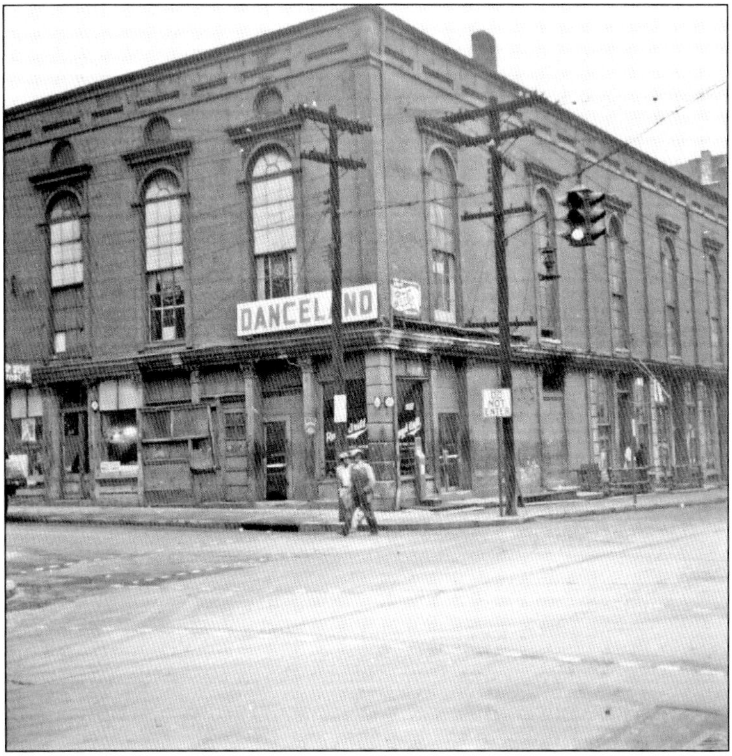

This 1951 photograph shows the Danceland Building at the northwest corner of Cedar Street and Fourth Avenue South in Nashville, just off the Dixie Highway. The first floor housed the Regal Café. (Courtesy of the Tennessee State Library and Archives.)

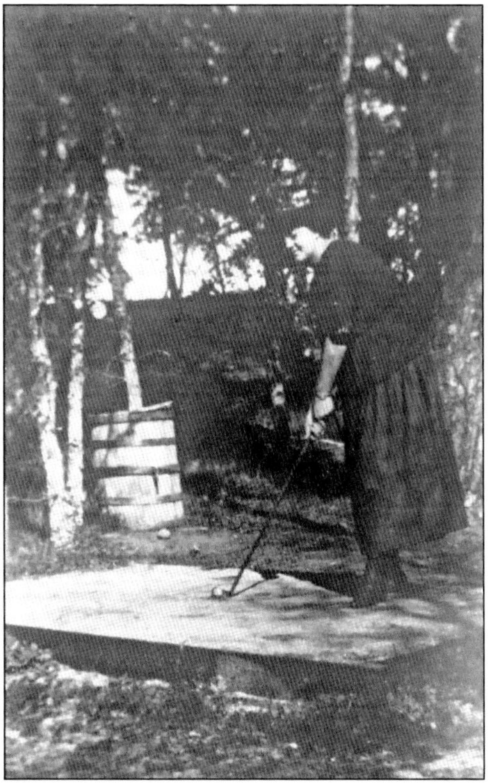

Garnet Carter of Rock City fame invented Tom Thumb miniature golf courses in the 1920s as a way to entertain his customers at the Lookout Mountain Fairyland Inn. Although no longer extant, Sanborn Fire Insurance Maps show miniature golf courses along the Dixie Highway route in Murfreesboro and in Winchester. This 1925 image shows Sarah Davis on a more traditional golf course in Smyrna. (Courtesy of the Albert Gore Research Center, Middle Tennessee State University.)

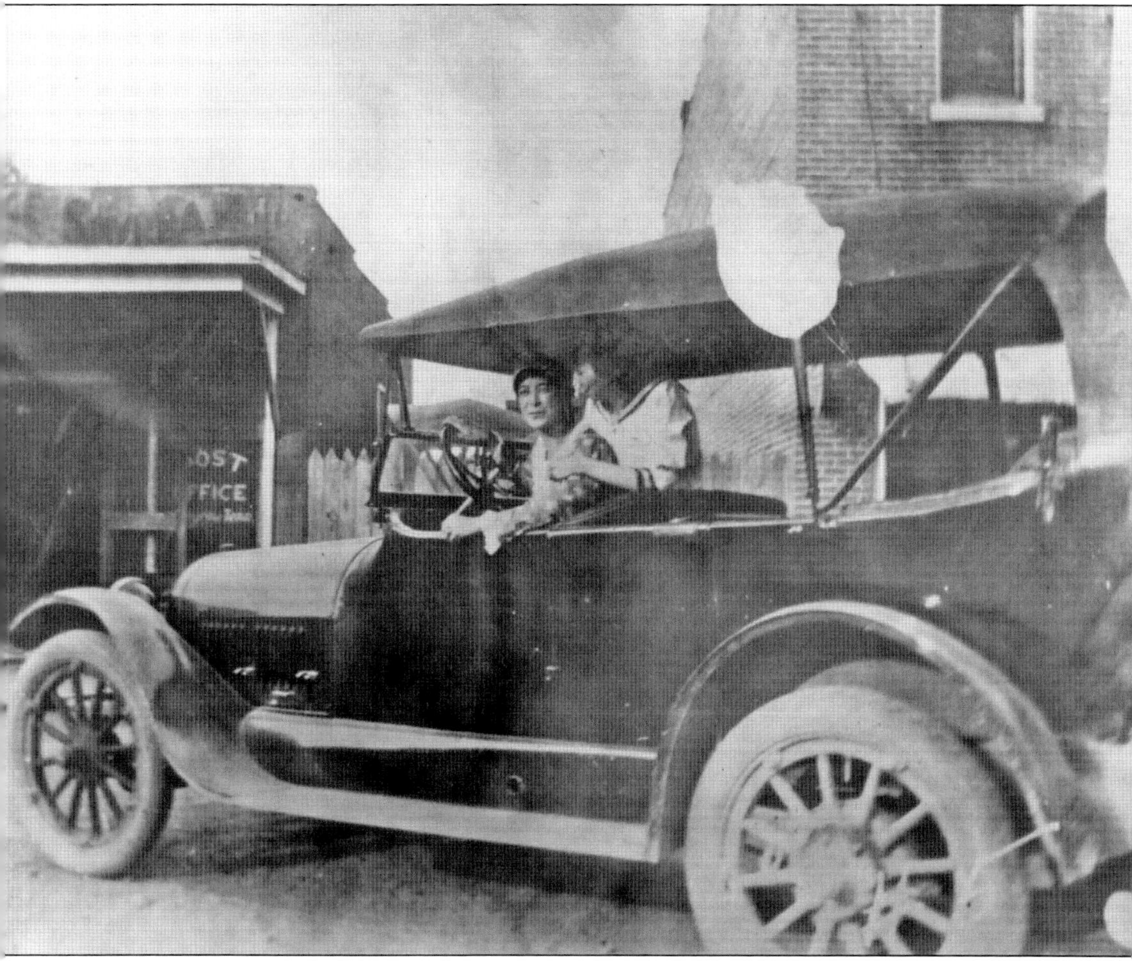


Whether going to town or driving for leisure, women used the Dixie Highway to get where they needed to go. Historian Virginia Scharff argues that early women drivers fought to overcome the image of cars as a male machine. And eventually, women found a new independence that came with the freedom of driving and even were instrumental in affecting changes in safety, comfort, and appearance of cars. This 1919 image shows Mellie Lannom Flowers in front of the Smyrna Post Office. She is driving with Cloe Gibbon in a 1918 Buick. (Courtesy of the Albert Gore Research Center, Middle Tennessee State University.)

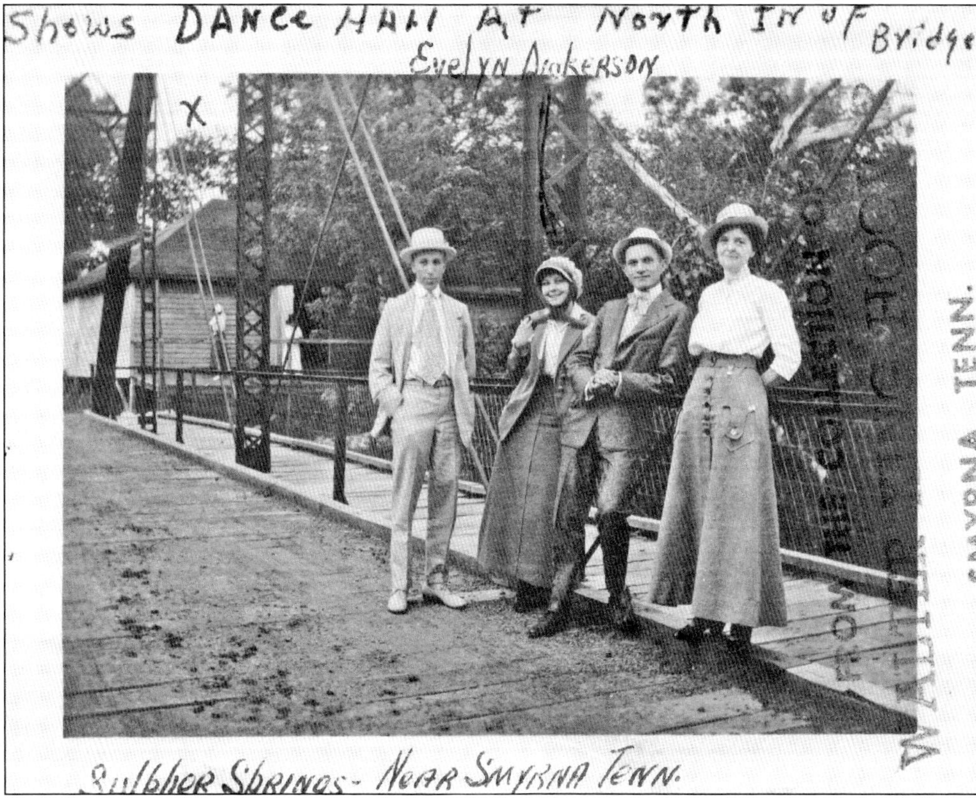


Four miles northeast of Smyrna is Sulphur Springs, also known as Jefferson Springs, which attracted visitors who wanted to swim, dance, and relax. Popular in the 19th and early 20th centuries, these resorts existed throughout Tennessee. This 1910s photograph shows the 1914 bridge and dance hall in the background. (Courtesy of the Albert Gore Research Center, Middle Tennessee State University.)

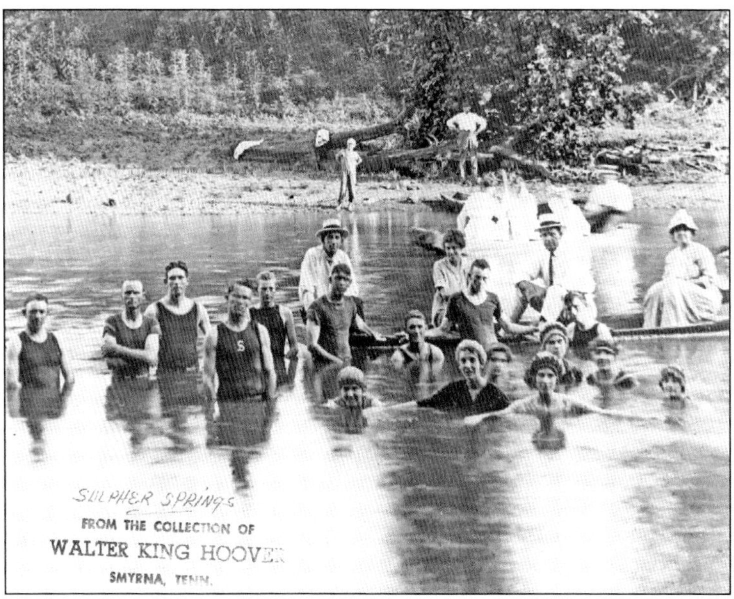


This 1910s image of Sulphur Springs shows guests swimming in the water. Legend has it that cows actually discovered these springs, which were destroyed when Percy Priest Lake was built. (Courtesy of the Albert Gore Research Center, Middle Tennessee State University.)

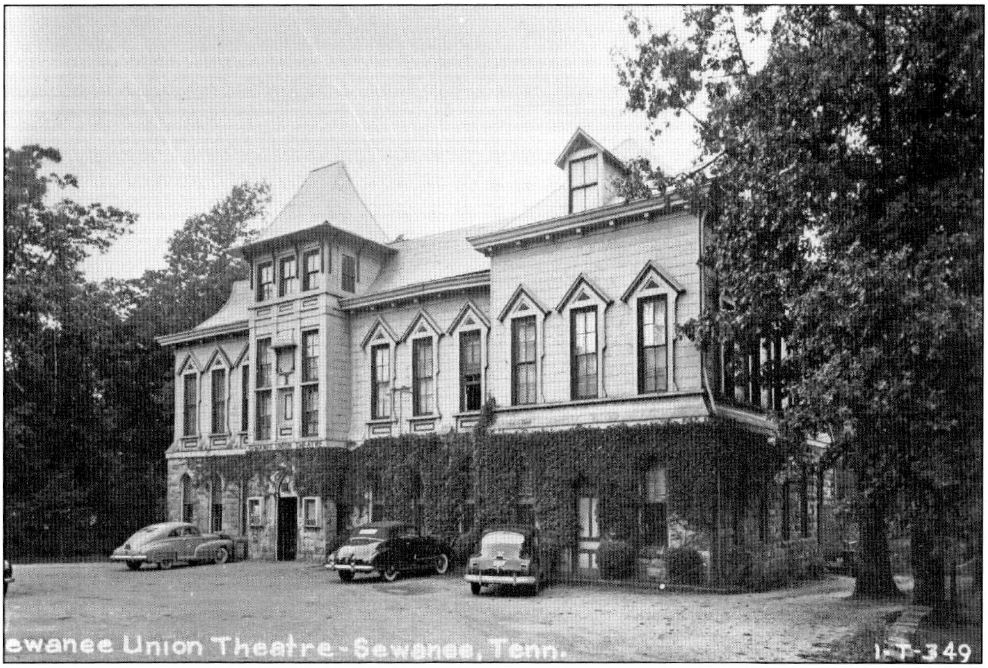


Located on the University of the South campus, the Sewanee Union Theater started showing movies in the 1920s, making it one of the oldest theaters in the South. The top image shows the theater in the mid-1940s. The second image shows the theater after it was destroyed by a fire in 1950. Currently, the Sewanee Union Theater is located in the Thompson Union Building on South Carolina Avenue. It still shows movies throughout the school year. (Both, courtesy of the Tennessee State Library and Archives.)

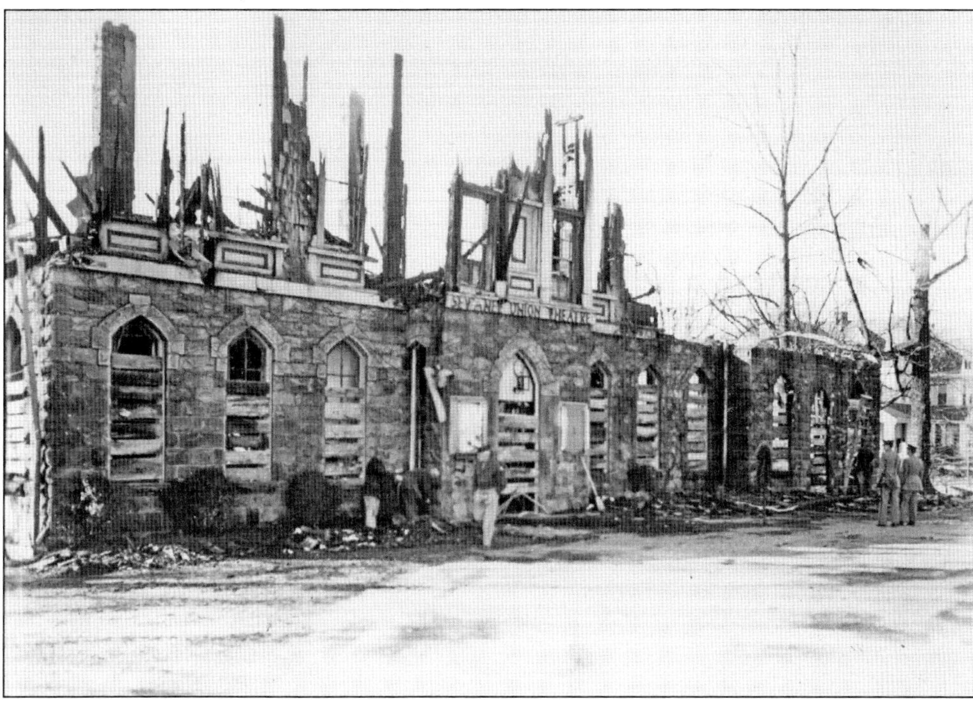

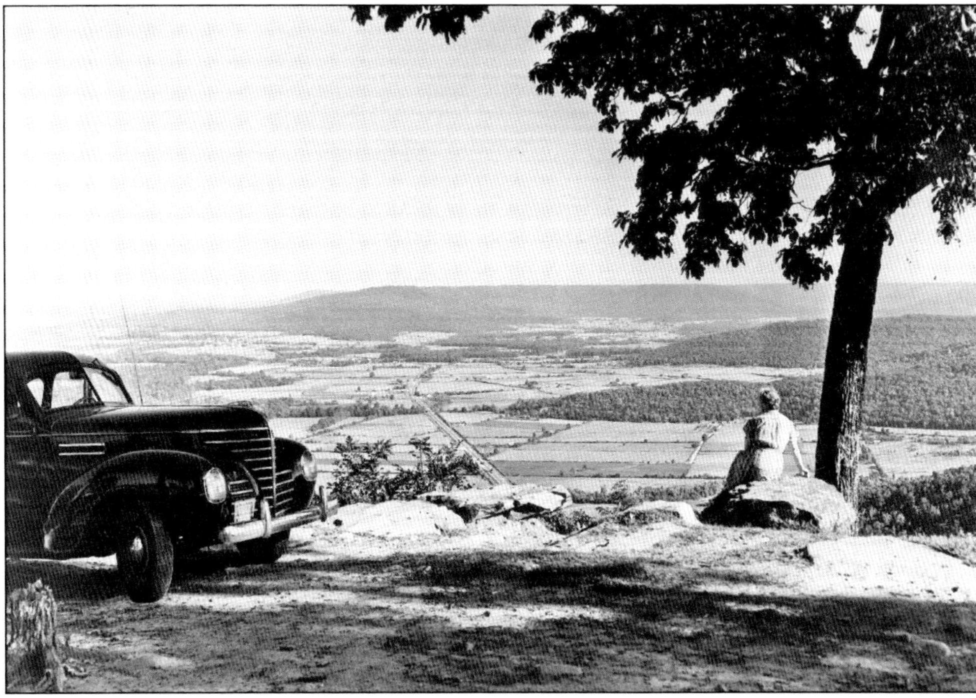

An unidentified woman is enjoying the million-dollar view in this 1939 photograph. Just outside of Monteagle, this spectacular vista is still a main attraction for automobile travelers out for a casual drive or on their way to another tourist destination. (Courtesy of the Tennessee State Library and Archives.)

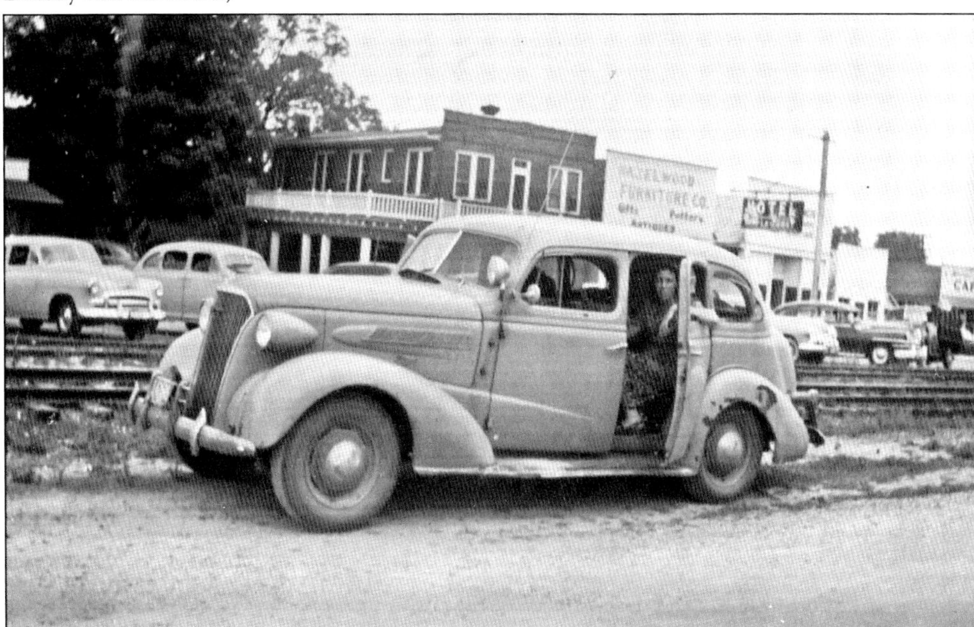

In this photograph, Frances Austin drives the family car in Monteagle. Taken in 1937, this image is part of the *Looking Back at Tennessee* photograph collection, which is housed at the Tennessee State Library and Archives. (Courtesy of the Tennessee State Library and Archives.)

Established in 1882 and chartered by the state as a Chautauqua—a place for spiritual enrichment and fellowship—the Sunday School Assembly at Monteagle was a destination for many seeking a renewal. Although no longer standing, the Victorian-era Assembly Inn depicted in this photograph served visitors to the assembly. (Courtesy of the Tennessee State Library and Archives.)

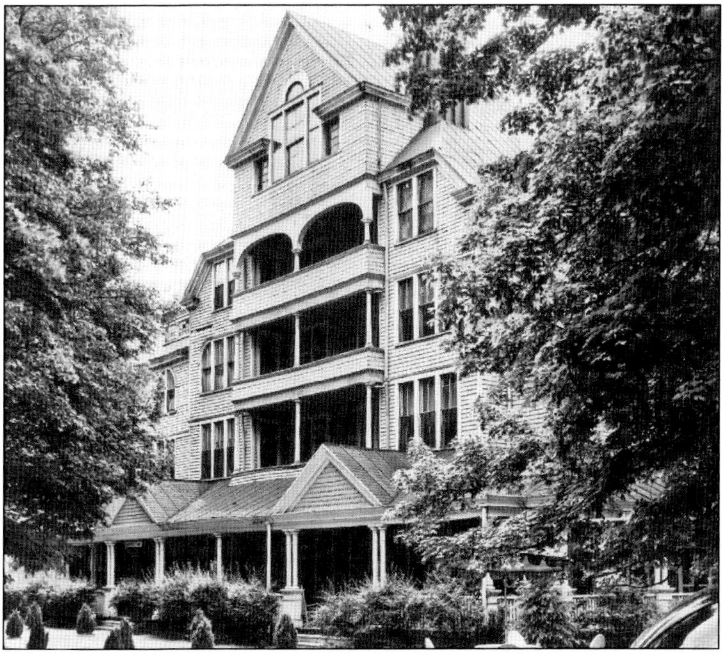

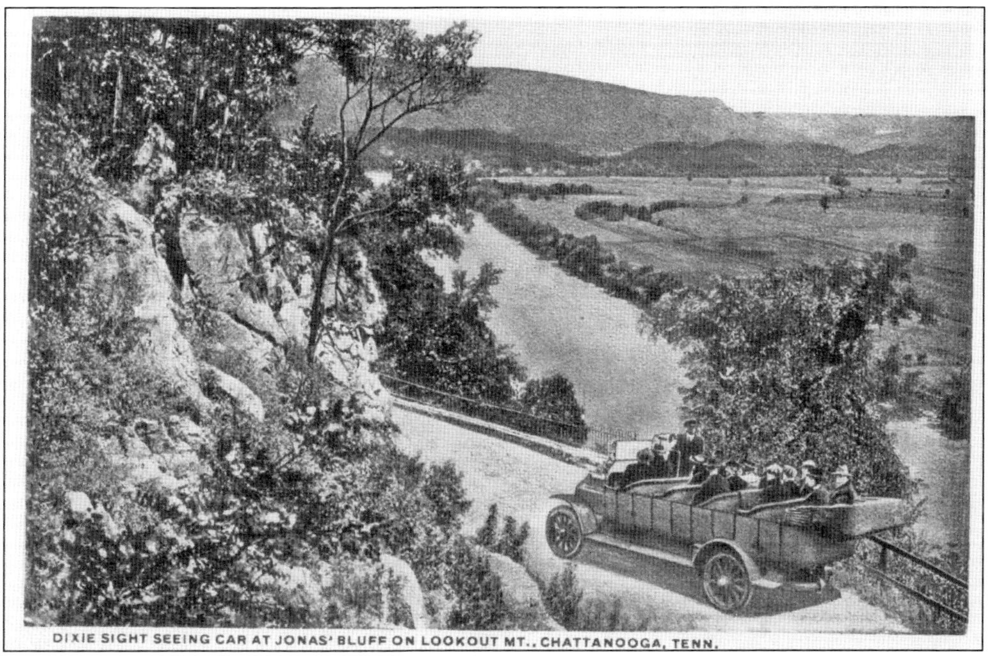


The Dixie Highway in Tennessee provided ample opportunities for people sightseeing either as individuals or as part of a tour group. This postcard shows a convertible sightseeing car riding along Jonas Bluff on Lookout Mountain. A tour guide is standing in the front of the car. (Courtesy of Jeffrey Lee Durbin.)

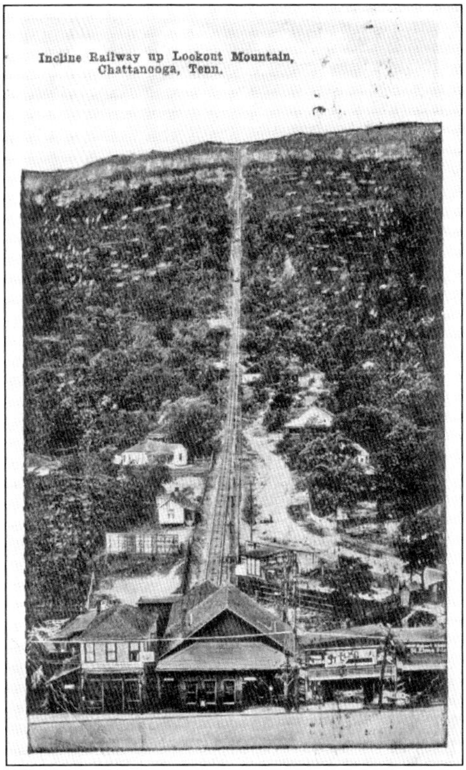


The Incline Railway carries visitors to the top of Lookout Mountain on what is allegedly the steepest railway in the world. Listed in the National Register of Historic Places and recognized as a Mechanical Engineering Landmark, the Incline Railway has been in operation since 1895. (Courtesy of Jeffrey Lee Durbin.)

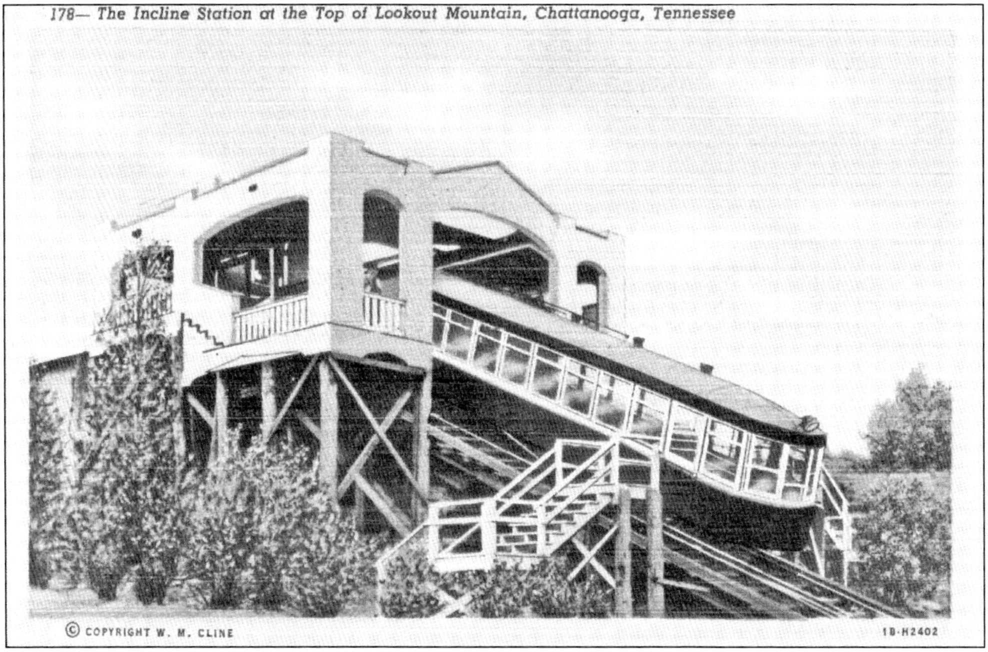


The incline station is located at the top of Lookout Mountain and is accessible by riding the Incline Railway up "America's Most Amazing Mile," as it is referred to in promotional literature. Visitors also can go inside the mechanical room to see the large gears necessary to take the train up the mountain. (Courtesy of the author.)

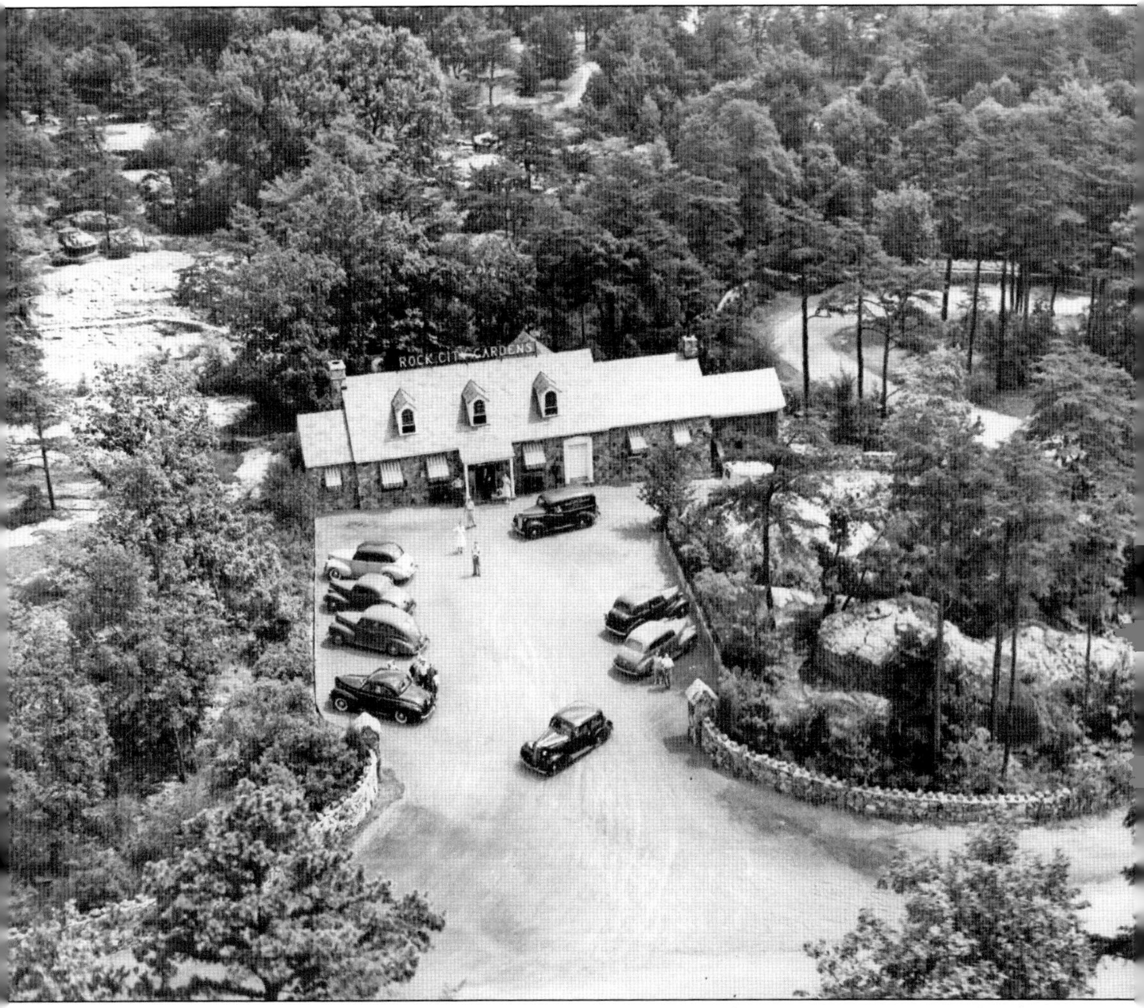


Rock City Gardens opened to the public on May 21, 1932, during the Great Depression as Frieda and Garnet Carter's dream of developing a golf course and residential community on Lookout Mountain faded. Carter had begun a new development called Fairyland in 1924; however, construction delays prevented it from being built. Carter then came up with the idea of miniature golf, and he founded the once-popular Tom Thumb Golf as the first of Rock City Gardens' attractions. Now one of the southeast's most popular tourist destinations, Rock City Gardens hosts more than 500,000 visitors a year. *National Geographic* named it one of "America's Iconic Places." This photograph from around 1940 shows the stone building entrance to Rock City Gardens, the parking lot, and the stone-lined drive leading to the attraction. (Courtesy of the Chattanooga–Hamilton County Bicentennial Library.)

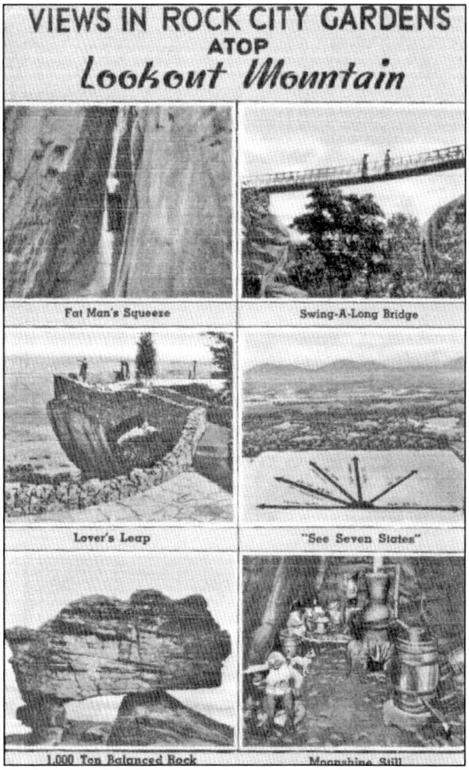


At Rock City Gardens, visitors can see outstanding geologic formations, plant life, and a 90-foot waterfall. Frieda Carter marked the path through the amazing rock formations with string and ended her trail at Lover's Leap. To help frame her trail, she transplanted plants and wildflowers. Carter loved European folklore and added German gnomes and fairy-tale characters throughout the trails. (Courtesy of Jeffrey Lee Durbin.)

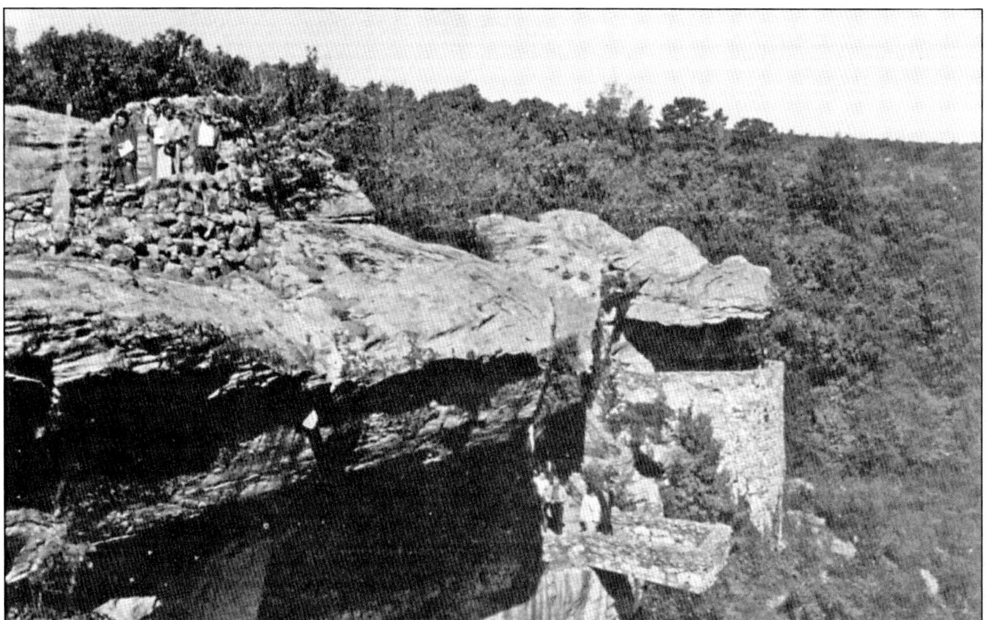

One of Rock City Gardens' claims to fame is that visitors can see seven states from one of the observation points. The states that can be seen are Tennessee, Georgia, Alabama, North Carolina, South Carolina, Virginia, and Kentucky. Rock City Gardens is actually in Lookout Mountain, Georgia, just 6 miles from downtown Chattanooga. (Courtesy of the author.)

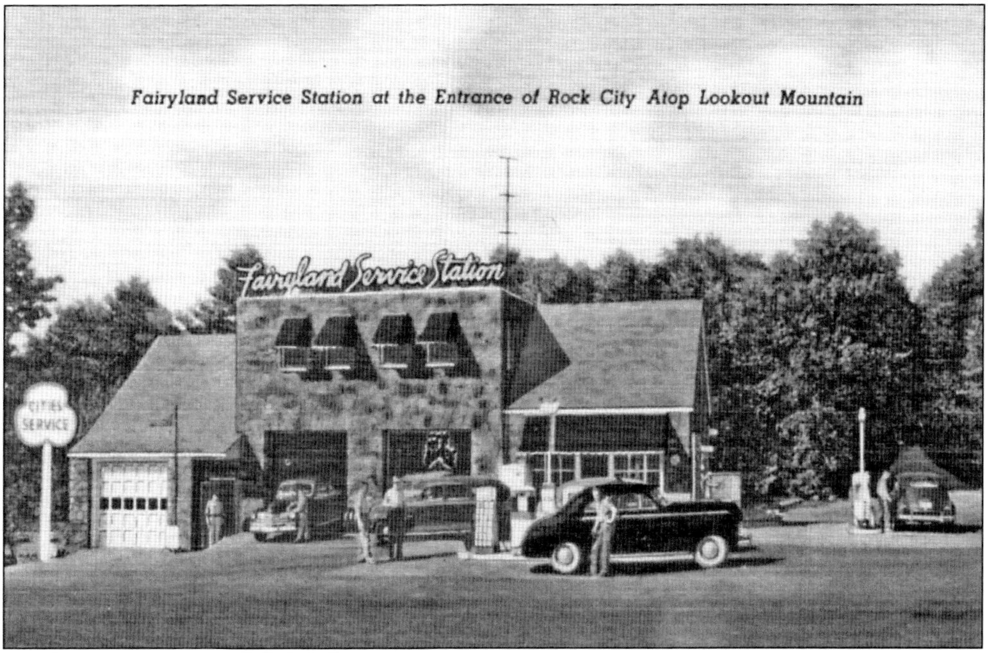


The Fairyland Service Station at the entrance of Rock City Gardens served the visitors to the attraction. Pictured in the early 1950s, this station was one of many tourist-centered businesses to come into the area that catered to the growing number of automobile tourists. (Courtesy of Jeffrey Lee Durbin.)

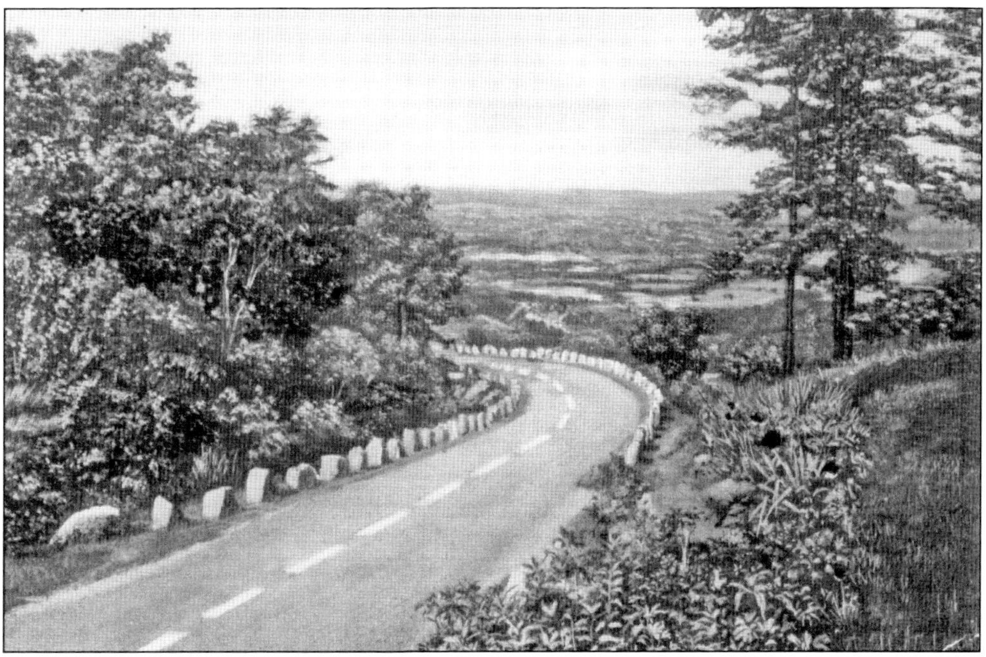

The drive up Lookout Mountain to the Rock City Gardens is spectacular, with views of Chattanooga and the surrounding countryside. On April 27, 1927, Lookout Mountain's road was surfaced in concrete, making it easier for automobiles to climb. (Courtesy of the author.)

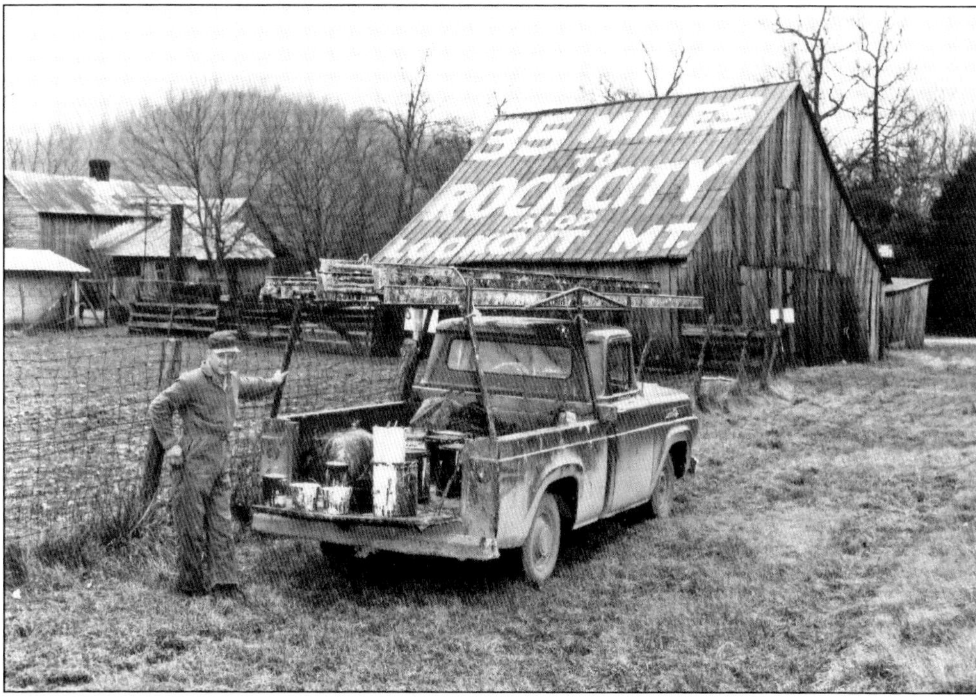

The natural-born promoter Garnet Carter found a clever way to advertise his attraction by hiring Clark Byers (1915–2000) to paint barns to read, "See Rock City." This image shows his first barn painted near Kimball, Tennessee, in 1933. It was torn down when Interstate 24 was built. Byers painted roadside advertisements for more than 30 years, including the roof of his home in Rising Fawn, Georgia. (Courtesy of the Chattanooga–Hamilton County Bicentennial Library.)

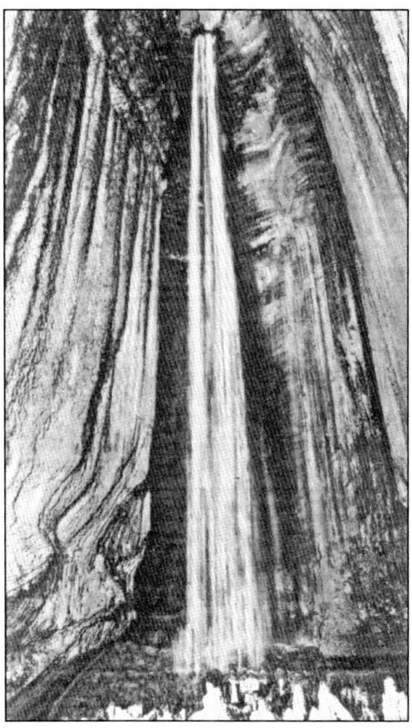
Ruby Falls and the Ruby Falls Caves have been open to the public since 1930 and have remained a popular tourist destination. The falls are located 1,120 feet below the surface of Lookout Mountain and are 145 feet tall. Local cave explorer Leo Lambert discovered the falls in 1928 and named them for his wife, Ruby. (Courtesy of the author.)

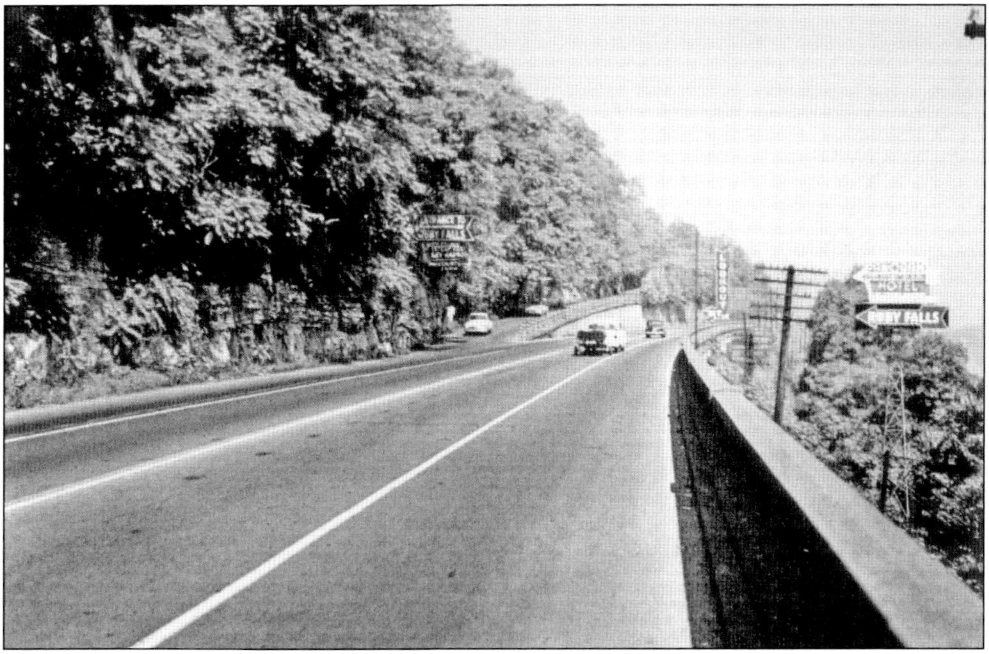


Like Rock City Gardens, Ruby Falls is well marketed by outdoor advertising. This image indicates the bold signage in which America's highest underground waterfall was and still is promoted along the highway. (Courtesy of Jeffrey Lee Durbin.)

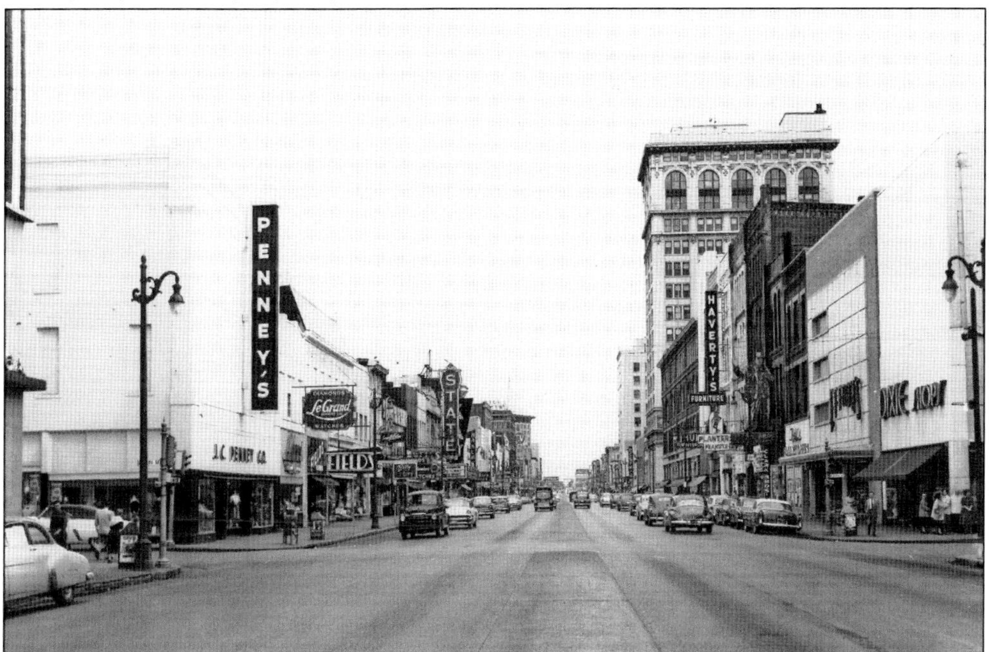


This view of Market Street in downtown Chattanooga captures the many places where shoppers could spend money, whether it was at Penney's, Haverty's Furniture, or the Dixie Shops shown in this photograph, which was taken around 1955. (Courtesy of the Chattanooga–Hamilton County Bicentennial Library.)

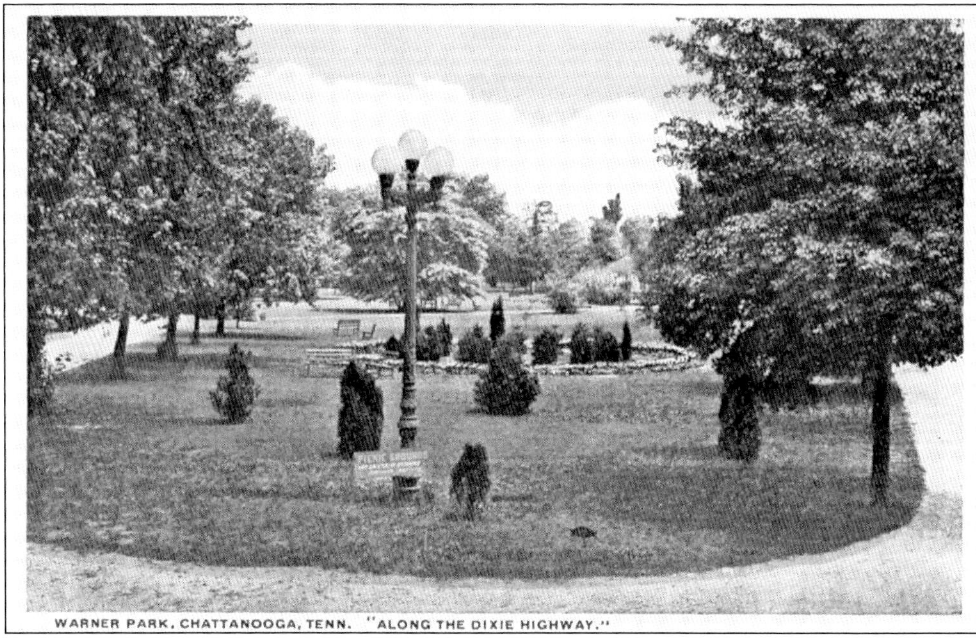


Today Warner Park, located on Third Street, is home to the Chattanooga City Zoo, playgrounds, softball fields, tennis courts, the Chattanooga Arts Center, and other recreational facilities. The zoo dates to 1937, and the park originated around 1895, when it was named Olympia Park. In 1912, the city purchased it and changed its name to Warner Park after commissioner Joseph H. Warner. (Courtesy of the Chattanooga–Hamilton County Bicentennial Library.)

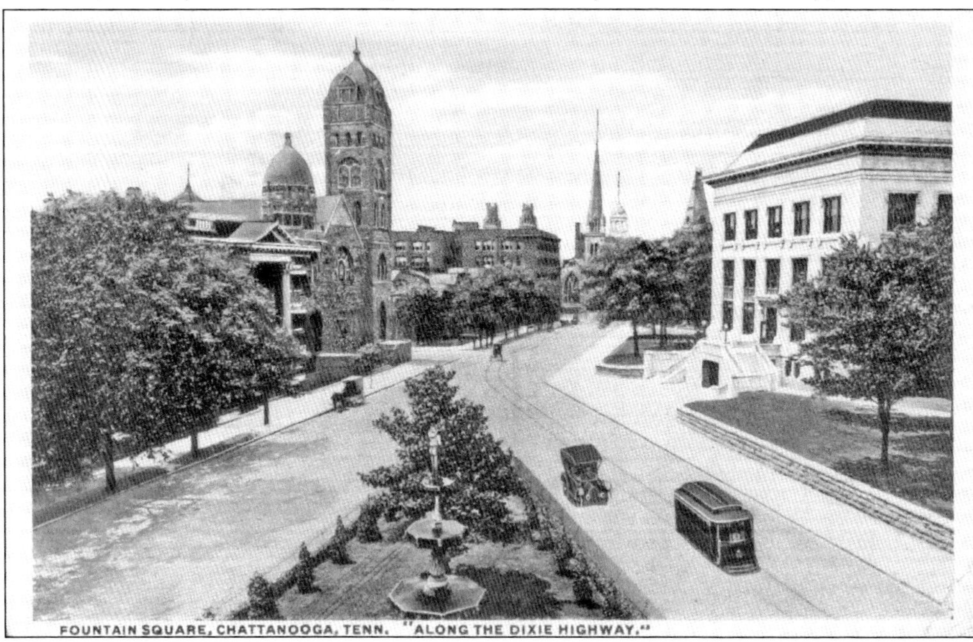


The historic Fountain Square dates to the first decade of the 20th century and is located "along the Dixie Highway" in the heart of Chattanooga. In 1979, the Fountain Square Historic District was listed in the National Register of Historic Places. (Courtesy of the Chattanooga–Hamilton County Bicentennial Library.)

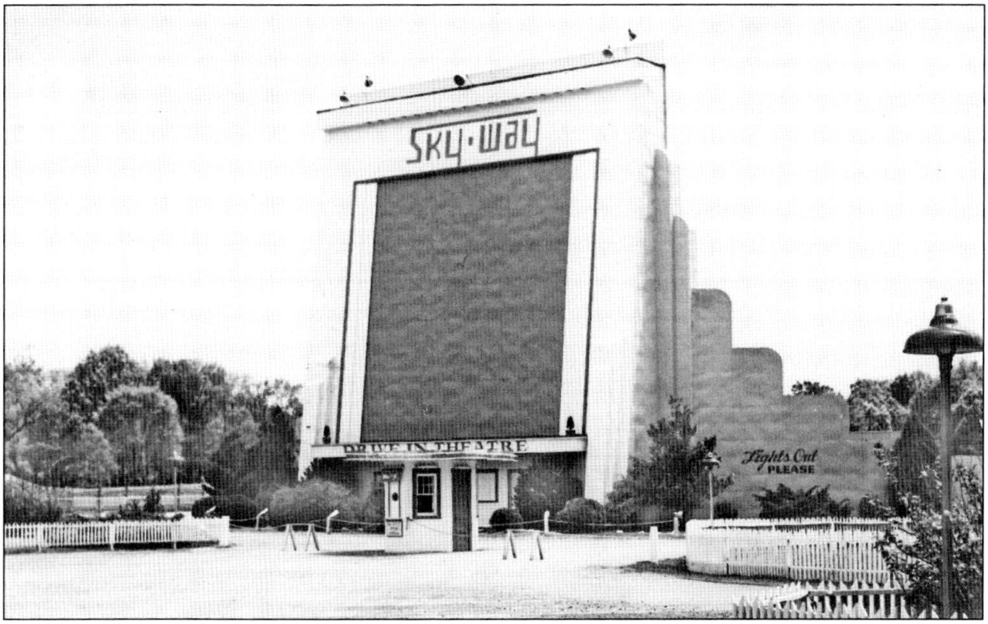


Drive-in theaters were one form of entertainment developed especially for the automobile. They were generally built on the outskirts of a city near other automobile-centered businesses. Built in 1941 and operating until 1959, the Skyway Drive-in Theater in Chattanooga was located on Brainerd Road. This photograph was taken in 1951. (Courtesy of the Chattanooga–Hamilton County Bicentennial Library.)

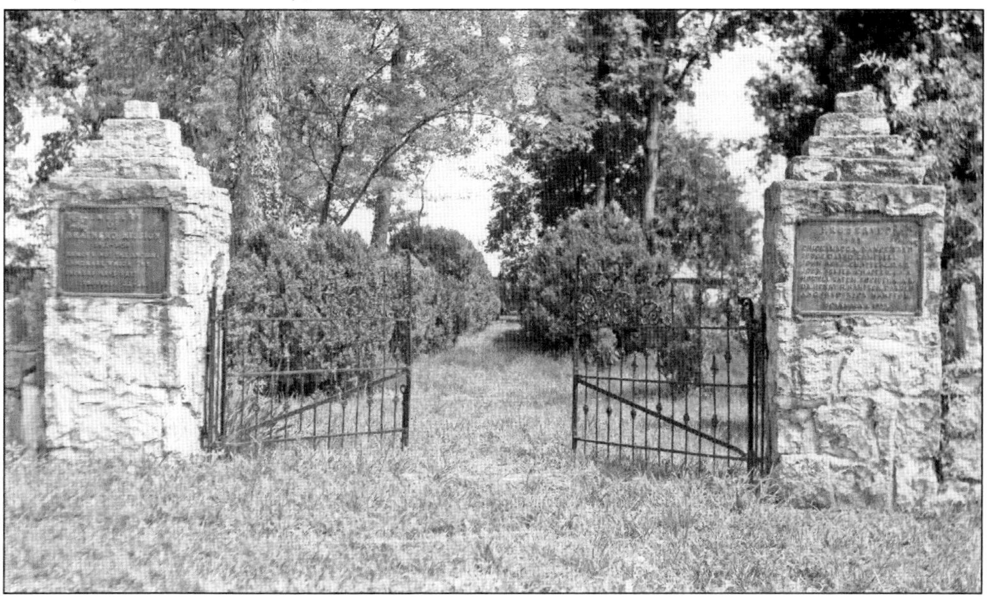

The Brainerd Mission School began in 1817 as a Cherokee Indian school named for missionary David Brainerd. It closed in 1838, following the forced removal of the Cherokee Indians during the Trail of Tears. The February 1924 issue of *The Dixie Highway* magazine promoted historic Chattanooga and nearby Brainerd School to attract history-loving tourists. Located 6 miles north of Chattanooga, the Brainerd Mission Cemetery is listed in the National Register of Historic Places. (Courtesy of the Chattanooga–Hamilton County Bicentennial Library.)

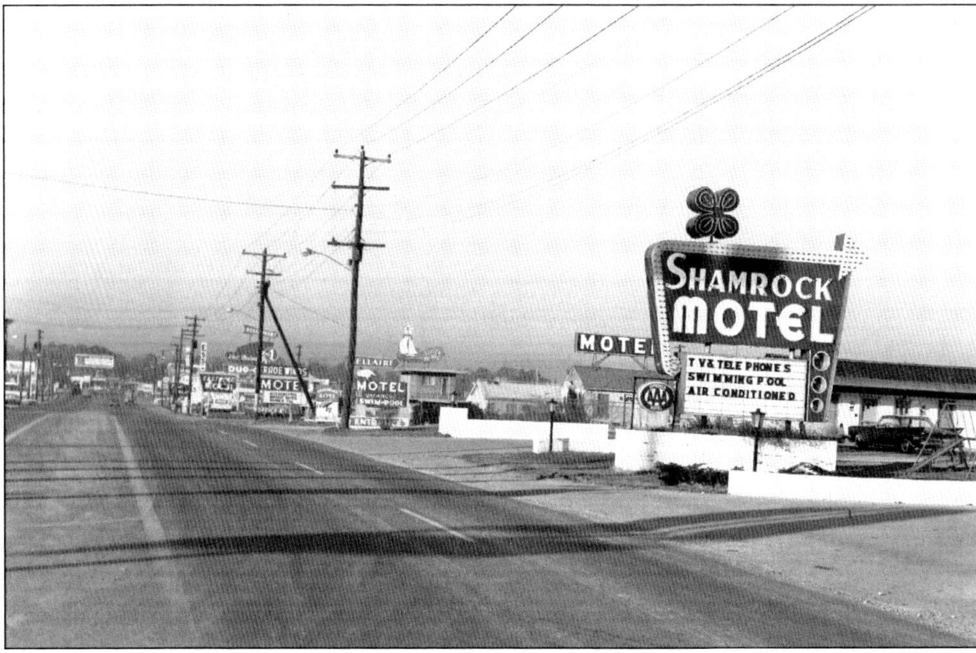


This image of Brainerd Road in Chattanooga, looking west from the site of the Brainerd Mission, shows how overnight accommodations followed the main routes in and out of cities. In this photograph, there are at least five motels—the Shamrock, Bellaire, Tradewinds, Eastgate, and Holiday Inn. (Courtesy of the Chattanooga–Hamilton County Bicentennial Library.)

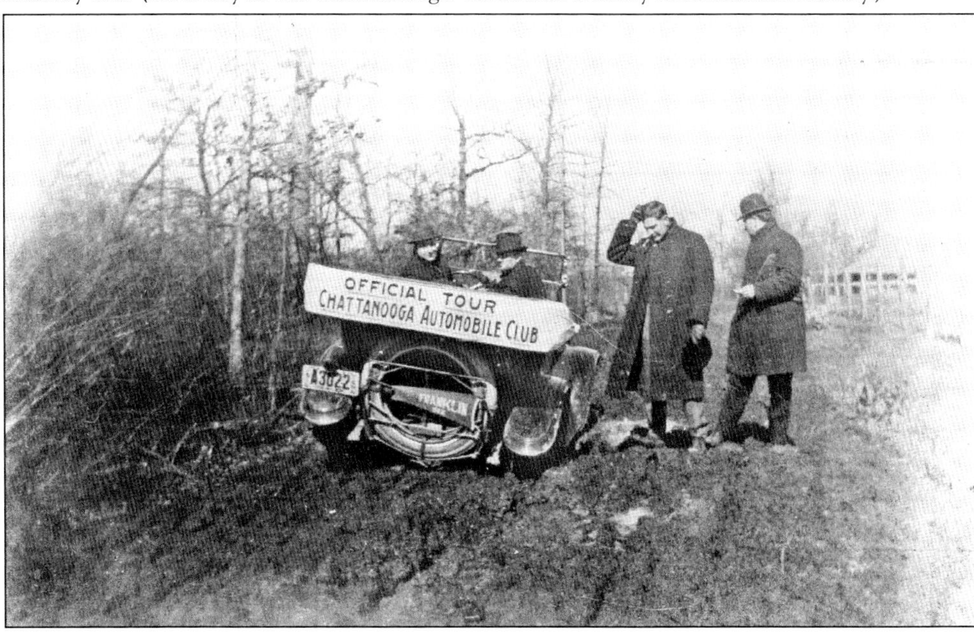


Touring the countryside was just one form of entertainment that the Dixie Highway provided. The Chattanooga Automobile Club hosted events during which its members made road trips throughout the region. In this photograph taken around the time that the Dixie Highway was developing, the members in their well-advertised club car appear to be stuck. (Courtesy of the Chattanooga–Hamilton County Bicentennial Library.)

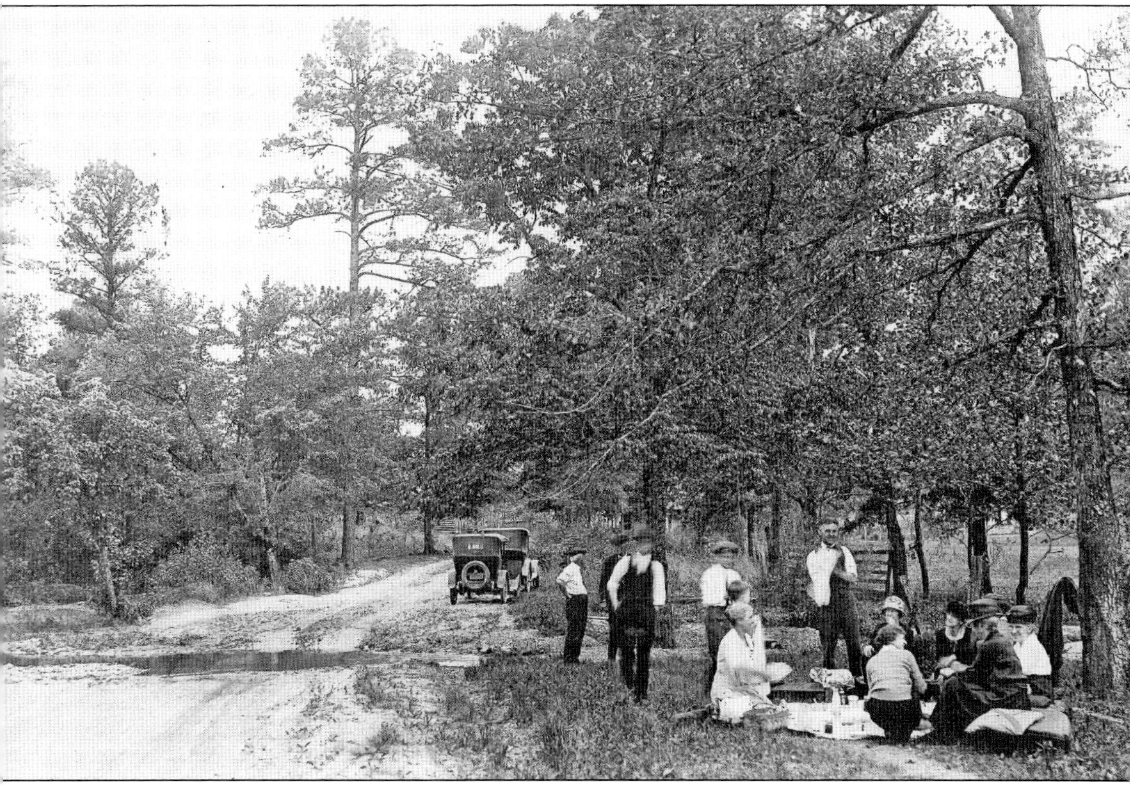

This 1930 image shows an unidentified group of people having a picnic along a dirt road. Roadside picnics could be planned social gatherings or an expedient way to get sustenance on a long trip in the middle of a rural area. During the early days of car travel, people picnicked and camped along the road. Some of these travelers were less than respectful of private property and left trash or took food from nearby gardens, orchards, and animal pens. To help address this issue, owners started charging people to camp, rented rooms, or put up no trespassing signs. Some local governments operated municipal camps for tourists that had bathroom facilities, trash cans, and camp sites. (Courtesy of the Chattanooga–Hamilton County Bicentennial Library.)

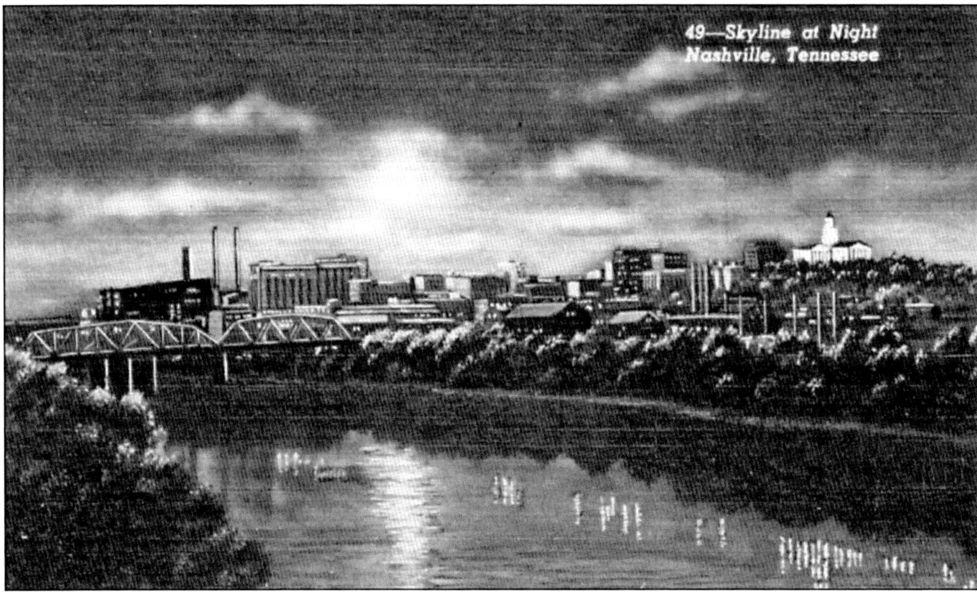


Following his victories at Forts Henry and Donelson, Gen. Ulysses S. Grant led a Union army and navy attack on Nashville, and on February 23, 1862, Nashville became the first Confederate capital to fall. Under Union occupation for the rest of the war, Nashville became the site of several contraband camps that eventually housed up to 2,000 refugees from slavery. (Courtesy of the author.)

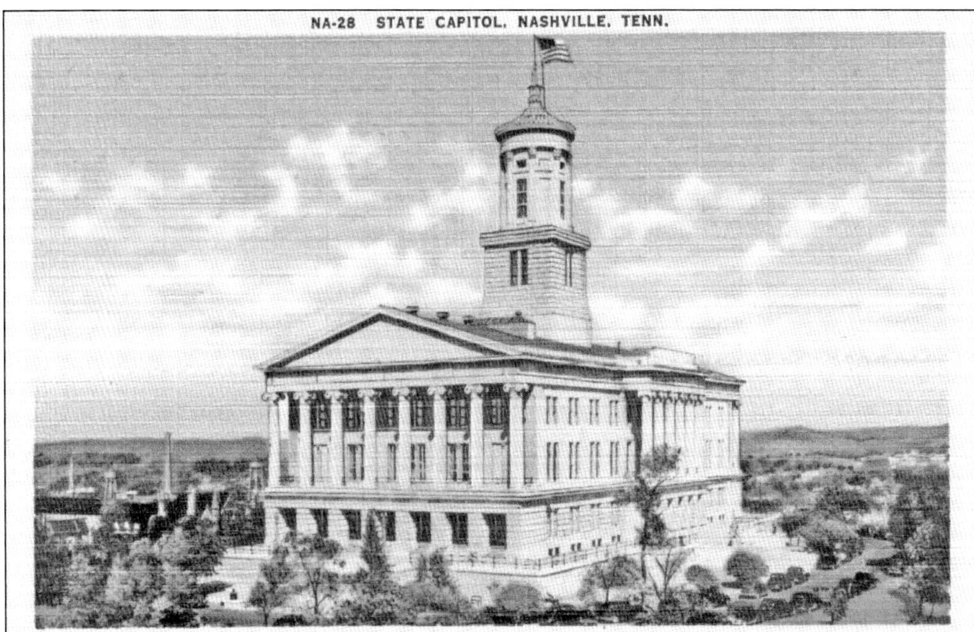


The Tennessee State Capitol, designed by noted architect William Strickland and completed in 1859 just before the Civil War, is one of many places in Nashville that reflects Nashville's Civil War history. Others include Fort Negley, Nashville National Cemetery, Belle Meade Plantation, Belmont Mansion, Travellers Rest, Tennessee State Museum, and the Confederate Circle at Mount Olivet Cemetery. (Courtesy of the author.)

# Six

# Remembering the Civil War

Tennessee played a significant role in the American Civil War (1861–1865). It was the last state to join the Confederacy, a reflection of its divided loyalties. Most of East Tennessee and parts of the Middle Tennessee Highlands were Unionists, while most of Middle Tennessee and West Tennessee supported the Confederacy. These split loyalties, as well as Tennessee being the gateway to the Deep South, added a complexity to the Civil War action in the state, in which all three divisions witnessed battles, occupation, and hardship.

People come from all over the United States to visit Civil War sites in Tennessee. Civil War tourism in Tennessee dates to just before the turn of the 20th century with the placement of monuments memorializing the soldiers from both the Union and the Confederacy and the creation of the first nationally recognized Civil War battlefield at Chickamauga and Chattanooga National Military Park in 1890.

The Dixie Highway provided access to many places associated with Tennessee's Civil War heritage, including the battlefields at Chickamauga-Chattanooga and Stones River, Lookout Mountain, the Sam Davis Home, and national cemeteries in Nashville, Murfreesboro, and Chattanooga that date to the Civil War. The major cities along the highway route—Nashville, Murfreesboro, and Chattanooga—all experienced occupation by Union troops and have their own distinct histories of how the war impacted their communities. In addition, there are many antebellum homes, buildings, and sites throughout the region that have a strong link to the Civil War story.

The significance of Tennessee's role in the Civil War was recognized in 1996, when the U.S. Congress designated the entire state as the Tennessee Civil War National Heritage Area (TCWNHA), the only national heritage area to include a whole state. The Center for Historic Preservation at Middle Tennessee State University administers the TCWNHA.

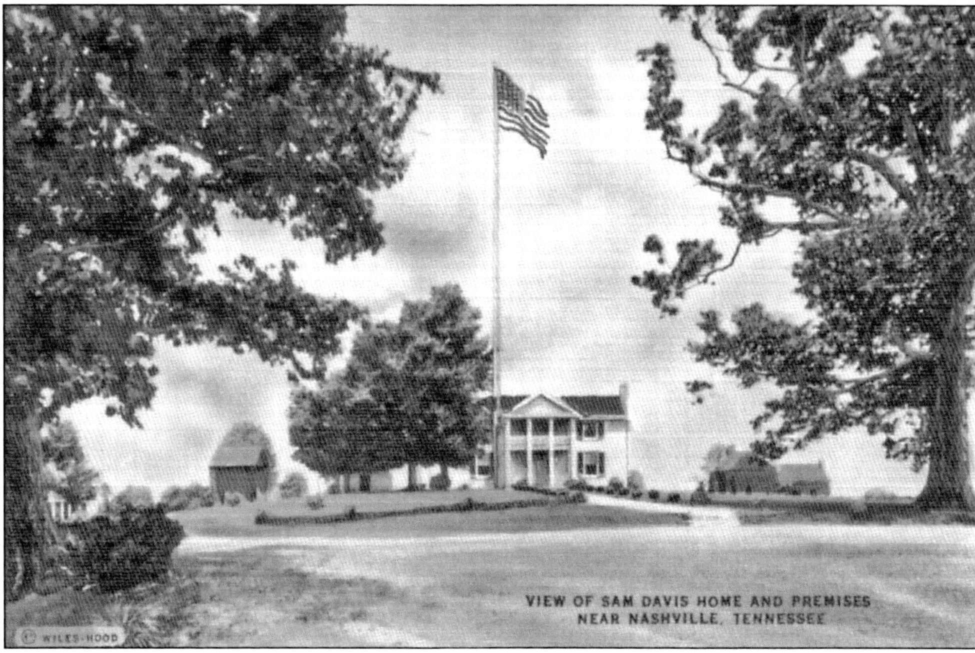


Located just east of the Dixie Highway in Smyrna, the Sam Davis Home and Museum tells the story of Civil War legend Sam Davis. Born in 1842, Davis enlisted in the 1st Tennessee Infantry Regiment in April 1861. By 1863, he was a member of Coleman's Scouts, who worked behind the lines gathering information and trying to interrupt Union communications. In November 1863, Federal troops captured Davis as he headed toward Chattanooga. Carrying papers about troop movements, several newspapers, and some personal belongings of Confederate general Braxton Bragg, Davis was treated as a spy even though he wore a Confederate uniform. When he denied being a spy and refused to divulge his sources, he was tried and hanged on November 23, 1863. His last words were, "I would die a thousand deaths before I would betray a friend." (Both, courtesy of Jeffrey Lee Durbin.)

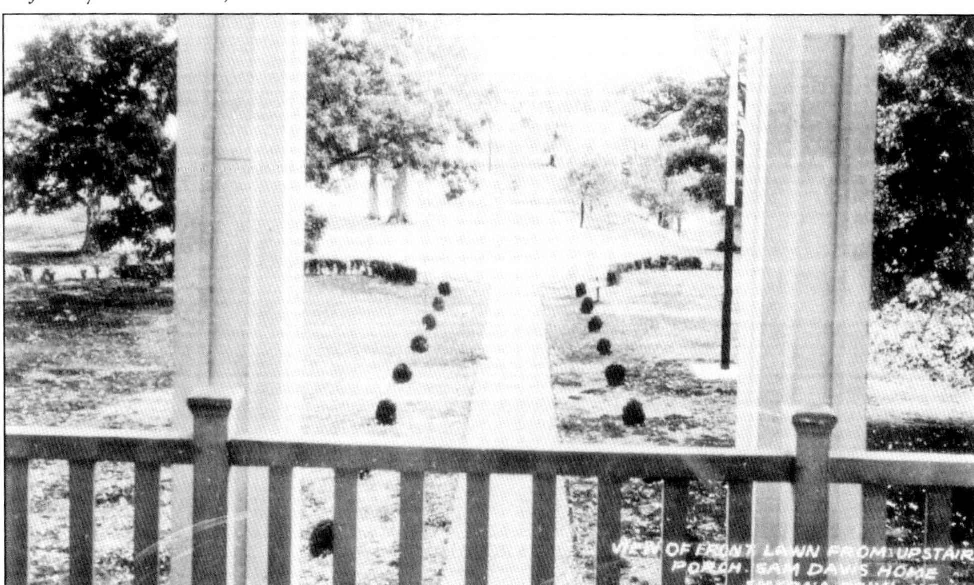

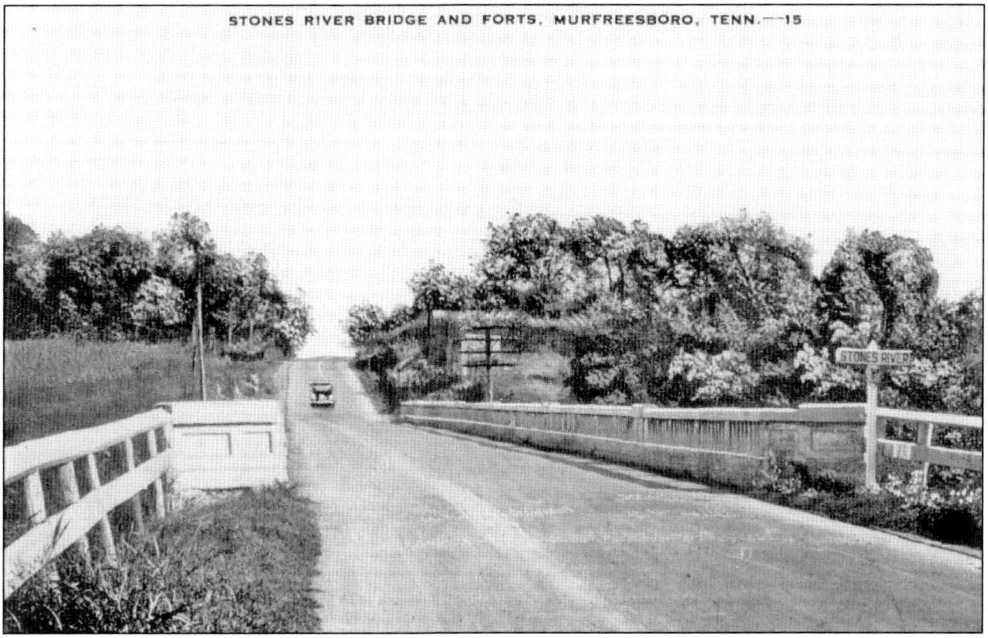


Located just north of downtown Murfreesboro along the route of the Dixie Highway on Old Nashville Highway, the Stones River National Battlefield commemorates one of the bloodiest battles of the Civil War and preserves about 570 acres that include a visitors' center, national cemetery, Redoubt Brannan, and portions of Fortress Rosecrans. (Courtesy of Jeffrey Lee Durbin.)

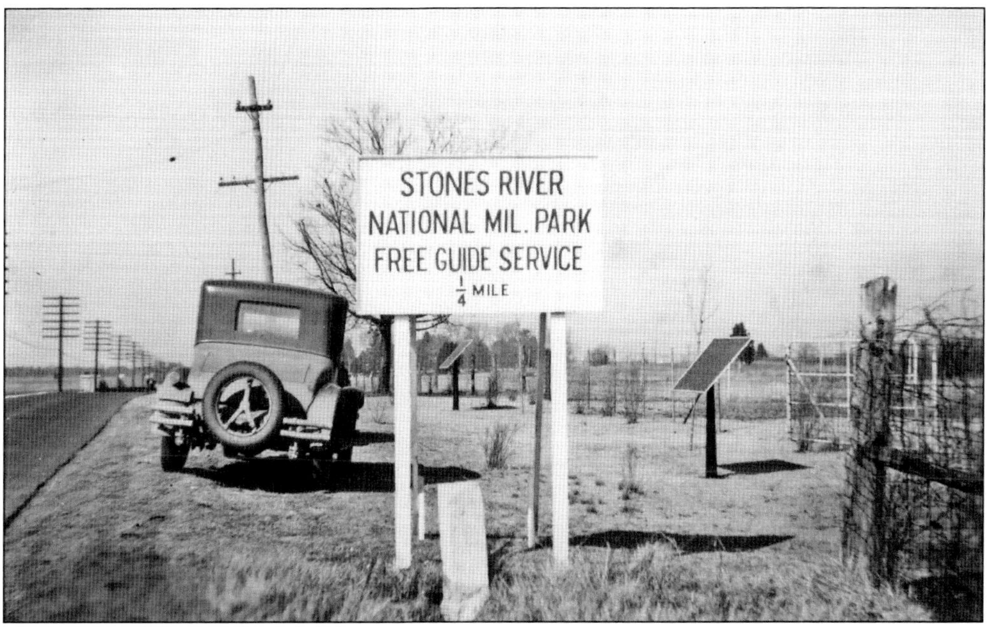


This 1930s photograph shows the character of the Dixie Highway as it runs through the battlefield. The battle included 43,400 Union soldiers from the Army of the Cumberland and 37,317 from the Confederate Army of Tennessee with a total of 23,517 captured, wounded, or killed. (Courtesy of the Tennessee State Library and Archives.)

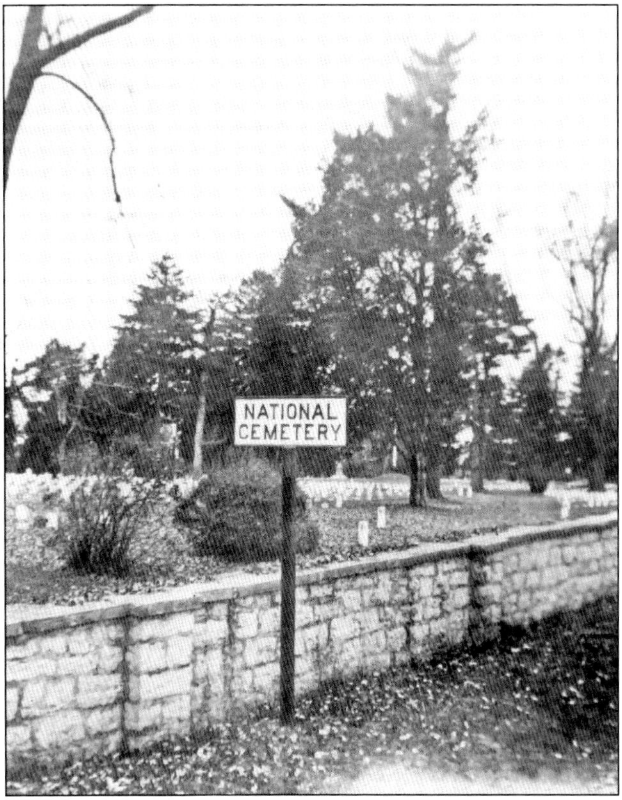


The men who built the wall that surrounds the cemetery were from the 111th United States Colored Infantry. They began the wall in 1866. More than 7,100 people are buried in this cemetery, including over 6,100 Civil War soldiers, approximately 100 veterans from other wars, and a few family members. The graves are marked with marble headstones. (Courtesy of the Tennessee State Library and Archives.)

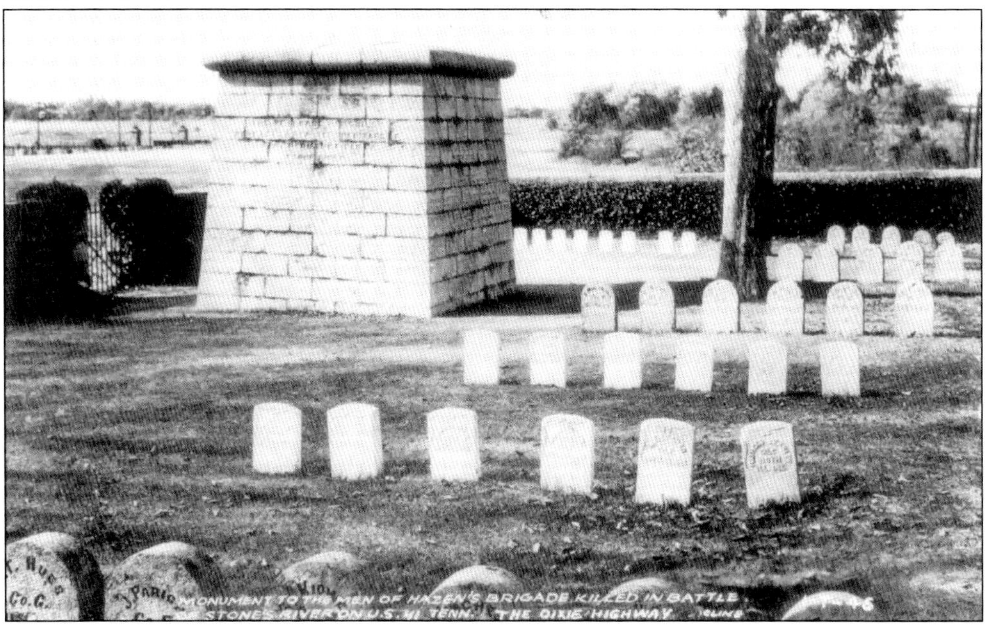


Hazen's Brigade Monument, located at the Stones River National Battlefield, is one of the oldest monuments to the Civil War. The soldiers of Union colonel William B. Hazen's brigade erected it in early 1863, just after the Battle of Stones River but while the war still raged, to honor the 45 men who died in the battle (409 others were wounded). (Courtesy of Jeffrey Lee Durbin.)

The Union army built Fortress Rosecrans—which includes Redoubt Brannan, depicted in this photograph taken from the nearby railroad tracks—following the Battle of Stones River. Rosecrans was the largest earthworks built during the Civil War. Just northwest of downtown Murfreesboro, portions of the fortress remain and are maintained by the National Park Service. (Courtesy of the Tennessee State Library and Archives.)

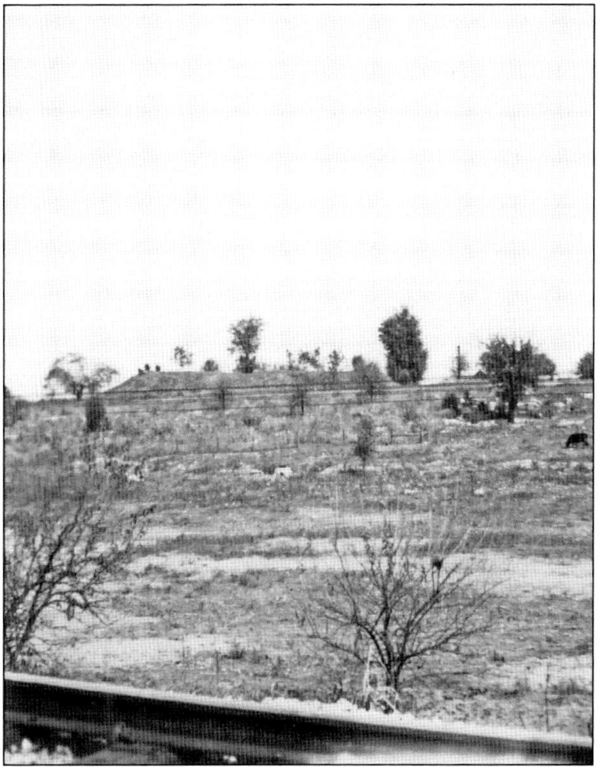

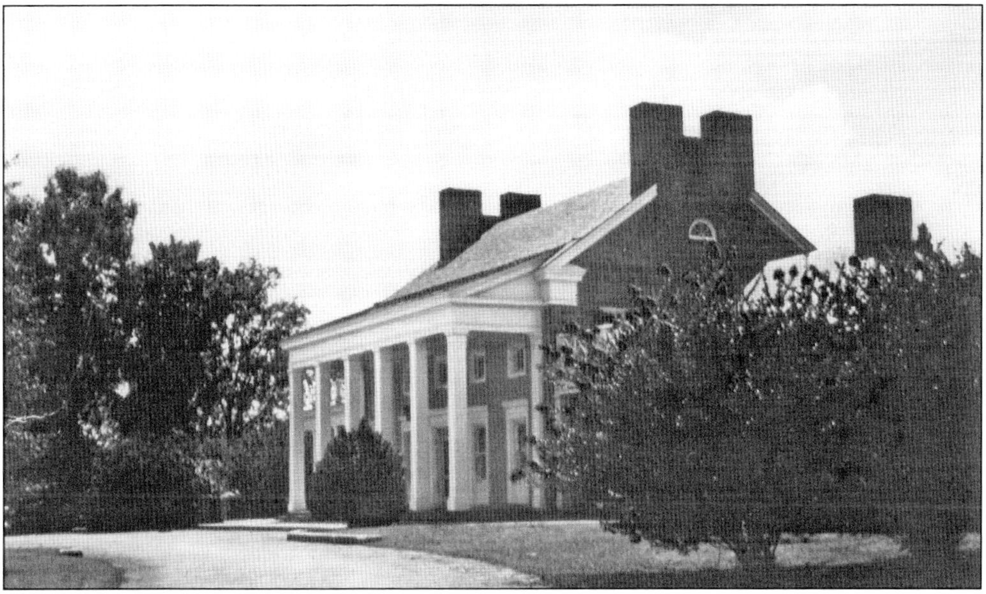

In 1890, the U.S. Congress designated the Chickamauga-Chattanooga National Military Park as the first federal military and historical site to be preserved. Veteran Union generals Henry V. Boynton and Ferdinand Van Derveer campaigned for the federal government to preserve land associated with the Civil War. Along the Dixie Highway, the visitors center is actually in Georgia, but it interprets the history of the multiple battles in and around Chattanooga and Lookout Mountain in Tennessee. (Courtesy of the author.)

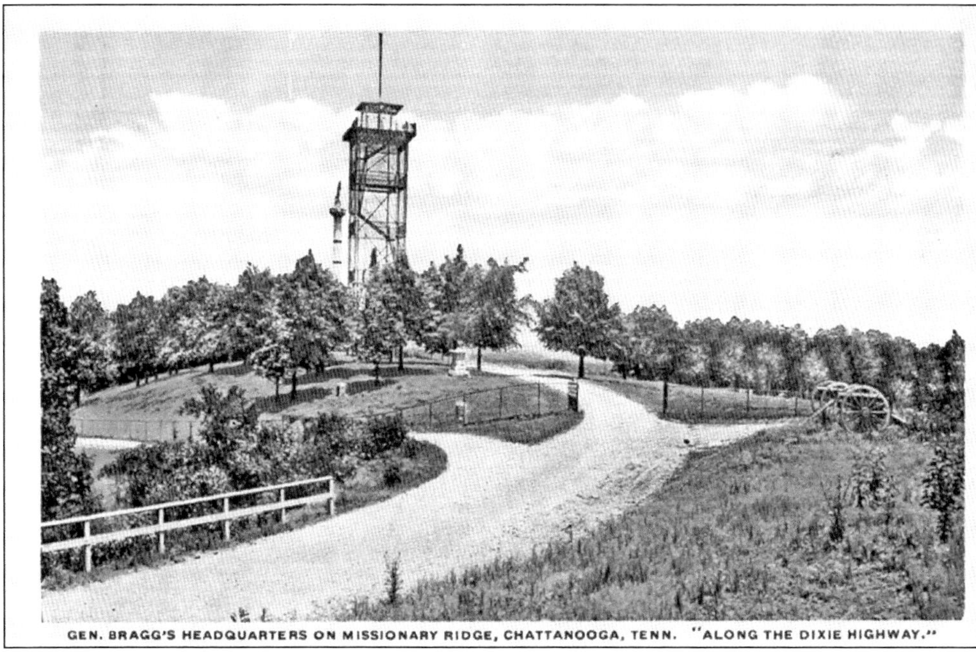


Confederate general Braxton Bragg (1817–1876) lost the Battle of Chattanooga at Missionary Ridge on November 1863 to Gen. Ulysses S. Grant. Located within the Chickamauga-Chattanooga National Military Park, this image shows the Illinois Monument, erected in 1899, and the Observation Tower for the Bragg Reservation. The tower was razed in 1941. (Courtesy of the Chattanooga–Hamilton County Bicentennial Library.)

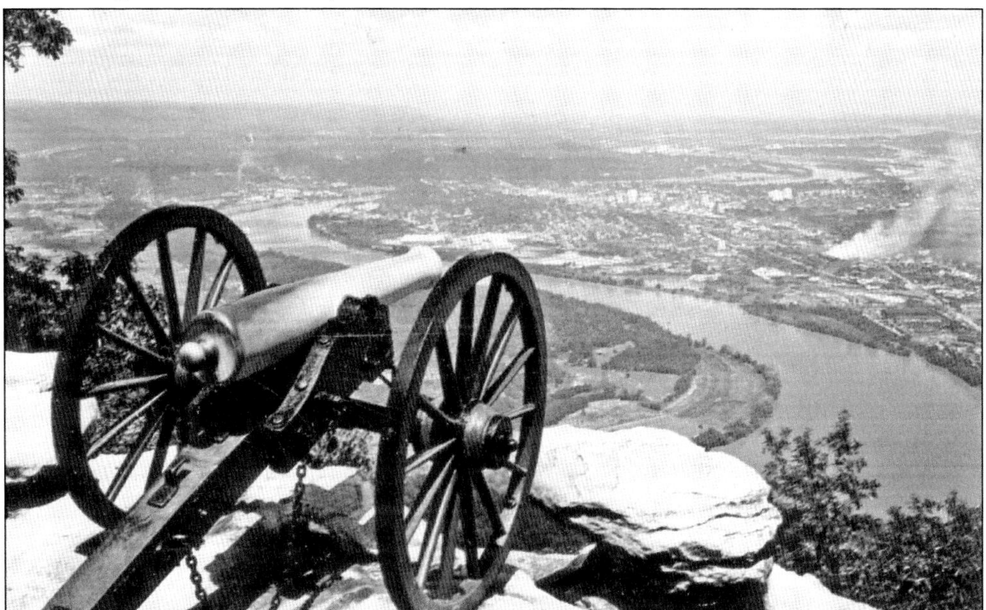

One of the best places for learning about Civil War history along the Dixie Highway is at Lookout Mountain, where the battles of Lookout Mountain, Chattanooga, and Chickamauga all took place. This photograph of the Confederate Battery on Lookout Mountain depicts how valuable the top of the mountain was as a strategic observation point. (Courtesy of Jeffrey Lee Durbin.)

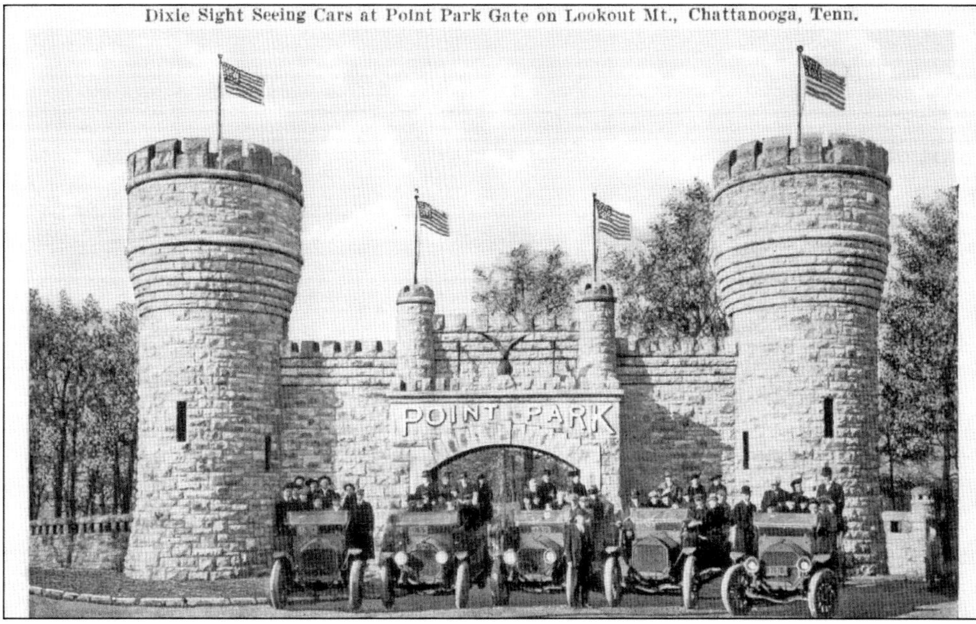


Completed in 1905, Point Park—formerly known as Whiteside Park—was completed to commemorate the Battle Above the Clouds. Officially a part of the Chickamauga-Chattanooga National Military Park, Point Park offers visitors access to excellent observation points, the Lookout Mountain Battlefield Visitors Center, multiple monuments, and the Craven House. (Courtesy of Jeffrey Lee Durbin.)

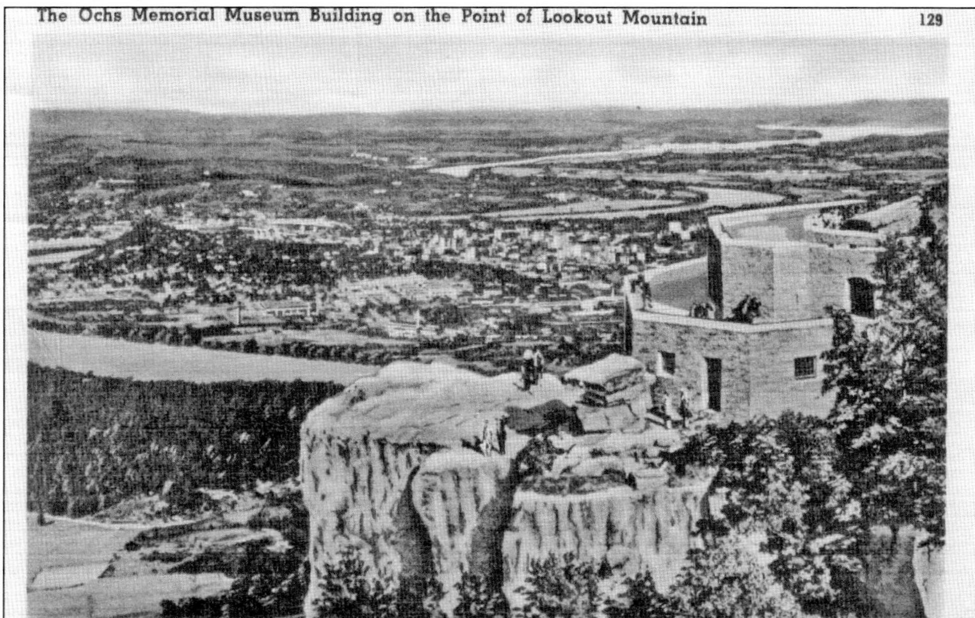


In 1898, Alfred S. Ochs, publisher of the *Chattanooga Times*, donated the land encompassing the Ochs Memorial Museum on Lookout Mountain and surrounding area to the federal government to commemorate and interpret the Civil War and the role in which Lookout Mountain played in the conflict. (Courtesy of Jeffrey Lee Durbin.)

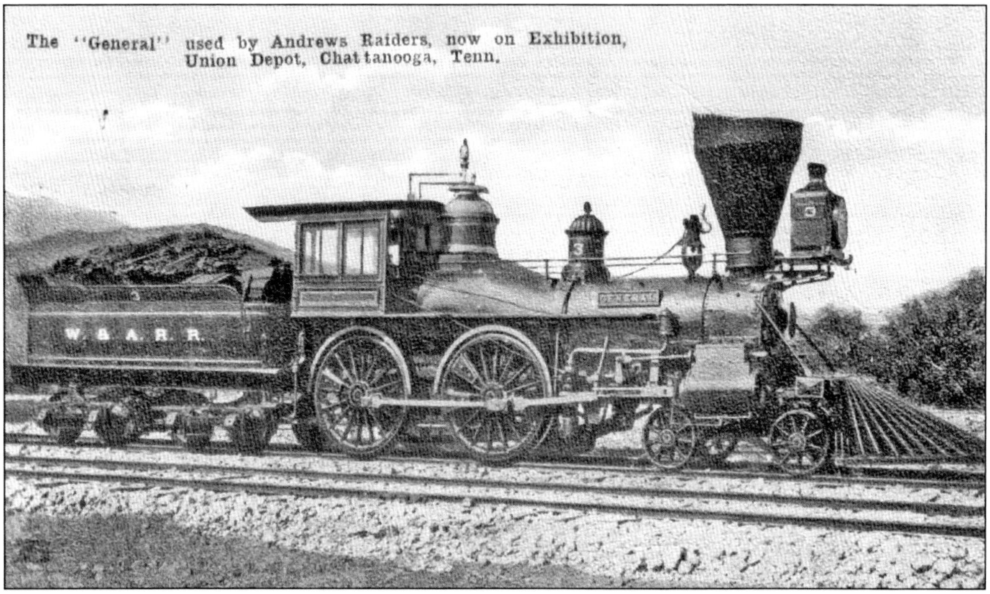


One of greatest Civil War stories, which also occurred along the Dixie Highway corridor, is that of the Great Locomotive Chase, or Andrew's Raid. On April 12, 1862, Federal raiders stole the *General* locomotive from the community of Big Shanty (present-day Kennesaw), Georgia, and a chase ensued that ended in Ringgold, Georgia. Following the war, the locomotive returned to service until the 1890s. In 1901, it was refurbished and housed at the Union depot in Chattanooga, as seen in this postcard. In 1972, after a legal challenge, Georgia brought it back to Kennesaw, one of the north Georgia towns along the route of the Dixie Highway. (Courtesy of the author.)

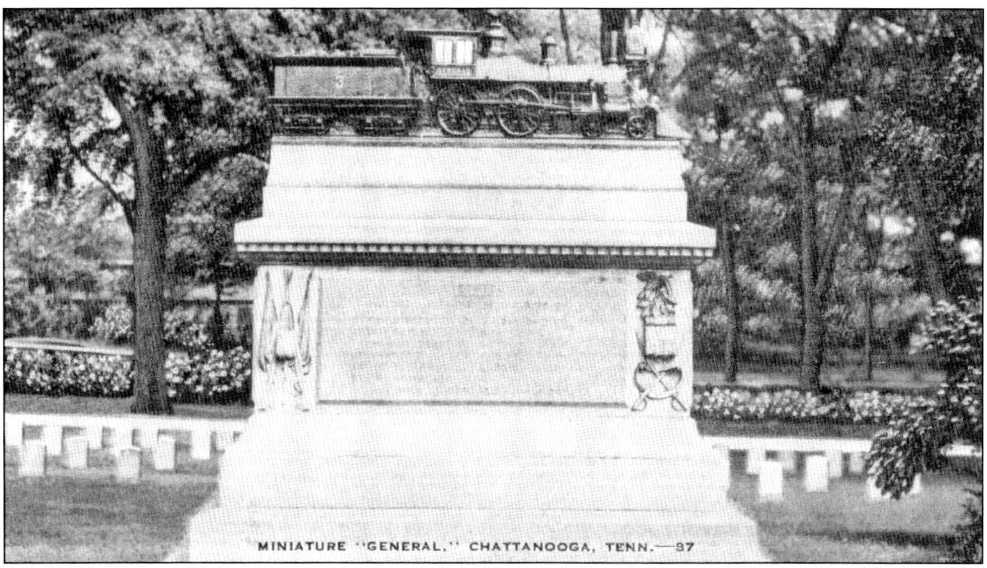


A miniature of the *General* locomotive rests upon the Ohio Monument in the Chattanooga National Cemetery to honor the six Medal of Honor winners who were hanged by Confederates for their part in the Great Locomotive Chase. Ohio gave the monument to the cemetery at a cost of $5,000 in 1891. The cemetery contains the remains of veterans from the Revolutionary War to the present, including 186 German prisoners of war—the only national cemetery to include foreign POWs. (Courtesy of Jeffrey Lee Durbin.)

# *Seven*

# DOCUMENTING THE DIXIE

Along the Dixie Highway, Tennesseans constructed gas stations, motor courts, stores, tourist destinations, and more to serve the car-traveling public. Known as "roadside architecture," these buildings created a transportation corridor affiliated with early automobile culture that was distinct from the largely rural landscape surrounding much of the roadway. Evidence of this significant turning point in American history is reflected in the man-made resources along the roads; however, the identity of this early transportation corridor is disappearing, as can be seen from looking at the Dixie Highway in Tennessee.

There are at least three components that contribute to the identity of a historic transportation corridor. These are the physical road itself (width, path, and character), the surrounding setting or context of the road, and the buildings and artifacts along the road. Just 20 year ago, the corridor between Springfield and Chattanooga was mostly a two-lane road with stretches of countryside dotted with development centered on the cities and towns. Today the original highway corridor has not fared well, and in fact, it has completely disappeared in sections. All three of these components of a transportation corridor have been adversely affected by double-digit population growth, developmental pressures, suburbanization, and transportation upgrades along the route. Documenting the Dixie Highway is an important step to identifying what is left in order to determine if any of this corridor is worthy of preservation action, and if so, what types of strategies can be undertaken to ensure that something is left in another 20 years.

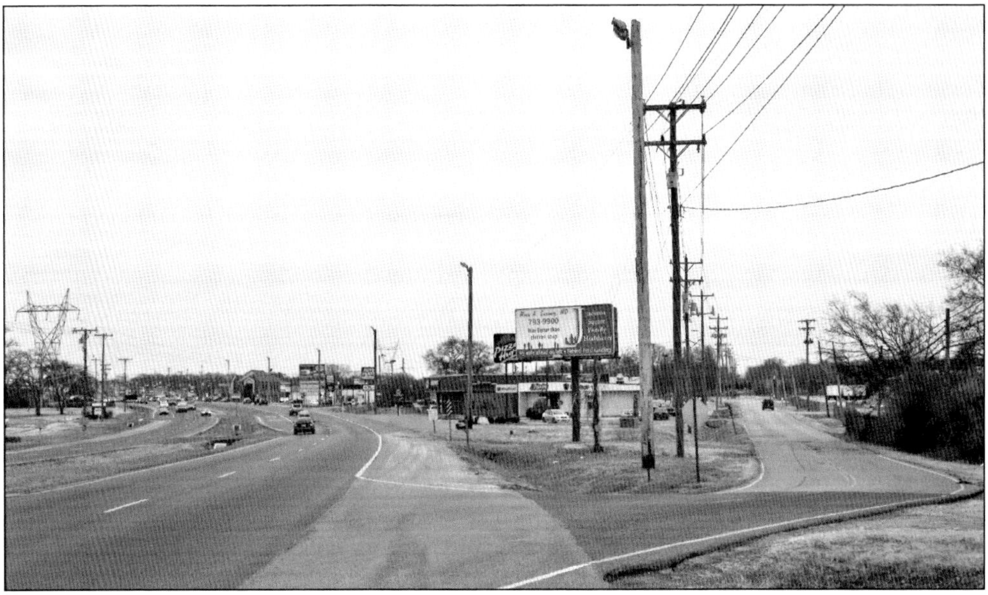

Between Nashville and Murfreesboro, a great many historic resources have been razed. Their demise can undoubtedly be linked to the developmental pressures brought on by the triple- and double-digit population growth in Rutherford and Davidson Counties from 1990 to 2009—more than 116 percent and almost 25 percent, respectively. This photograph shows the bypassed Old Dixie Highway to the right and the modern U.S. Route 41 to the left. (Courtesy of the author.)

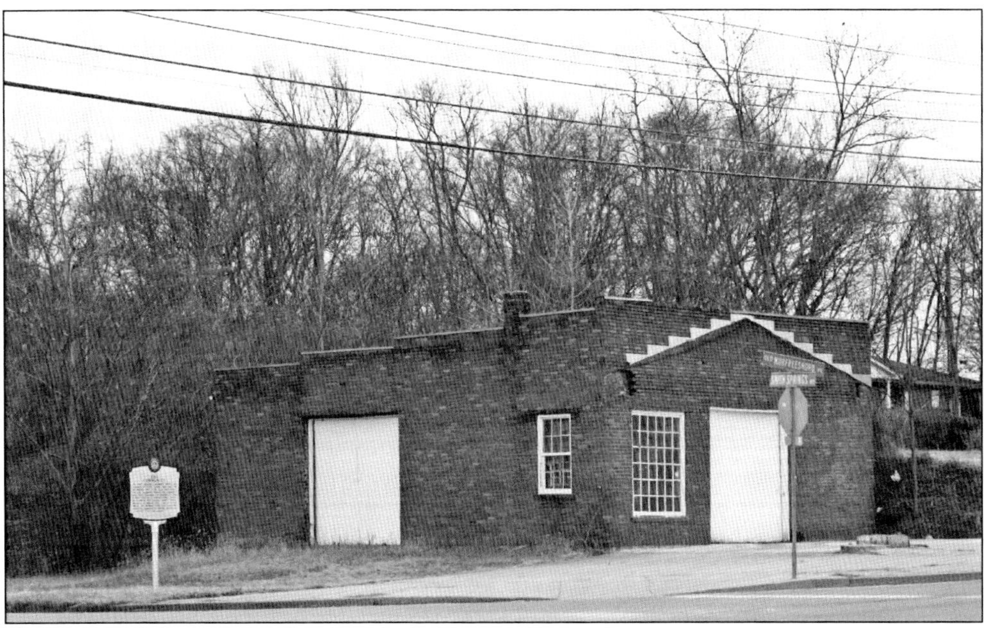

In the community of Una in Davidson County, the road and two buildings marking its early history as a crossroads have been impacted by modern road expansion and curbing. The I. M. Smith and Sons General Merchandise Store has been torn down, and the Ellis Garage, which is listed in the National Register of Historic Places and is shown in this photograph, has had its canopy removed and its integrity jeopardized. (Courtesy of the author.)

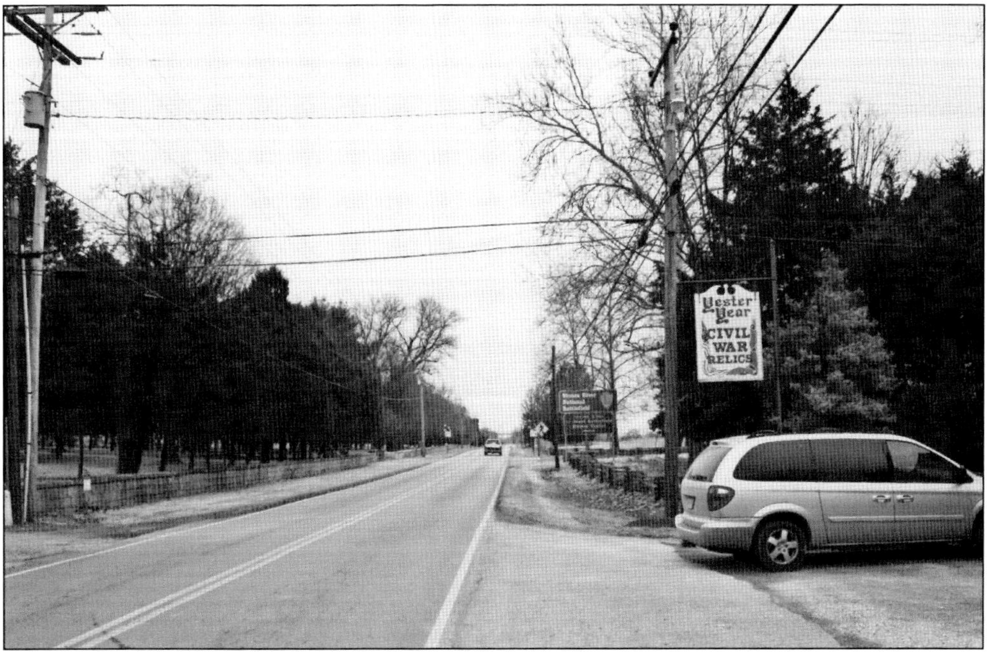


One portion of the Old Nashville Highway that retains much of its character has been preserved because of its proximity to the Stones River National Battlefield and National Cemetery. Along this section, there are some family farms, the Stones River, and several railroad overpasses and bridges that contribute to the historic setting of the area. (Courtesy of the author.)

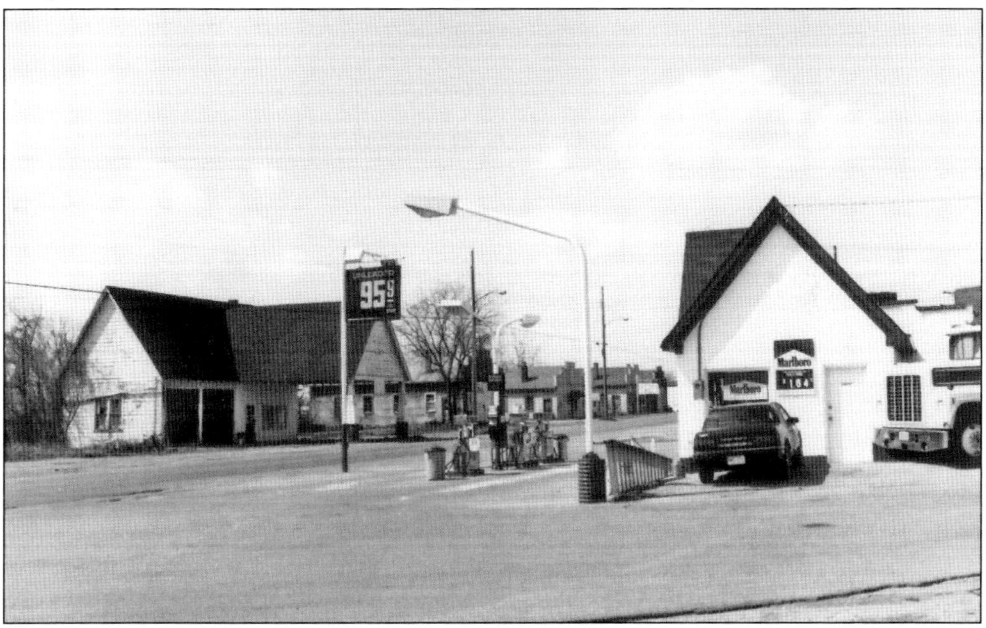

West College Street in Murfreesboro was once a "gasoline alley" with at least 14 automobile-related businesses in a two-block area. Of the six properties documented in 1992 that made up the alley, only two are still in use, one as a gasoline station and the other as a motor repair shop. While they remain in good condition, three other properties are gone, and one is vacant and altered. (Courtesy of the author.)

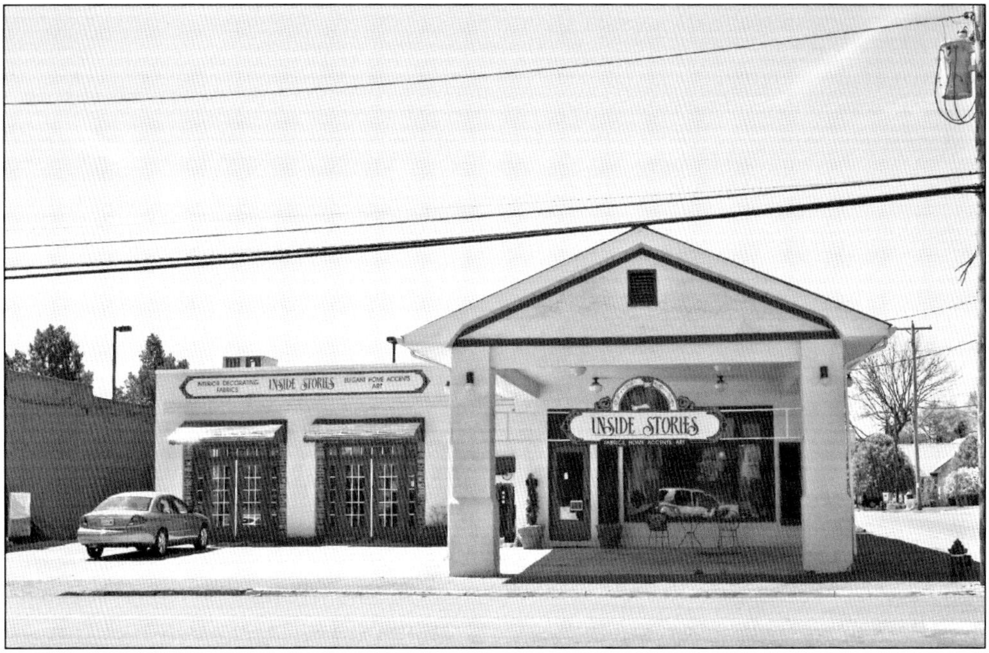

Each of the downtown areas along the route has several resources that date to the development of the Dixie Highway. In Winchester, there still remains an automobile dealership, theater, and gas station that date to the 1920s and 1930s. The gas station shown in this photograph has been converted to an interior decorating and furnishing store. (Courtesy of the author.)

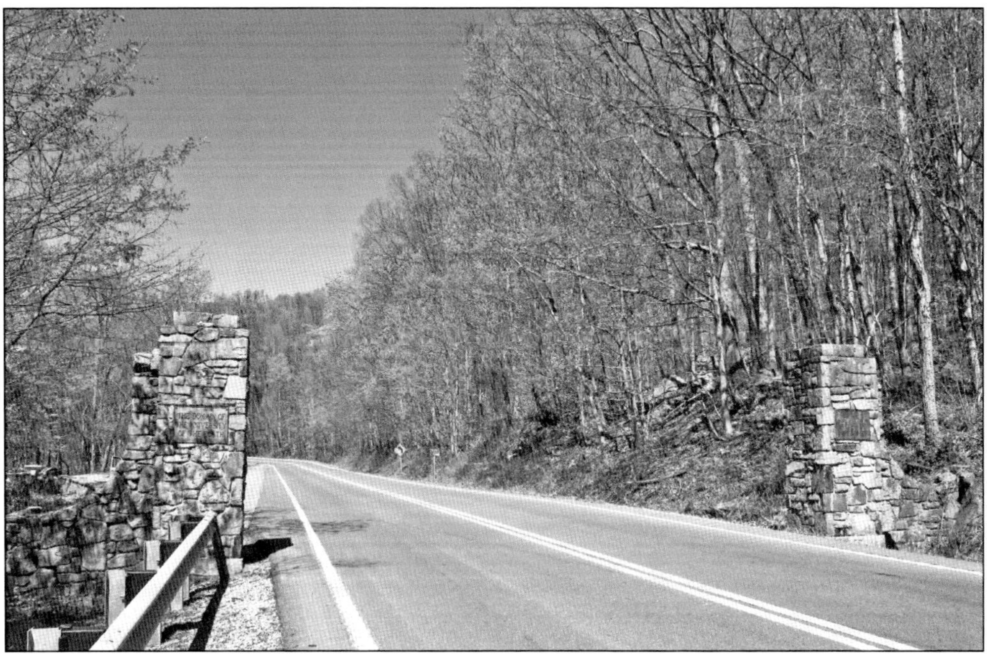

The terrain has helped preserve the scenery and maintain the feel of the road in the more mountainous sections of the highway. Heading toward Sewanee, the road and its original setting are still intact, as demonstrated by the well-kept overlook at the entrance of the Domain—a 13,000-acre tract of land owned by Sewanee University. (Courtesy of the author.)

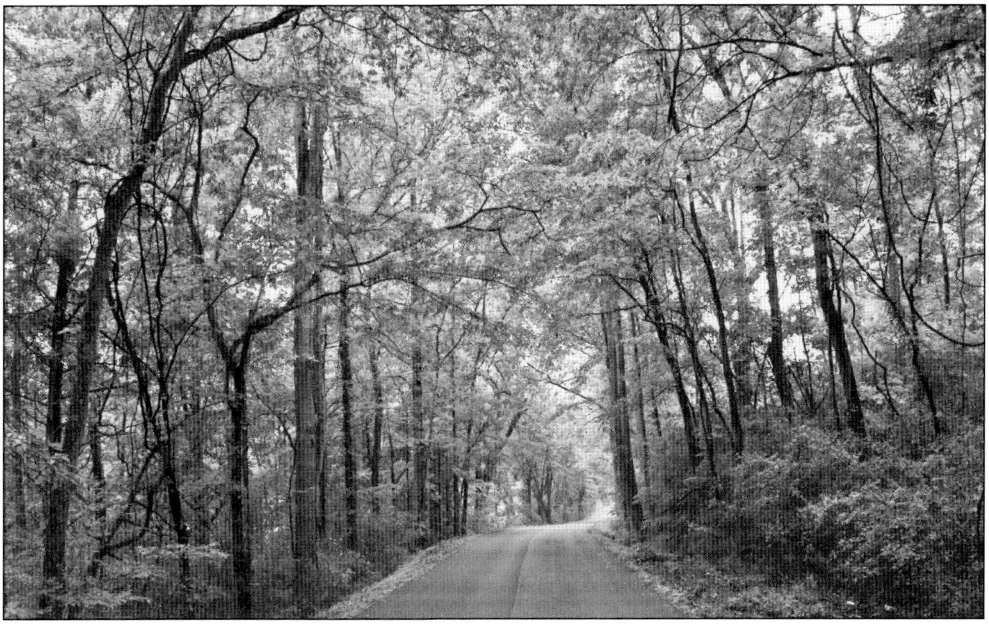

Between Monteagle and Kimball, Interstate 24 overlapped or bypassed sections of the original road. These bypassed portions—some of which retain the name "Old Dixie Highway"—are the most historic-feeling segments of the original road. It is here that one gets a sense of what the 1920s traveler experienced: few cars, curving roads, steep climbs, farms, and not many roadside businesses. (Courtesy of the author.)

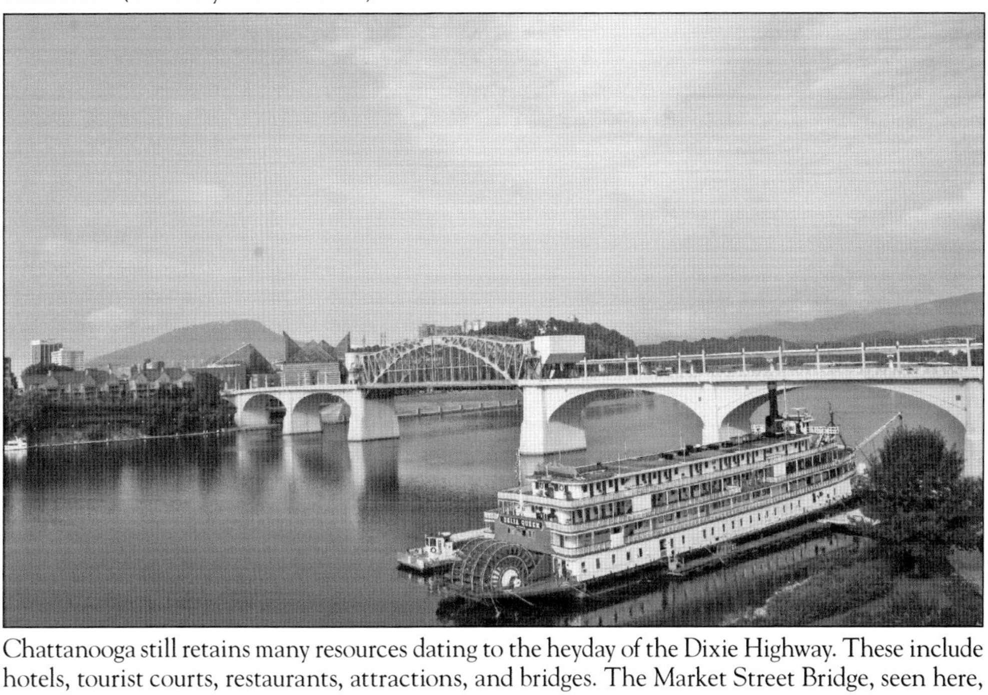

Chattanooga still retains many resources dating to the heyday of the Dixie Highway. These include hotels, tourist courts, restaurants, attractions, and bridges. The Market Street Bridge, seen here, was called the "million-dollar bridge" because the large amount of money it cost to build caused such a stir. It is still used for Market Street traffic and is a reminder of Chattanooga's pivotal role in the development of the Dixie Highway. (Courtesy of the author.)

# Bibliography


Ash, Stephen V. *Middle Tennessee Society Transformed, 1860–1870: War and Peace in the Upper South*. Knoxville: University of Tennessee Press, 2006.

Carver, Martha, preparer. *Tennessee's Survey Report for Historic Highway Bridges*. Nashville: Tennessee Department of Transportation, Ambrose Printing Company, 2008.

Durbin, Jeffrey Lee. "Survey Techniques for Roadside Architecture: The Gas Station, Murfreesboro, Tennessee, as a Case Study." Master's thesis, Middle Tennessee State University, 1989.

Ingram, Tammy Leigh. "Dixie Highway: Private Enterprise and State Building in the South, 1900–1930." Ph.D. dissertation, Yale University, 2007.

Lowry, Amy Gillis, and Abbie Tucker Parks. *North Georgia's Dixie Highway*. Charleston, SC: Arcadia Publishing, 2007.

O'Brien, Tim. *Tennessee: Off the Beaten Path*, 6th ed. Guilford, CT: The Globe Pequot Press, 2002.

Preston, Howard Lawrence. *Dirt Roads to Dixie: Accessibility and Modernization in the South, 1885–1935*. Knoxville: University of Tennessee Press, 1991.

Sharp, Leslie N. "Down South to Dixie: The Development of Dixie Highway from Nashville to Chattanooga, 1915–1940." Master's thesis, Middle Tennessee State University, 1993.

Stager, Claudette, and Martha Carver, eds. *Looking Beyond the Highway Dixie Roads and Culture*. Knoxville: University of Tennessee Press, 2006.

West, Carroll Van, ed. *The Tennessee Encyclopedia of History and Culture*. Knoxville: University of Tennessee Press, 1998. Revised electronic version available at http://tennesseeencyclopedia.net.

———. *Tennessee's Historic Landscapes: A Traveler's Guide*. Knoxville: University of Tennessee Press, 1995.

# INDEX

Consistent with our mission to preserve history on a local level, this book was printed in South Carolina on American-made paper and manufactured entirely in the United States. Products carrying the accredited Forest Stewardship Council (FSC) label are printed on 100 percent FSC-certified paper.

MADE IN THE USA